THE
SOLITUDE
OF THE
OPEN SEA

To John,
Fellow traveler
+
Adventurer!
All the
Best!

Gregory
Newell
Smith

THE
SOLITUDE
OF THE
OPEN SEA

SEAWORTHY PUBLICATIONS, INC.
Port Washington, WI

The Solitude of the Open Sea

Copyright © 2005 by Gregory Newell Smith

For rights inquiries, or to contact the publisher:

Seaworthy Publications, Inc.
207 S. Park St.
Port Washington, WI 53074

Phone: 262-268-9250
Fax: 262-268-9208
E-mail: publisher@seaworthy.com

Visit us on the Web: www.seaworthy.com

Library of Congress Cataloging-in-Publication Data

Smith, Gregory Newell, 1953-
    The solitude of the open sea / Gregory Newell Smith
        p. cm.
    ISBN 1-892399-22-9 (alk. paper)
    1. Smith, Gregory Newell, 1953---Travel. 2. Seafaring life. 3. Sailing, Single-handed. I.
Title.

G540.S617 2005
910.4'1--dc22

                                                                2004065394

Cover and map design by Todd Goehner
Book design and composition by John Reinhardt Book Design

CONTENTS

ACKNOWLEDGEMENTS

Writing a book and sailing around the world may be tests of self-reliance, but neither could happen without the help and encouragement of many others. On the sailing side, I extend my sincere thanks to my brother Dave Smith for teaching me to sail and inciting me with stories of foreign shores; to George Galpin, for selling me *Atlantean* and knowing she'd bring me home safely; to Sam Swihart, the jack-of-all-trades and dear friend who helped me get *Atlantean* ready to sail; to Willi and Lou Schmidt, aboard *Whirlwind,* Hilton and Melva Ward aboard *Spindrift,* and Brian and Mary Alice O'Neill aboard *Shibui,* for being part of the community of cruising sailboats, without whom few of us would have the courage to face the open sea; and to my Welsh friend Ioan Price, for being the best crewman a captain could ever want.

I couldn't have begun this book had not Wayne and Joy Attwood offered me their Lake Coeur d'Alene house for a long, quiet winter, where the first drafts of these accounts took shape; I offer them my eternal gratitude for that and more, and only wish all writers and artists could be privileged to know such kind and generous benefactors. Thanks, too, to Julie Titone, friend, journalist, and fellow writer, who labored through every draft and convinced me to stay the course; to Carol Rosenthal, Bob Marks, and Craig Smith, for their careful readings and many helpful suggestions; to Jonathan Johnson, John

Keeble, and all of the writers and teachers of the Inland Northwest Writers Center.

I also thank my family for their support and encouragement, and for being patient with a poor relation who hasn't had a "real job" for so long. And finally, I thank my beloved wife of just over a year, Elaine Green, whose introduction to ocean sailing was accompanying me on a twenty-six day yacht delivery, Hawaii to San Francisco. Thank you, Elaine, for believing in me even when I no longer believed in myself.

Moscow, Idaho 2004

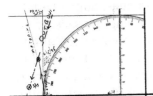

THE SOLITUDE
OF THE OPEN SEA

WHAT'S THE LONGEST ANY of us can say we've been truly alone? I'm a sailor, at home in the practical world of physical forces, of wind, weather, and waves, so I'm not talking in existential terms, alone within the shell of the body, or locked in the prison of the mind. Rather I'm referring to the conventional notion of aloneness: by oneself, cut off from human contact, completely isolated from the sight or sound of another person.

Whenever I ask this question, the initial answer is generally, "I've spent a lot of time alone." But after thinking it over, few people can come up with even a twenty-four hour stretch during which they saw no one, talked with no one, when the phone didn't ring and they didn't turn on the television or radio. Before I embarked on this life of ocean sailing, I could recall only a single incident when I'd had a day all to myself—a solo backpacking trip in the North Cascades, twenty-six hours between the Tuesday morning I left the trailhead and the next afternoon when a ranger wandered through my camp.

My longest encounter with extended solitude begins on a sultry morning in mid-May, when I set out from the Pacific-side of the Panama Canal en route to Hilo, Hawaii, about to cross more than 5,000 miles of ocean. Already behind me are three years and 37,000 miles aboard this 39-foot sailboat, *Atlantean*, during which I've explored iceberg-choked bays in Alaska, basked in Mexican sunshine, island-hopped the South Pacific, sojourned among kiwis in New Zealand and koalas in Australia, transited the Indian Ocean, rounded the Cape of Good Hope, and cruised the Caribbean coast of South America. Family and friends have joined me for parts of the trip, and pick-up crews have helped out on the long ocean passages. Single-handing a few short hops has taught me the tricks of getting the sails up and down by myself (*Atlantean* has two autopilots, one electrical and the other a mechanical Aries windvane, so I'm rarely stuck behind the wheel), but no matter where I've dropped my anchor, I've always been part of the cruising community, an armada of several hundred sailboats all heading in roughly the same direction, like a moveable small town where everybody recognizes most everybody else.

The Hilo passage will be different; I'll be alone, forty days if *Atlantean* maintains her daily passage average of 125 miles per day, but certainly longer since the old clipper ship route I plan to follow adds nearly 1,000 miles to the journey. Hurricane season is already underway, and I know of no other boats headed to Hawaii with whom I might maintain single-side-band (long-range) radio contact. Prevailing winds and currents make the alternative of sailing up the coast of Central America impractical.

I'm ready to test myself. An extended solo passage represents the last great challenge on this trip that is rapidly drawing to a close. My health is good, *Atlantean* is as sound as a boat can be after sailing eighty-percent of the way around the planet, and I'm anxious to get home to Seattle. And though having another body on board would be a convenience, for sharing watch duty and dealing with emergencies, being alone obviates the human conflicts that invariably arise from sharing close quarters—a bit of wisdom practiced by that most solitary of sailors, Joshua Slocum, who wrote of his own voyages aboard *Spray*, "There was no dissension amongst the crew." Now the only company I have to complain about is my own.

Being alone is the furthest thought on my mind this morning as I motor away from Panama; I'm too busy dodging freighters and peering through the curtain of low cloud and constant rain. The Canal is both a funnel and a spigot, channeling a non-stop flow of commercial traffic out of one ocean, and spewing an equally steady stream into the other. All day long ships pass like ghostly shadows as one squall after another washes over me, leaving me huddled under *Atlantean's* dodger and sweating inside my rain parka. When night falls, the rains ease, making it easier to track the freighters' lights in the distance. The wind picks up, and I'm able to shut down the engine.

Sleep is a serious issue for the solo sailor, primarily because of the risk of a collision at sea. The common wisdom is that it takes twenty minutes for a commercial vessel to appear from over the horizon and run you down, so most single-handers sleep in the cockpit in brief snatches, alternated with sweeps of the horizon to determine all is well. By midnight, I'm seventy miles out of Balboa, and traffic has dwindled. I can keep my eyes open no longer, so I set my wristwatch alarm for twenty minutes and curl up on the cockpit cushions. Each time I wake up, there is a ship in sight, but never on a threatening course. This works until around 0400, when the wind dies and the drenching rains resume, forcing me to fire up the diesel and retreat to my bunk. I continue to rise every twenty minutes for a quick look around before collapsing back into nervous sleep inside the noisy sweatbox of my cabin.

By 0630 dawn has arrived as a mere glimmer in the otherwise monochromatic murk, and I'm completely wrung out from worry and lack of sustained sleep. I drop onto my bunk with the engine roaring next to my head and don't wake again until forty minutes later—after sleeping through one of the alarm cycles. While I'm sitting up and shaking loose the cobwebs, *Atlantean* rocks so suddenly and violently that I'm thrown backwards against the bookshelf. The instant rush of adrenaline rockets me out of my cabin and up the companionway ladder, where I'm met with the sight of a wall of black steel sliding by in the early morning mist, less than a hundred feet away. "Holy shit," I say aloud, and for a long moment all I can do is hang on to the binnacle and stare in gape-mouthed wonder. *Atlantean* gradually stabilizes as the ship's bow wave passes, and I don't need binoculars to read the name: *Gaston*, out of Sebastopol. The frothing wake curves sharply away from her rounded stern and traces the emergency course change that probably saved my life.

I dash below to hail *Gaston* on the radio, but there's no answer, perhaps because the helmsman doesn't speak English, or is embarrassed about not maintaining a more vigilant radar watch (*Atlantean* has no radar, but is equipped with a radar reflector). The ship soon vanishes in the foggy drizzle, and I'm disappointed not to be able to thank some ex-Soviet seaman for looking up in time to avoid hitting a blue and white sailboat chugging blindly out of the Gulf of Panama.

This has been a brush with death, one that has surely cost me one of my dwindling supply of lives. I'm shaken, but the incident isn't worth berating myself over. Rather, it's one of those random events, like getting struck by lightning or winning the lottery. What else could I have done? I took the precautions I thought were necessary and had merely succumbed to the need for sleep.

But what if I hadn't been lucky? Part of being alone is that nobody knows what happens to you. If *Gaston* had run me down, it's unlikely the crew would have noticed; a freighter hitting a sailboat is the equivalent of an eighteen-wheeler bouncing a rabbit on the interstate. And since nobody is planning on hearing from me for seven or eight weeks, my family would have no idea where to begin looking when I didn't show up in Hilo. I would simply have vanished from the face of the Earth.

Sometimes all you can do is take a deep breath, be glad you're still alive, and move on. In my case, that means grabbing a quick swig out of the whiskey bottle, offering a dram over the side in a prayer of thanks to the Old Man, scanning the horizon, and going back to sleep for another twenty minutes, this time with my watch propped next to my ear.

The next several days pass in a groggy blur. There's very little wind, so most of the time I keep the engine running on low-rpm to increase the distance between me and Panama. On day three I spot two sailboats, also motoring, and when I hail them on the radio, I learn they're Germans, *Helios II* and *Taurus*, bound for the Galapagos Islands. They remain in sight for several hours, but after a light wind rises and I shut down the engine, they quickly disappear over the horizon.

I haven't seen a freighter since *Gaston*, and gradually lengthen the time between alarms, to thirty minutes, then forty. By the end of the first week, the rains are gone and my alarms are an hour apart. I'm still in a daze almost all the time, and sometimes when my alarm goes off, I only dream I get up and look around. I don't have much desire to do anything but lie in my bunk. Raising and lowering the sails to address the constantly changing conditions saps what little motivation I can muster.

But the human body can adapt to almost anything, and soon I've developed routines to occupy myself during the ten or twelve hours per day when I'm not working on sleep. I practice my flute and guitar, recite my French lessons, and read the mystery novels I've picked up in book swaps. The highlight of each evening is marking my progress on the Eastern Pacific chart (a thumb-print's width if the wind has been good, a little finger's if it hasn't), though the tiny cluster of Hawaiian islands nestled along the chart's left-hand margin often looks impossibly distant. Another ritual is listening to the high-seas weather broadcasts out of Honolulu; I always breathe a sigh of relief when the computer-generated voice addresses my little piece of the Pacific and says, "Warnings: None." The broadcasts come every six hours and are my only regular link with the civilized world.

Conditions vary from almost no wind to rainless twenty-five knot squalls that last an hour or two before dying away to nothing. I keep busy figuring out new sail sets and ways to minimize the slatting and crashing when there isn't enough wind to fill the canvas, which is most of the time. When all is well, I feel wonderful, in love with *Atlantean* and the sailing life.

From the log:

> *May 20, day eight: Yesterday has to go down as one of my best sailing days ever. Everything worked right—good course, comfortable seas, good progress, good weather. Just before sunset I got a little worried when the wind eased, then it came right back.*
>
> *As a bonus, dolphins visited me. I saw one leap completely out of the water in a 180° flip. "Good trick," I called out. "Do that again." Within minutes a dozen of his buddies were leaping and splashing all around the boat, small ones of a species I don't think I've seen before. After dark another group turned up, a larger species that swam in the bow wave, leaving stardust wakes of bioluminescence as bright as I've ever seen.*

Other days are not so cheerful:

> *May 23, day eleven: After a restless night, a wind shift to the west, and two hours of motoring (surely the last my dwindling supply of fuel can afford), I finally gave up. All the sails are down except the staysail, sheeted in tight to cut down on the rocking. The autopilot, set for west/southwest, has the boat pointed roughly south. Rocking, rocking, rocking, southeast swell mixed with southwest chop, made worse by what little west/northwest wind puffs through. Everything in the boat slides its maximum allowable distance, generating the maximum possible noise, and then slides back to where it started, generating the maximum possible annoyance.*

On day fifteen I see a ship in the late afternoon, the first since *Gaston*. It's a Japanese car carrier, a monstrous orange box that towers so far above the water it's a wonder it doesn't capsize. I hail them but they ignore me, as Asian vessels always do. I thought I was out of the shipping lanes, but perhaps they're hauling a load of Nissans to Santiago. That same night when I get up to pee, I spot another set of lights slipping over the horizon behind me. I slept right through its passing—how close, I'll never know.

Two days later I have to climb the mast to replace a halyard that chafed through from all the slatting (a halyard is a line that runs through the turning blocks at the top of the mast and is used to hoist sails). It's fifty-six feet to the masthead, and I climb on stirrup steps I installed before leaving Seattle. Although the mast swings like a pendulum with any passing wave, the seas are relatively calm and the winds light. I focus my attention on careful hand and foot placement and make it up without undue difficulty. With two feet planted firmly in the steps and one hand holding tight, I double-wrap my safety harness tether around the hollow aluminum spar and clip the carabiner to a sturdy padeye. It's time for a look around.

It's surprising how vast the ocean appears from on high, where there's far more than the customary deck-level four miles to the horizon. Looking down on the water rather than across it makes the Pacific a deeper and more vivid shade of blue—*Indigo? Sapphire? Azure? Or is this what they call cerulean blue?* I choose cerulean, an appropriately noble name for the unbroken expanse of ocean that spreads before me like a magnificent carpet, richly textured by the ripplings of long, lazy swells stretching forever in all directions, until the weave merges into the powdery hues of the sky. There is nothing as far as the eye can see but ocean, and sky, and cottony puffs of cloud with their little blobs of shadow trailing beneath them like faithful dogs.

Biblical verse comes to mind: "And the Spirit of God moved upon the face of the waters." I am alone, totally and assuredly alone, but alone in the midst of such an unbounded beauty that it would have made the poet Rilke weep for joy. There is no feeling of despair or loneliness, no existential isolation, only the thrilling freedom that comes from unity with one's surroundings, a sense of communion, a liberation so overwhelming it approaches rapture. I am completely unconstrained, as if I could unhook myself and soar like a bird in a complete merger of body, spirit, and the world around me. Is this how sailors on the old sailing ships felt when they watched from the crow's nest or tended the sails on the upper spars? Could this splendid blend of solitude and union be part of the siren song that has always drawn humans to the sea?

My aerial reverie doesn't last long. The wristwatch alarm beeps, signaling the next Coast Guard weather broadcast, which of course

I'll have to miss. It raises a chuckle—where else on a thirty-nine foot sailboat could I be sixty feet away from the radio?—but it also reminds me there's work to be done. After an hour and two more trips up the mast, *Atlantean* is again sailing under a full suit of sails.

Pleased with my day's work, I treat myself to a bottle of South African wine, with which I toast the sunset and another fruitless search for the green flash, and later polish off under the stars. Drunk and happy, I stay up late and dance around the cockpit to the strains of the *Rocky Horror Picture Show* soundtrack coming from the tape player strapped to my hip. In spite of the aches and bruises from my climbing expeditions, I sleep through the night, only getting up once to empty my bladder and check the horizon. A saltwater shower in the morning, followed by aloe and talcum and the bliss of fresh underwear, eliminates the slight hangover.

Life is good.

Twenty-nine days out of Panama, the ocean is flatter than I would have thought possible; the surface is an oily sheen so unrippled that the puffy cumulus clouds are reflected as if in a mirror. For the last eleven days I've been drifting back and forth across the Equator, eased along by the current and hoping to find the southeast trade winds, sometimes making as little as twenty-eight miles a day. The needle on the wind speed gauge bounces from five to zero to five as the masthead rocks in the long, slow swell, spinning the anemometer cups aloft. The afternoon is hot and humid, and I'm frustrated with the lack of progress. There's no excuse not to go for a swim. I take down the limp sails, hang the swim ladder over the side, don my mask, snorkel, and fins, and take the plunge. I don't even bother tying a safety line around my waist; *Atlantean* certainly isn't going anywhere.

This is my first free swim in ten thousand feet of water. After I clear my mask, what captures my attention is the startling clarity; the length of *Atlantean's* white-bottomed hull stands out as if seen through glass. I rotate through a complete circle, and though there is nothing else to focus on, I'm under the impression that the visibility is hundreds, if not thousands of feet in any direction.

By far the most compelling view is down. I have no idea how far the sun's light actually penetrates, but there is the unmistakable sensation of depth, incredible depth, as if I can trace every shade of blue through its various gradations until everything disappears in the inky purple abyss. There have been many times I've snorkeled or scuba dived when I couldn't see the bottom, but I've never experienced this sensation of vertigo, unable to even *imagine* the ocean floor almost two miles below. It's unsettling, the opposite of that powerful sense of communion atop the mast when I felt as if I could gather the whole of creation into myself. "And the earth was without form, and void, and darkness was upon the face of the deep." No wonder the ancients always located hell in the underworld. Gazing with such clarity below the surface, the ocean is distressingly featureless, immeasurable and unknowable. There is no orienting myself in the face of such immutable darkness, no direction towards which I might find refuge, except upwards, to the air and light. And though my rational mind has always known it, I'm at once viscerally aware that the surface of the ocean is only the merest part of it, the scant margin on which we hover suspended in our fragile air-filled vessels and bodies, blocked from experiencing even an inkling of what lies hidden beneath. Looking down, I peer into the void, as if floating in an intergalactic space so empty that there aren't even the distant stars to reassure me I'm not alone.

But happily the sun is warm on my back, my snorkel is my link to precious air, and *Atlantean's* comforting presence is only a turn of the head away. Out of curiosity, I test my nerve by seeing how far from the boat I can swim. Fifty or sixty feet are all I can manage. With each stroke my feelings of vulnerability and foreboding within this now suddenly uninviting environment are magnified and grow, until I'm like a helpless toddler who's discovered his mother has vanished. A glance over my shoulder at the hull bobbing peacefully in crystalline relief is enough to make me hurry back.

Work provides a comforting focal point after having faced the unfathomable, and a quick inspection reveals there is much to be done. *Atlantean's* hull is a field of gray-brown stubble; it's alive with thousands of gooseneck barnacles, some almost three inches in length. With a small plastic scraper I quickly clear the area around the knotmeter, as well as the depthsounder transducers and the propeller shaft, which are totally encrusted. The barnacles release their grip easily enough, but each time the creature's little foot takes a smidgen of bottom paint with it, convincing me to go after only the heaviest concentrations. I work for twenty minutes, enjoying the exercise, until there's a long trail of dislodged goosenecks drifting slowly downwards and out of sight.

It's time for a break, so I climb the swim ladder for a drink of fresh water and a rest. Afterwards, I'm poised to jump back in when I hear a splashing sound behind the boat. I look over the stern pulpit and spot the unmistakable elongated gray body and pointy fins and tail of a shark—at least nine-feet long, the largest shark I've seen in the wild. "Whoa," I say aloud, "so much for swimming."

He (or she) is an impressive creature, nosing up against the windvane's servo-rudder as if to sniff it. *Atlantean* is still not moving, so the shark snakes back and forth to keep the water flowing over his gills, giving me ample opportunity to admire his ominous dorsal fin, the gimlet eyes, and the three-foot remora attached to his side, along for the ride. I would like to admire the shark's sharp teeth, but I can't get him to bite at any of the Ritz crackers I toss at his head. He stays with me for fifteen minutes, long enough for a snapshot and to wonder what a reef-feeder is doing a thousand miles from the nearest reef. Whatever the reason, my paddling around must have sounded like a wounded fish and an easy meal.

I'm not so alone after all.

Each time a little breeze picks up, I let it push me to the northwest, back across the Equator and closer to Hawaii. When it dies, I drift to the south, vowing that I'll keep heading that way until the southeast trades return. How far south could I sail? My chart says I'm closer to the Marquesas Islands than Hawaii. Why not go back there, to rest and refuel before resuming my journey? For that matter, why not simply stay in the South Seas? Bernard Moitessier did it; only a few thousand miles away from an easy victory in the 1968 Golden Globe Race for the first solo non-stop circumnavigation, he abruptly changed course and spent another three months sailing to Tahiti. Like me, Moitessier may have thought, "The sailing life is the life I know, and what awaits me back home?"

But returning to the South Seas isn't an option I seriously consider. Sailing has had a lot to teach me about the world and about myself, and now it's time for a change. The problem with staying out here, with never coming home, is that it's a dropout lifestyle, a way to run away from the world rather than embracing it. A round-eye with a sailboat and a modest bank account can always find some little island to waste away his days, and maintaining boat and body will provide enough challenges to satisfy the human need for productive work. But in the end, those people are lost souls, adrift, belonging to no one and to no place.

For me, life on land isn't all bad. There's much I miss: music, art, literature, the lively exchange of ideas among inquiring minds. Relationships that matter, family and friends, and a special person with whom to share my life, a partner for future quests. And not least by far, I miss a sense of place, the feeling of home. I've visited dozens of different countries, but nowhere has resonated so deeply within me as does my beloved Pacific Northwest—not New Zealand, not South Africa, not even Southeast Alaska, though they are all beautiful in their own ways and have much to offer. I'll leave those places to their own natives, to those people who, as Terry Tempest Williams writes, naturally comprehend their landscapes and hold them as sanctuary inside their unguarded hearts. Verdant forests, rugged mountains, and sparkling waters are the landscapes I hold in my own heart: the Mt. St. Helens area where I grew up before the great eruption, and Puget Sound where I've spent most of my adult life.

No, I'm not headed for the Marquesas. Been there, done that, as the saying goes. For now I'll keep my sights set on Hawaii, and afterwards, Seattle.

June 13, a day of light but steady winds, marks an entire month at sea. Dolphins and pilot whales show up just before dark; the dolphins come to play and the whales keep their distance. During the night I hear the pilot whales' squeaks sounding through the hull, and the next morning they're swimming with the boat. It's a good omen. The winds build to a steady fifteen knots, and that day *Atlantean* covers 138 miles, including 124 miles of westing. I'm almost to 125° west longitude, well west of Seattle, and past the point I've arbitrarily designated as halfway to Hilo. Hopefully the second half won't take so long.

I let the wind push me northward, and by June 16 I've reached 5° north latitude; that night Polaris glimmers briefly through the haze, low on the horizon. The distance to Hilo is down to two thousand miles and I'm only twelve miles from crossing my outbound track—the course I followed from Mexico to the South Seas more than two years ago—and the official completion of my circumnavigation. Unfortunately the wind goes back to zero and I drift eastward, caught in the Equatorial Countercurrent. The culprit is the intertropical convergent zone, the Pacific equivalent of the doldrums, a band of dead air and thunderstorms north of the Equator. When the good winds started a few days before, the mechanical radio voice reported the zone had slid up to 9° north. Now it's back down to 4°, and I'm in the middle of it. To make matters more interesting, the radio also reports that the season's first official hurricane, Adolphus, has formed off the coast of Mexico, with sustained winds of 120 knots. I'm glad it's 2,000 miles away.

The sails stay limp all night and the morning fix reveals I've drifted to the northeast—my outbound track is now farther away than it was twelve hours before—and the course line on my Pacific Ocean chart takes a discouraging kink to the right. It's time to start burning my precious fuel. After what I used escaping from Panama, plus intermittent battery charging, I calculate there are forty-five hours of low-rpm motoring left in the tank, forty of which I'm willing to commit to crossing the ITCZ. I start the engine, and the "iron genny" pushes *Atlantean* due north, with the electric autopilot doing the driving. I continue through the day and night across the placid, windless seas until the course lines on my plotting sheet finally come together—at approximately 0800 on June 18, I cross my outbound track, latitude 7°28' north, longitude 125°04' west—thereby completing the circumnavigation. Next to the thrill of arriving in Cape Town at dawn, it's the most satisfying accomplishment of my trip.

The celebration begins that evening with my ritual watch for the green flash (as usual, nothing to report). The engine has allowed me to run the refrigerator all day, making a tray of ice cubes and chilling my last can of Coke. The bit of vodka my rowdy Panama Canal crew left behind is enough for two big cocktails. The precious Maker's Mark bottle is down to its last inch, and after sunset I follow a generous swig with a dram over the side in thanks to the Old Man (there's enough left for a final thanks offering in Hilo). When the last of the vodka goes into my glass, I compose a note commemorating the circumnavigation and launch it in the vodka bottle, including my sister's address and telephone number, and a promise to send the finder fifty dollars.

I've done it. Sailed around the world. Sailed west and come back to a place I've been before. So much has happened during the three-plus years since I left Seattle, so many trials and tribulations, so many people and places trailing in my wake. But I haven't really done it alone; *Atlantean* has been with me every inch of the way, has made it all possible. Perhaps I really do love her best. I raise my glass in a toast. "I couldn't have done it without you, old girl." She remains silent, as always, though over the years there's been more than enough *Atlantean* luck to prove she really cares about me.

But knowing I've sailed around the world isn't the same as telling somebody about it. Perhaps Mallory really was the first man up Everest, and maybe he, too, had launched a message in a bottle, but nobody ever found it. A few nights later, after I've crossed the convergent zone and the trade winds have returned, I'm scrolling through the various frequencies on the SSB radio and hear the high seas operator's voice coming through loud and clear. He's just signed off from a call with an Alaska fishing boat, so I hail him with my boat name and position. Radio propagation must be perfect tonight, because he answers immediately, and I'm able to place a long-range telephone call on the radio, to my sister, collect.

After a few rings an unfamiliar voice picks up and accepts the charges. "Hello," I say into the microphone, "this is Greg calling from the middle of the ocean. Is Carol home?"

"Oh gosh, oh gee," the woman says when I release the transmit button, "They're not here right now, oh no, can you call back? This is the baby sitter, they'll be back in a couple hours. Oh, they're gonna be so sorry they missed you, I wish they were here, they talk about you all the time, are you okay?"

I've flustered the poor woman; how often does someone get a radio call from a sailor on the Pacific Ocean? But it doesn't matter. I'm overjoyed to hear a friendly voice connected to my family, even if I don't know her. Baby sitting: this simple reminder of domestic routine brings with it an almost overwhelming longing for the comforts of family and home. I reassure the woman that I'm fine, ask her to write down my latitude and longitude (which I have to repeat several times because she doesn't understand what the numbers mean), and tell her my ETA in Hilo is July 3.

"Tell them I love them," I say.

"I will," she says. "They love you, too."

I'm still in the mood to talk (the first I've spoken with anybody since the Germans on day three) and have the high seas operator on the line, so I give him the number for George, *Atlantean's* former owner, who has been a faithful correspondent over the years and even joined me on a couple of ocean passages. Once again I hear the telephone ringing, and after the operator goes through his spiel, George's patrician voice says, "Hell yes I'll accept the charges."

"George," I shout, scarcely able to contain myself, "I did it, I sailed around the world! I crossed my out-bound track three days ago in the middle of the Pacific!"

"You son of a bitch," he laughs. "All right! I've been thinking about you. How's *Atlantean*?"

"*Atlantean's* great. I'll be in Hilo July 3. How about sailing home with me to Seattle?"

There's a long pause. "Damn it, Greg, don't tempt me," he says, followed by another long pause. "Damn. This isn't a good time, but let me think about it. Call me when you get to Hilo."

I pass on my position, and we soon ring off. But it's been enough. I've been at sea over forty days, and now at least people know where I am, know I'm safe, and when I'm expected. It's a comfort to me and surely to my family. Forty days isn't an unusual amount of time not to hear from somebody, but most people aren't crossing oceans on small sailboats.

But equally important, if not more so, is the feeling that telling George about my feat has validated my efforts, as if an accomplishment can't be properly appreciated until it's been shared. No matter how accustomed someone has grown to solitude—and by now I'm very comfortable being alone at sea—humans are social animals and crave attention from others. It's a way of saying, "Look at me. I'm not another face in the crowd. I matter." There may have been ascetics who spent years living as hermits in caves, but they didn't achieve sainthood (and thereby become an inspiration to others, which is after all the point of saints) without the world hearing about them.

Over the next few nights I'm encouraged to give the high seas operator another try, but the ionosphere isn't cooperating and I'm never again able to make contact.

Hawaii is drawing closer, but as it does, the winds gradually fade and more rainless squalls blow through. One night there is so little breeze that I'm back to dropping the main, sheeting in the staysail, and going to bed. The sound of a low mechanical rumble brings me on deck, but instead of another *Gaston* bearing down on me, I spot a freighter's distant lights disappearing over the horizon; the conditions must have been right for carrying the sound of the engines over the miles. Though there is bound to be more shipping traffic in this part of the ocean, I don't change my routine of going to bed at night with the masthead light on. I'm willing to accept whatever fate sends my way, and besides, every couple of hours my subconscious senses some subtle change in the feel of the boat—in the heel, or the pull of the sails, or the sound of the bubbles gurgling past the hull—and it wakes me up for a quick look around. Other than the one freighter, I sight no other passing vessels, either day or night.

The calendar turns over to July and I'm only 350 miles from Hilo. With steady wind I could easily cover that distance in three days, but the breeze goes into the east and stays below ten knots. The current is pushing me along, but the sails aren't doing much. I fuss with the rig almost constantly, even gybing now and then to see if I can improve my course; *Atlantean* has been heeling on starboard tack for so long that the goosenecks are above the waterline when I put the wind to port. Hurricane Barbara is seven hundred miles off and headed towards me, but it's steadily losing steam. I tell myself it can't possibly last all the way to Hawaii.

The big island of Hawaii has two mountains in excess of 13,000 feet, which I should be able to spot from quite a distance. On July 3, however, clouds stack up to the west and a few sprinkles fall, the first rain I've had since the Gulf of Panama, and not enough to clear the sheen of salt off the deck. I gaze through the binoculars as the sun sets—I'm still a hundred miles out—but there's no sight of the mountains.

The next morning I'm down to seventy miles, and a few hours later I catch my first whiff of the damp, earthy smell of growth and rot that tells me land is approaching (unlike the seashore, there's no smell of the ocean, at least not for human noses). My nostrils flare and twitch at the hint of sulphur from the active volcano on the island's eastern flank. And at 1310, twenty-eight miles east of Cape Kumukahi, I spot it, an unmistakable solid curve rising above a break in the clouds. "Land Ho!" I shout to nobody in particular, before the clouds regather and the mountain disappears.

At 2100 it's full dark and I'm practically drifting, twenty miles from Hilo. Lights are visible on shore, but I don't have a detailed chart of the island, only the little hand drawn diagram of Hilo Harbor in *Charlie's Charts* ("Not Suitable For Navigation," the caption never fails to remind me). While I'm peering into the night, a series of brightly colored flashes appear, low on the horizon. I climb the mast as far as the spreaders and for the next twenty minutes watch the distant sparkle and glitter of the Hilo Harbor Fourth of July fireworks display. A burst of patriotic pride and nostalgia for the land of my birth wells in my chest.

Dawn finds me five miles from the entrance to the harbor in a light drizzle under a totally overcast sky. This is Hilo after all, on the wet, windward side of the island, where the trade wind clouds stack up on the mountains' flanks and plenty of rain falls. The ceiling is nevertheless high enough that I'm dazzled by the sight of so much green; after weeks of nothing but blue, it's as if I've awakened to a vibrant world of intense and vivid color, even in the gray light of dawn.

It's time to find out if I have enough fuel to make the harbor. Although I haven't run the engine in over two weeks, it immediately kicks to life on the charge the solar panels have maintained in the batteries. I putter through the entrance to Radio Bay Harbor, waving happily at the few fishing boats heading out; they must think I'm crazy, sailing so early in the morning. I raise the Harbor Master on the VHF, and he directs me to the inner yacht basin. By the time I arrive, most people aboard the half-dozen sailboats lying at anchor are up and about. A couple of them climb into a dinghy and help me stern-tie to the quay. "Where are you coming from?" they shout.

"Panama!" I call back, pleased to see the surprise on their faces.

My longest passage is complete. After factoring in the six time zones I crossed, I've been at sea fifty-three days, seven hours, and thirty-seven minutes.

When I tell people about my Hilo passage, their most common questions are, "Weren't you lonely?" and "Didn't you get bored?" My answers generally prove to be so unexpected—an unqualified "No," to both—that I've learned to avoid confusing my listeners by steering the conversation towards other aspects of the journey. Our culture is highly suspicious of solitude, to the extent that many people cannot comprehend how being alone on a small sailboat could be anything but the equivalent of a jail sentence. If prison punishes criminals with long periods of boredom, then solitary confinement is even more cruel, depriving the prisoner of the balm of social intercourse.

Modern society affords few opportunities for people to be truly and peacefully alone. Faced with life's daunting complexities and the nearly constant onslaught of useless information, we cope by "turning down the volume," erecting a protective filter between our brains and an otherwise overwhelming quantity of sensory data. We retreat inside our heads and only come out when our defense mechanisms tell us it's safe. The more carefully we guard ourselves, however, the more superficial our interactions with the outside world will be. To satisfy the universal hunger for meaning, many try to fill the void not by increasing their awareness and searching out meaningful connections, but rather by grasping for ready amusements and constant companionship. Approaching these diversions with the same guarded superficiality may produce a temporary solace, but it cannot compensate for what is missing in their lives.

I can think of no more *immediate* experience than sailing by oneself (the word "immediate" is from the Latin, "without mediation or an intervening agent"). Alone on the sea, every moment occupied my attention: there was always a sail to trim, a line to check, a squeak to investigate, the course and wind to monitor, equipment to maintain and repair, or simply the waves and clouds to watch. I might say there was no time to be bored, but there was more to it than that. Boredom and loneliness are really two sides of the same coin: we feel bored or lonely when we are no longer living in the present moment. We want a change of circumstances, to be somewhere else or doing something else. We separate ourselves from our immediate reality by positing an alternate. We react rather than respond.

A sailboat forces one to work with the natural environment instead of against it. Sailors may challenge temporary obstacles with judicious use of a diesel engine, but for the most part we rely on whatever winds and currents Nature provides. The key is acceptance: eventually the sea will get you to admit that one of the few things you can change in life is your attitude. A successful ocean passage is therefore nothing short of the union of the boat and its crew with the natural environment, and exemplifies the difference between reacting and responding. When we react to the outside world, we objectify it; the world becomes something we wish to tame and subjugate to our own purposes, whether it's a poorly designed turning block, a clumsy crewman, or wind that won't blow the way we want. On the other hand, when we realize we are intimately connected with our surroundings, we work with them rather than against them, responding in ways that are cooperative, not combative, finding solutions that don't force the elements into behaving other than they would naturally. Reacting, we try to shape our environment. Responding, our environment shapes us.

And therein lies the answer to avoiding both boredom and loneliness. Turning our attention away from ourselves and the alternate reality we uselessly wish for, and towards the actual reality in which we live our lives, we enter into what I call communion, the immersion of ourselves in an intimate and profound interchange with the world around us. Loneliness is nothing more than the universal craving for communion, which many believe can only be found in the company of others. Yet we are never so alone, never so excluded from the connection we desire, than when we're surrounded by the nameless, faceless mob of modern humanity.

It took the sea's total freedom and the solitude I found there to finally achieve the communion I'd sought for so many years. When I found that communion, it was not with another soul, as I had so long dreamed it must be. Instead, it was a communion with Nature, with the universe beheld each day, with the wind, the waves, the sky, and the creatures of the sea, and with dear *Atlantean*, that fragile product of human craftsmanship and ingenuity that kept me alive to enjoy it all. And perhaps most importantly, I achieved communion with myself. For a brief time I was at peace. There was nothing I truly desired, no other person I needed to make me feel whole. My world was complete.

Sailing a boat across a wide expanse of ocean, or even all the way around the world, is no great accomplishment, not in the grand scheme of things. One lesson the sea has taught me is the relative insignificance of human accomplishment. At any moment Nature could have squashed me like a bug: a chance slip on deck might have spelled disaster, or hurricane Barbara. But I believe in Edward Abbey's maxim that though Nature may be indifferent to our love, she is never unfaithful. We humans are a part of Nature, and her faithfulness means that she treats us with the same care and respect she affords to all. Nature provides the stage on which we play out life's brief flicker, and allows us to accomplish what we might. She promises only to be fair, no matter that it might result in our ultimate failure. Because even failure would be another of life's great experiences: proof of the miracle of our existence.

Life is ultimately a quest for personal satisfaction, and the tests to which we subject ourselves are not to prove we can survive anything and everything that might come our way, but rather are means of assessing how we individually measure up against standards we set for ourselves, standards that have relevance to our individual beliefs and values. A successful life doesn't have to include climbing Mt. Everest, or winning an Olympic gold medal, or finding a cure for cancer. Everybody's circumstances are unique, and each of us has the right to choose how we will judge our successes and failures, to choose the goals against which we will measure our achievement, whether it be in pursuing a career, raising a child, loving another human being, or sailing across an ocean.

There is much I still hope to accomplish in my lifetime, many more tests that I will find for myself, and countless undreamt dreams waiting to be followed. Yet I can think of nothing I would trade for those fifty-three days, alone, at sea.

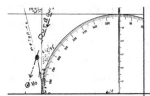

KAVA ON KANDAVU
(OR, KANDAVU ON KAVA)

"IF YOU'RE GOING TO KANDAVU, you'd better be prepared for sevu sevu," Brian says. He and Mary Alice, my cruiser friends from the yacht *Shibui*, have been to Fiji before and know the routine. Kandavu is one of the country's less visited islands, despite such attractions as the excellent diving around the Great Astrolabe Reef. It's south of Suva, Fiji's largest city and port of entry, and requires a day of beating into the trade winds to get there. "You have to ask the locals' permission wherever you go," Brian continues. "Everything belongs to the village, not just the land. The water, the reef, the fish, probably even the air, it's all theirs."

"What if they say no?" I ask.

"They won't. Not if you do sevu sevu. You give the headman a little yaquona, be polite, and you're in. They'll treat you like one of their own. You won't have to worry about a thing."

"This yaquona," I say, following Brian's pronunciation, yan-GOH-nah, "that's what they make kava out of, right?"

"They'll probably expect you to tip a few bowls," Brian says.

My traveling companion aboard *Atlantean* for the next few weeks is Beth, the more pleasant half of the cruising couple on *Silk*. I met Beth and her partner Evans during Happy Hour at the Royal Suva Yacht Club (not nearly as pretentious as its name), and when Beth heard I was solo sailing to Kandavu, she asked if she could come along.

"How do you feel about that?" I later asked Evans.

"I could use a break," Evans said. "I'm going to stick around Suva, maybe rent a car. If Beth wants to go sailing, that's her business. Have a good time." I can sympathize with Evans. Sometimes all I really want is to hang out and do nothing. Sailing means boat maintenance—stitching the sails, patching the leaks, rewiring, polishing, and lubricating—all of which can be put off for another day if you're not going anywhere. Only I'd rather hang out on some out-of-the-way island like Kandavu than stay put in Suva harbor, where I spend too much money on spicy restaurant food, where the Indians stand up and shout at the screen during the movie, and where *Shibui* was recently broken into, the thieves making off with all of Brian and Mary Alice's clothes and two spare sails.

Evans and Beth are a rare commodity in the cruising community, a young couple with an expensive boat, a trim Halberg Rassey ketch they purchased new in Sweden, then sailed across the Atlantic and through the Panama Canal to the Pacific. They're taking a three-year hiatus from their successful MBA careers to see the world. Evans is the closest I've come to somebody who shares my relative youth, professional background, and variable taste for adventure. Beth, however, is congenial company. A rosy-cheeked blonde with a propensity to bake too many cakes and ginger snaps, she's a knowledgeable sailor and stimulating conversation partner.

After a couple of overnight stops at Beqa and Yamanutha islands, and following an all day beat to the south, Beth and I anchor *Atlantean* shortly before dark in a narrow bay inside the reef joining the southwestern end of Kandavu with tiny Denham Island. The next morning while we're preparing to go ashore, a steady stream of boat traffic motors past us and disappears around the point. The boats resemble Mexican *pangas*—about eighteen feet long with high bows and sturdy Mariner outboards—and are loaded to the gunwales with native men, women, and children who stare at us, as if they're not sure what to make of a cruising sailboat anchored in their bay. When I wave, only the women smile and wave back.

We're about to go to the village for our first round of sevu sevu (there were no villages where we anchored the last two nights), and we're a little anxious. Along with the cruising permit and letters of introduction written in Fijian I obtained through the Ministry of Culture, I have four kilos of yaquona, purchased at the market in Suva. The yaquona is a tangled mass of dried roots and stems, divided into bundles and bound together with several wraps of pink Christmas-present ribbon.

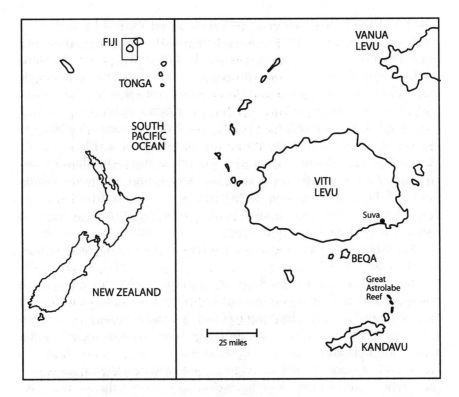

"Is this modest enough?" Beth asks as she opens the door to her cabin in the forepeak. She's wearing a flowered pareu wrapped around her waist over her sailing shorts, and a loose white peasant blouse. Her long hair is pinned behind her head.

"It'll do," I say. "We wouldn't want to raise any libidos by showing a little leg." Mary Alice said the Fijians on the outlying islands are touchy about women's appearance—no shorts or bathing suits, and definitely no skimpy tops. I've put on a clean button-up shirt for the occasion, but in this heat there's no way I'm going to wear long pants.

We dinghy to shore where trails lead left and right away from the beach. We choose the right-hand trail, the direction of crowd noises and activity, and soon come to a large athletic field, at the far side of which are two school buildings. Probably three hundred people, at least half of them children, are gathered around the field, where a running track has been chalk-striped on the tufty grass.

"It's a kid track meet," I say. "That explains where all the people were headed." We stand on the slope overlooking the field and watch a few races, which happen every couple of minutes and are accompanied by haphazard applause and varying amounts of attention.

The children—sometimes, but not always, segregated by gender or age—run distances ranging from around fifty to two hundred meters. A tall Fijian wearing a gray warm-up suit and a Batman ball cap starts each race by clapping two boards together. The finish line is a red ribbon held by young girls for the victor to run through. Nobody keeps a stopwatch, and most of the racers run without shoes.

Though we're the only non-Fijians present, we seem to attract no notice. "I would have thought we'd make more of a splash," I say. "It's not like we blend right in." Maintaining my most cheerful demeanor, I approach three men perched atop an overturned fishing boat. "Hello!" I say in English. "We are here to perform sevu sevu." I speak slowly and clearly, and hold up our yaquona bundle. "Can you tell me where I might find the..., uh, the headman?" I was going to say "chief," but that didn't sound right, nor did "mayor," or "take me to your leader."

The men discuss my question among themselves in Fijian, then point across the field to where a group of men sits in the shade of a concrete porch running the length of the main school building. It's also the direction from which a steady *Gong! Thunk!* is coming, sounding like a dull bell, rung and then choked off.

We walk around the field, navigating the crowd of spectators, nearly all of whom are women. Now that we're among them, the women offer us big smiles and say, "Hello, how are you?" and "Bula," a universal Fijian friendly-word, like the Hawaiian "Aloha." They respond to our own greetings with "Very fine, thank you, goodbye."

"Goodbye?" Beth whispers. "Are they telling us to leave? We just got here."

"Maybe that's how they learn it in school," I say. Our guidebook says instruction in Fijian schools is exclusively in English, which must be something of a challenge to the pupils since English is hardly the mother tongue.

We discover the source of the ringing, a man standing in front of a heavy cast iron bucket, which is welded to a broad circular base. His hands grip a thick iron bar, rounded on one end, wedge-shaped on the other, and nearly as long as the man is tall. He lifts the bar, clangs it against the inside rim, then tamps it into the bucket's curved bottom. *Gong! Thunk! Gong! Thunk!* Another man comes by, takes a few handfuls of sawdust-like powder out of the bucket, and throws in a pile of roots. The man working the bar temporarily shifts to the sharp end of his tool, and resumes the monotonous pounding. *Gong! Thunk! Gong! Thunk!*

"This must be how they crush the yaquona into powder to make the kava," Beth observes.

"Do you suppose there's any significance to the rhythm?" I ask, assuming the role of culturally curious tourist. "Maybe it's part of some sacred ritual."

A man steps off the porch towards us, wearing khaki slacks, rubber flip-flops, and a cut-off faded orange sweatshirt. His most striking feature is a pair of Revo mirrored sunglasses, the first sunglasses I've seen on a South Seas islander. Also out of the ordinary is his oiled wavy black hair, instead of the normal tightly kinked burr (Fijians are not Polynesians, but rather Melanesians), reminding me of a fifties nightclub musician with a process. Typically South Seas, however, are his teeth—crooked, yellow, and with generous gaps on one side.

We shake hands. "I am Abel," he says, pronouncing it AH-bull. "Where you from?" He spies my bundle. "You wanna do sevu sevu?" I tell him we're Americans from the sailboat in the bay, and yes, we want to present the headman with our yaquona. "Put it over there," Abel says and points to a place on the concrete porch steps.

I set the offering down with both hands, as the guidebook instructed, and look up with what I hope is a humble expression, searching among the faces on the porch for the man in charge. Those who bother to notice my arrival regard me with about as much interest as they'd give a sea gull who'd landed in their midst. "Hello," I say, feeling like a nervous Jaycee about to deliver his rehearsed speech, and get a few mumbled hellos and bulas in return. "We wish to offer sevu sevu for permission to stay in your bay, to visit your village, to fish, and to meet with your people." It's not great, but I expect more of a response than the indifferent silence that follows.

"Where you come from?" one of them finally asks.

"America, aboard a sailboat," I say.

"Ahhh," some of them nod, and that loosens them up for the normal questions: "How long you here? How many on boat? First time to Kandavu?" I respond slowly and with a courteous smile, using the indeterminate foreign accent non-native English speakers seem to find more intelligible than my customary Americanese. The men, who are mostly older, sit in small school-children chairs leaned back on two legs against the wall. During my interview, a young man walks up with two woven mats, places them at the men's feet, and gestures for us to sit down.

"You wanna sit over there instead?" Abel asks, and points to a group of women sitting under some trees near the track. His eyes, invisible behind his Revos, provide no clue as to how I should answer, so I look at Beth, who looks back at me. Neither of us wants to commit some breach of etiquette at our first Fijian village. "Your sevu sevu is already accepted," Abel says, as if to answer our question. The man who brought the mats picks up our yaquona bundle and casually drops it on a pile of roots near the pounding bucket.

"We'll stay here," I say, and take a seat on the mat.

Within a few minutes, the men lose all interest in us. I surreptitiously look them over to figure out which one is *el jeffe*, and decide on an older fellow towards the middle who's neither spoken to us nor acknowledged our presence in any way. Now and then he leans to the man sitting next to him and they exchange a few quiet words and edentate chuckles.

Beth's nudge calls my attention to a shirtless young man offering me a coconut shell bowl in which sloshes a generous portion of muddy brown liquid. *Kava!* I wasn't expecting this, at least not at 11:00 in the morning. My brain races, trying to remember the guidebook's description of the ceremony for drinking kava. I take the bowl in both hands and ask, "Is it okay to drink?" meaning, "Am I supposed to say something before I drink?" but it comes out sounding like maybe I'm supposed to toss it out or hand it back. The man stares at me, looking a little impatient, so I tip the shell to my lips.

The first thing I notice is that kava doesn't burn or taste medicinal; it's more like I'd expect a lukewarm mud puddle to taste. The only way to go at it is in big, steady gulps. Halfway through the bowl, I'm wondering if I'm going to get it down without retching, but it does go down, perhaps because of its numbing effect on the gag reflex. After several swallows, I recall something about leaving a little in the bottom of the bowl, perhaps as an offering to the gods, or maybe just to avoid the sludge. I hand the man the bowl, with a good mouthful still in it. "I'm supposed to leave some, aren't I?" The man glances at the bowl. Seeing some left over, he tosses the dregs in the bushes and walks away.

Hmmm, I think. *So much for ceremony.*

The effects are almost immediate, though hardly overwhelming. Numbness creeps into my mouth and tongue, along with a sense of mild euphoria, similar to the painkillers a dentist uses. I understand kava is thought to be alkaloid in nature—the yaquona plant belongs to the pepper family—though nobody has really bothered to investigate it thoroughly. It's not a get-down-and-party-hearty kind of drug.

We sit on our mats while the kava bowl makes its way around, a coconut shell communion cup, first to Beth, then among the men on the porch. *Gong! Thunk! Gong! Thunk!* The man pounding the roots lays down the beat, and the laughter of the women and children provides the background music. *Clack!* Batman cap starts another race. The men around us certainly seem relaxed, which is how Beth and I are beginning to feel. They converse in subdued murmurs if they speak at all. Before accepting the bowl some of them clap their cupped hands together in a hollow *pop!* Some raise their voices slightly and say, "Ho!" after drinking.

Beth leans close, looking like she just woke up from a satisfying afternoon nap and hasn't stretched yet. "What now?" she breathes.

"As near as I can tell, this is it."

A few children walk by, stealing shy glances and hiding embarrassed smiles when we smile at them. I entice a few to come over with an offer of the hard candies I carry in my pocket, but they snatch the candy out of my hand and run away. Elsewhere in the South Pacific, children flocked to us wherever we went, tussling with each other to hold our hands and prattling on in their unintelligible dialects. Perhaps the presence of the men intimidates them.

Before long, a second cup of kava appears, then a third. We sit for almost an hour, any need for conversation long since forgotten. I don't feel any particular resolve to get away. Where would we go? What would we do? With kava, any sort of initiative seems like too much work. I think of the British trying to persuade these people to cut sugar cane.

The men gear up for yet another bowl, but Beth's eyes are losing their focus. "I don't think I can take any more kava right now," she says. It's noon and the games dribble to a halt. The women break out food baskets and set up lunch for themselves and the children.

"Let's get some food," I suggest. "It might sober us up. We need some of that outer-island hospitality we've heard so much about."

"Do you see any place that might be serving?" Beth asks. We're willing to buy our lunch if nobody's sharing, but there are no signs of commercial enterprise.

I turn to the man sitting behind me. "We need to get something to eat. I think we go back to the boat." I'm hoping he takes the hint and makes a suggestion.

The man seems surprised, showing more animation than we've seen all morning. "You come back?" he asks.

"Later. Maybe for dinner." The man nods and sits back, satisfied with my answer. None of them appear the least bit concerned about eating, nor about anything else, for that matter. We walk away amid a chorus of "Bula, how are you, very fine thank you, goodbye" from the women and children.

"They're probably happy we left," Beth says. "They don't know what to do with us."

"You really think so?" I say. "We weren't exactly cramping their style."

Fiji is a former British colony, and though there's little evidence of it on Kandavu, the country's continuing political turmoil is a direct consequence of the colonials' failures of policy. When the English decided to claim Fiji for their own, one of their first discoveries was Fiji's suitability for growing sugar cane, and they promptly set about appropriating and clearing vast tracts of land for plantations. The native population of Fiji, however, wasn't interested in the long hours of toil under a hot sun that sugar cane requires (sugar cane is of dubious value as a food crop), and couldn't be induced to supply the muscle needed to further the causes of economic imperialism. To fill the void, Britain turned to another of its colonies, India, and there found a work force all too eager to relocate to foreign shores. Once their terms of indentured servitude were up, the industrious Indians stayed on and became the colony's merchant class of shopkeepers, bureaucrats, and skilled craftsmen. Because the native Fijians were content with their mostly rural lives in the small villages and on the outlying islands, and the Indians collected in the towns and cities founded by the colonials, conflicts were minimal, at least so long as the Redcoats were there to maintain order. There was very little intermarriage between the native Fijians and the Indians, and few attempts to assimilate the two cultures. With the apparent blessing of their overlords, the Indians quickly assumed control of almost every aspect of Fiji's non-traditional economy, which the Indians themselves had largely created. They prospered and multiplied, and now make up almost exactly half of the country's population.

Independence accompanied Fiji's foray into the modern world, along with a rising tide of material wants and needs, and the no-longer-content native Fijians found themselves at the economic mercy of the not-so-benevolent Indians. Democratization led to representative forms of government, and since the Indians were better versed in Western ways, they soon dominated the political environment as well. The practical and money-minded Indians, however, neglected to consider the advantages of careers in the military, and left the army the one profession controlled by the Fijians, to the Indians' lasting detriment. Military coups have kept a strong-man Fijian in power during most of the last several decades, accompanied by periodic threats to send the Indians back to India, though they've now been in Fiji for generations and really have no home to return to. (The latter fact alone should render the terms "Fijians" and "Indians" impolitic distinctions, since Fiji is the birth country of the Indians as much as for the ethnic Fijians, but the signifiers are useful for describing the lines along which the racial and economic conflicts are centered). Because Fiji's economy would collapse utterly without the Indians, the Fijian dictatorship is content to leave them be for the most part, other than cutting down on their freedoms and imposing punitive taxes and take-overs now and then.

Our first taste of the Indianization of Fiji came the morning I tied onto the Suva customs wharf after a passage of several days from Tonga. The British may have taught the Indians about bureaucracy, but it was the Indians who perfected it. It took me all day to complete the paperwork and make the required rounds through the city, filing multiple copies of crew and equipment lists, and obtaining stamps for customs forms and health certificates. The most absurd exercise was having to fill out the paperwork for the woman crewing for me, going through an equally cumbersome procedure to discharge her, then repeating the filing process with a revised crew list. At one point I was second in a long line of supplicants at a government office window when the noon bell rang. The Indian behind the counter pushed the nearly completed forms back at the man in front of me, told us to return at 1400, and slammed the window in our faces.

The city of Suva was much larger and even more of an assault on the senses than the Polynesian capital of Papeete. All of the businesses seemed to be run by Indians, and I had the impression that every street was an aisle in some gigantic Wal-Mart, surrounding me with goods for sale. Along the waterfront were broad boulevards and stately stone buildings, remnants of the British era, but the rest of the city might as well have been Bombay: narrow cobblestone lanes choked with people, smoky automobiles and bicycles, mysterious spices and cooking smells, and every available inch of space dedicated to commerce. A few ethnic Fijians were on the sidewalks near the waterfront, or sat on park benches like the forlorn homeless back home, or worked as clerks in some of the more tourist-oriented shops, the kind that sell tee shirts, post cards, and bags of shells. But most of the people I saw were Indians: men in long dark pants and loose, carefully pressed short-sleeved shirts, their hair and mustaches trimmed; purposeful sloe-eyed women with red dots on their foreheads, dressed in colorful saris, and shawls that sometimes doubled as head scarves, wearing hooped bracelets, earrings, and gold necklaces.

But now we're on Kandavu, which is so far removed from life in Suva, it might as well be a different planet. There's not an Indian in sight.

After lunch aboard the boat, I snorkel the reef in an unsuccessful attempt to spear a good-sized fish for dinner, followed by a few stabs at scraping the accumulated growth from *Atlantean's* hull. Beth takes a nap, but neither of our perk-up strategies works. By late afternoon we're both feeling hazy and lethargic from the lingering effects of the kava.

"So this is what we do," I say. "We'll go to the village, see about buying dinner or otherwise getting invited to sample the local fare. Then we find the headman and tell him, '*Bula vinaca*, we're sailing out in the morning.'"

"And no more kava," Beth adds.

Clad once again in our visiting attire, we climb the steep left-hand path leading to the village. Along the way is a small, isolated house, and a man shouts "Hello!" from the open door.

"Bula!" we wave and continue up the trail.

A minute or two later the man strides past us and speaks to us over his shoulder. "You are going to the village?" he asks, still walking.

"Yes, we must talk with the headman," I say, "to tell him we are sailing away in the morning." We then answer the usual questions about where we're from, how long we've been in Fiji, and so on. He tells us he is a school teacher, and explains how the school we saw today serves four surrounding villages, for children up to the age of fourteen. He stays several steps ahead of us, even after we quicken our pace to keep up, as if headed for some destination other than our own. When he turns away from the path that leads into the center of the village, I remind him of our mission, to find the chief.

"Oh yes," he says. "I am taking you there."

The village is on the undulating hilltop, and consists of fifty or sixty rough houses facing in all directions, not arranged in rows or along identifiable pathways. Houses have one or two rooms and sit on cinder-block foundations, with walls of plywood, cinder blocks, or corrugated metal. All have corrugated metal roofs, which must be incredibly noisy in Fiji's regular downpours, and they're topped with more cinder blocks to hold the sheets in place against the wind. Doors aren't common, nor is there glass in any window, and we note that most places have wooden floors, though some are only packed dirt.

The village is neither tidy nor dirty, neither overly prosperous nor destitute; every house is in about the same somewhat disheveled state. There are no automobiles and few western goods, other than western clothes, which everybody wears. Now and then wires run overhead to some of the houses, or to three or four outdoor light fixtures. We pass several outhouse-sized structures, which are what we assume they are, though they don't appear to be associated with particular dwellings. In front of most houses women tend pots over open fires, engaged in an activity that looks and smells more like boiling laundry than cooking, although it's surely approaching dinnertime. We smile at everybody and say, "Bula!" Our guide keeps up the brisk pace on the meandering paths.

We finally come to an unpainted wooden house with no windows and a closed door on the side facing us. The teacher stops twenty feet away. "This is the chief's house," he says.

"Should I knock?" I ask.

"No," he says. "You go right in." He seems uneager to join us.

Just then Abel comes around the corner, still wearing his Revo sunglasses and carrying a clear plastic bag containing twenty or thirty packs of cigarettes. "You are back," he says pleasantly. We shake hands, exchange smiles and nods, then tell him our story about leaving. While we talk, the teacher slips away without saying goodbye. Abel seems disappointed about our decision. "I thought you were going to stay longer."

"We are meeting friends from another yacht at Ndaku," I say. Ndaku is at the other end of Kandavu. It's not true, but it sounds better than telling him we don't see much point in hanging around here slurping kava all day.

"Two yachts visited our village last year," Abel says. "They anchored in the bay across from my house. Maybe you know them?" It's a common misconception I've heard on the more remote islands of the South Pacific. If a boat passed their way a year or two before, they ask, "They were from America. Do you know them?" The breadth of America seems beyond their comprehension.

After a few minutes, topics of conversation run low, so I remind Abel we're here to see the chief, to say goodbye. "We have to go back to the boat for our dinner, though we had no luck fishing in the bay today." Maybe this time he'll get the hint and tell us where we might find some food.

"Yes, yes," he says. "You will see the chief. But wait a little bit. They are making the yaquona. If you go in now, you only sit."

I hear Beth's low groan and pretend to laugh off the idea. "I don't think I can drink any more kava," I say. "I am still weak from three bowls today." Maybe if Abel thinks I'm a wimpy round-eye, he'll cut us a break.

He chuckles politely. "Only one bowl, then you go," he says.

I look at Beth, who sighs and nods.

"Okay, one bowl."

We go to the side of the house, where the sturdy metal bucket sits, this time pounded by the tall Fijian with the Batman cap. *Gong! Thunk! Gong! Thunk!* in the same, slow rhythm. A man scoops out handfuls of powder and another throws in more roots. Nearby are low platforms covered with sheets of corrugated metal, under which thousands of inch-wide disks of light-colored woody material are drying. "These are stems for kava," Abel explains. "We sell them to Suva for money. We drink only yaquona, the roots. It is better, stronger. Stems are for Suva people. They don't know better."

"I didn't know the Indians drank kava," I say.

"No, not the Indians," Abel says. "Suva people," and leaves it at that.

When it's time for us to go inside, Abel opens the side door. "Leave your shoes and bag out here," he says.

I hesitate, but a man seated on the floor nods reassuringly. "They okay," the man says. "No worry."

There are maybe two dozen men inside the single room, all sitting on the wooden floor, which is about fifteen feet wide and twenty-five feet long. The only illumination comes from a doorless floor-to-ceiling opening in the front wall, before which is the room's single furnishing, a mustard-colored woven mat running nearly to the back wall. A few men sit on or near the edge of the mat, but mostly it's empty. On the side of the room where we entered, the younger men sit cross-legged, and in their midst, next to the mat, is the wooden kava bowl. It looks like a shallow salad bowl or a wok, about thirty inches in diameter, smoothly polished and without decoration, and stands on four squat legs. Around the far sides of the mat are the older men, most slumped comfortably against the back wall, some with their legs stretched out, occasionally joking quietly amongst themselves and teasing one another, unlike the younger men who are nearly all silent and seem deferential to the elders.

We pick our way along the front wall to where we're shown a spot at the corner of the mat, near the large opening and opposite the elders. A man slides to one side to allow Beth to sit down, just off the mat. There were no other women in the room when we entered, but now two women, perhaps brought in for Beth's benefit, are led through the corner door to sit among the younger men.

I seat myself cross-legged on the corner of the mat. It doesn't seem to satisfy my hosts, and a few men grunt and gesture for me to move a little more off the corner, crowding me into another man who makes no effort to move and doesn't seem to mind my being practically on top of him. My neighbors scrutinize me silently, and then another man reaches over and shifts my angle slightly so I'm more perpendicular to the mat.

We have no idea who the chief is. The most likely candidate is an older fellow who has a tiny plastic radio next to him that plays soft, static-filled traditional Fijian music. Everybody is a little glassy-eyed, which isn't surprising considering they've been drinking kava all day.

A man next to me nods in a friendly greeting. I quietly tell him our story about wanting to thank the chief and saying goodbye. In a low voice he introduces himself as Sere, SAY-ray, or something like that, and asks me the usual questions. He's older, but not as old as the elders. His skin is very dark, and deep cracks crisscross the thickly calloused soles of his bare feet. He slouches lazily on one elbow, in a more casual posture than almost anybody else in the room. Like many of the elders, he wears a sleepy smile and looks to be enjoying himself, in contrast to the quietly serious younger men.

Abel moves freely through the group, still wearing the Revos and guarding his bag of cigarettes, as if he carries some higher status or is the most clear-headed. He comes and goes several times, then finally shows up with two plastic jugs, one blue and one black. Both jugs are smudged with greasy dirt, and, from the heavy way he handles them, are apparently full of some liquid, maybe water for the kava. While I watch him set the jugs on the mat near the bowl, another man tugs my sleeve and points to a spot an inch to my right, adjusting my position one more time. I slide over, imperceptibly, and he nods in approval.

Conversation stops. The old man with the radio starts to mumble quietly, and stares through the open door, at nothing I can see. The man next to him shuts off the radio. Everybody listens, and at the first break in his speech, they all say, "Vinaca," which we've been using with the understanding that it's a word of thanks. He goes on like this for several minutes, in Fijian, and at each pause the men say something, sometimes in unison, other times not. Beth and I sit reverently, our heads half bowed in case this is a blessing or prayer, though not everybody in the room has a lowered head.

At the end of this speech, Abel slowly claps his cupped hands together several times, making a muffled popping sound. He recites a few phrases that are followed by murmured responses from the men, and then prostrates himself before the two jugs with his arms extended and his hands laid across their tops. After a lengthy pause, he raises his head. Everybody says "Ho!" and there is more hand popping, in which we join. Most of the clapping is together, but several clap to rhythms of their own.

Abel leaves with the two jugs and another young man brings in an even larger jug, this one translucent and about three-quarters full of murky water. The man tending the bowl reaches into a plastic bag and takes out a handful of yaquona powder, which he places in the middle of a large square of torn rag, then folds the rag and holds it with one hand in the bowl. While the other man slowly pours, he kneads the rag and sluices it through the water, which turns from merely yellow-brown to full-blown muddy brown.

When they've prepared four or five liters, another man fills a coconut bowl and presents it to one of the elders. The elder pops his hands once, accepts the bowl and drains it while the bearer stands to the side, popping his hands together slowly. The elder finishes it, grunts "Ho!" and hands the bowl back. He concludes by popping his hands together twice. Another young man dips a bowl, and the two bowl bearers work their way around the room, in opposite directions, starting with the men on either side of the first elder. Eventually it's my turn. I imitate the procedure, draining the bowl, saying "Ho!" and popping my hands together. I'm immediately buzzing again.

Beth whispers to me she only got a half-bowl. "Low tide," she says, a term Mary Alice told us about. "Probably the women's portion. Thank goodness."

Though everybody has been served, it doesn't seem the appropriate moment to jump up and excuse ourselves. Quiet conversations resume, so I turn to my mat-mate, Sere. "How often do you do this?" I ask.

He seems puzzled. "Every day," he says, as if, what did I expect?

"Really?" I ask. "Every day?"

"Yes, every day. After we go to the fields or go fishing."

"So work first, then kava," I say. "How late does this go on?"

"Oh, eight o'clock, nine o'clock. Maybe later. After dark."

That's a lot of kava, I think to myself. "All the men?" I ask.

"Yes," he says, "all the men."

Not true; the school teacher, probably one of the more educated men in the village, isn't here, and seemed decidedly uneasy about getting too close to the chief's house lest he get pulled inside. While we were talking with Abel, we saw him kicking the soccer ball with the kids.

"Women, too?" Beth asks. Earlier we wondered how the women felt about all this kava quaffing.

Sere laughs. "Yes, some women drink kava!"

It's a light laugh. Kava is a gentle high. Mild. Quiet. I can't imagine a Fijian coming home after a night around the kava bowl and beating the wife and kids, which might be the case with alcohol abuse.

Perhaps these sessions are integral to the village's sense of community. If so, it's a male-dominated community. Even at the track meet, the men stayed apart from the women and children. What kind of community is that? Wouldn't it be better if the kava drinkers were home with their families? Of course not many women drink kava. They have to take care of the kids, since the men aren't doing it.

It's time to go, I think, yet I don't make any move to leave. In fact, I don't feel like doing much of anything except sitting here and listening to quiet voices purling me away. The room darkens. Abel appears again, carrying what looks to be a large, curved tooth, attached at either end to a woven reed necklace. He places the tooth and necklace on the mat, and everybody stops talking. Able inspects the necklace, and then moves it a little further onto the mat. After a few more delicate adjustments, he's satisfied and backs away. My legs are going to sleep, but I'm afraid to shift them, in case I'll be out of position again.

Another elder starts a low-volume mumble and we go through the responsive chant routine again. It seems like some kind of ritual, spiritual in nature, but I also suspect it's as much a way to pace themselves between hits out of the kava bowl. After a round of hand pops, Abel approaches the tooth and prostrates himself. He sings a single tremulous tone that gradually drops in pitch and fades away. As it ends, everybody says "Ho!" and does a few more hand pops. Abel scoops up the tooth and leaves.

I turn to Cracked Feet, which is how I've begun to think of my mat-mate. "Sperm whale tooth?" I ask. The guidebook said such items were considered among a village's most prized possessions.

The gears grind behind Sere's eyeballs while he thinks over what I said. He deciphers it and smiles. "Yes!" he nods. "Sperm whale tooth!"

"Was that a blessing?" I ask. He cocks his head and blinks. "Like a prayer?"

"Ah, yes," he says. "Like a prayer." From his expression, I suspect it wasn't really a prayer, which reaffirms my suspicions that this is something they do to spread out the kava drinking.

Another round of bowls makes its way through the group. I drain mine and turn to Beth. We have to leave or we'll never make it back to the boat; I don't want to sleep on the floor, even if it is the chief's floor. "Outta here?" I ask. She nods. I tell Cracked Feet we need to go while it's still light enough to find our way down the trail.

"Okay," he says, unperturbed. "Shake hands around the circle."

We still don't know who the chief is as we work our way through the room, careful not to step on the mat. The men are gracious, and we say thank you and bula and goodbye on our way out the corner door. After recovering our shoes and pack, we retreat through the village where the kids and women call out goodbye and hello and very fine, thank you. There's still no sign of food being prepared. When do these people eat?

We reach the beach. The sky is a blend of peach and magenta, silhouetting the lacy palm trees on nearby Denham Island like a painted diorama. Graceful *Atlantean* bobs contentedly on the purple and silver ripples. Peace and well-being suffuse the warm evening air, and the dinghy glides through the water, effortlessly. Beth and I exchange no words, offer no commentary. There's no need.

It's the kava glow.

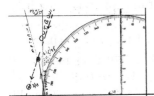

THE
HORSEWOMAN'S TALE

CARVED INTO THE MOUNTAINSIDE above Zihuatenejo, overlooking the bay, is a villa as opulent as any on the French Riviera, with gleaming white walls, red-tiled roofs, terraces, fountains, and a swimming pool. Dark green hedges, trimmed palm trees, and flowering plumeria bushes stand in verdant contrast to the surrounding dry, rocky hills. Several hundred meters down the villa's steep entrance drive is a gate, where armed soldiers maintain a watch and patrol the grounds, towed by vicious dogs. According to my fellow cruisers, the villa once belonged to the recently deceased Commandant of the Mexican Federal Police. On an annual salary equivalent to US $25,000, he was able to amass seven such residences throughout the country. While the Commandant was still alive, Mexico's much ballyhooed anti-corruption forces were unwilling to go after him. Now that he's dead, the government has made a show of seizing the residences. The man's widow has filed suit, no doubt inspired by Imelda Marcos, pleading impoverishment, and demanding the return of her "homes."

Late one afternoon Joel drives *Atlantean's* inflatable yellow dinghy past the broad beach near the corner of the bay, where Mexican fishermen gather to unload their catch, mend their nets, and socialize. The descending sun, still hot, glitters red and gold from the villa's west windows. We weave our way through the high-prowed *pangas* and dilapidated motorboats moored in the flat-calm, smelly inner harbor. When the murky brown water is only six inches deep, Joel kills the outboard and tilts it forward so its propeller won't drag in the sand. Luke and I jump out as the dinghy slows and grab its side ropes to pull it ashore. Before we've gone more than a few steps, a half-dozen young boys, as dark and lean as a handful of twigs and wearing only ragged shorts or bathing suits, run toward us, laughing and splashing.

"No, gracias, no necessario, no amigos, gracias," I tell them. The boys ignore my protests and jostle for position on the dinghy's sides and behind it, getting in our way as we carry the dinghy above the high tide mark. They prance around us while we gather up our shoes and daypacks, and the younger ones horseplay, slapping each other and kicking sand.

"One dollar," the oldest urchin demands for ushering our dinghy safely to shore.

"No, muchachos, no dolares. Dulces." It's important to keep laughing so they won't take revenge on the inflatable after we're gone. I toss a handful of cellophane-wrapped candies onto the sand. The boys fight for them happily and run away when another cruiser's dinghy approaches, except for the youngest, who's no more than five or six. He's come up empty-handed in the scramble and now beseeches me with sad brown eyes. I regard him with a solemn frown and hold out my closed fists. When I open them, in one is a candy and in the other a peso. The boy shrieks with delight, grabs the candy, and runs off to join his friends.

The beach is next to the concrete pier used by the larger fishing boats, at the head of which is the office for the fishermen's co-op. A metal spiral staircase winds around a pole on the outside of the building, leading to a gated second-story balcony facing the bay. PRI flags—green, white, and red—the emblem of the country's powerful "Revolutionary" party, flutter from the balcony's wrought-iron railing. Leaning against the staircase is a cocoa-colored man in dark corduroy pants and a red ball cap, who cools his belly in the Mexican fashion, rolling his clean white tee shirt above his little beer paunch. Behind the fishermen's pier is an open sewage ditch leading to a fetid lagoon. The cruiser scuttlebutt says there are ambitious plans to dredge the channel and the lagoon, and build yet another marina complex for the gringo yachties. There's little doubt the proper *mordida* will be paid, the government will provide financing, and marina construction will commence. Whether it's ever finished is another question.

We rinse the sand and sludge from our feet under the water tap next to the co-op office, and put on our sandals. Though the street kids drink out of the tap, I've decided not to trust it. The government's policy is to invest in water treatment facilities for the marinas and fancy hotels, rather than a reliable municipal water supply. Residents of Zihuatenejo who can afford it buy bottled water.

Joel and Luke, the two young Canadians who have signed on to crew for me as far as Tahiti, are playing basketball this evening at the lighted courts along the waterfront, near the town square. They're talented athletes and taller than most Mexicans, and have become regular participants in the constant stream of pick-up games, where their jump shots communicate better than the Spanish they don't speak. They set out after agreeing to meet me at the dinghy at 2200. I've decided to treat myself to a rare restaurant dinner, after which I plan to stroll through the town, when it will be cool and the streets will be alive with people.

All around are banners (in English) announcing the "International Fishing Contest" going on this week. Several large sportfishing boats with triple-decked flying bridges are tied up alongside the pier. Young men wipe down the brightwork and arrange sturdy gold- and silver-reeled fishing poles, working only hard enough to appear busy. I walk down the pier a little way toward a flatbed truck onto which four men, wearing heavy gloves and stained work clothes, are heaving huge fish.

Every day this week dozens of magnificent marlins, dorados, and rainbow runners (wahoo) have been brought to the pier where they're measured and weighed, then dangled beside *norte americano* fishermen posing for photographic proof of their prowess (and thus no doubt compensating for the tiny appendages cowering inside their undershorts). There are daily prizes for the biggest catch (by species), the most fish (by weight), and grand prizes for both categories over the course of the tournament, thereby maximizing the slaughter. After the judges' review and the photographs, the fish are forgotten, left in the sun to stink and to provide a feast for the flies. At the end of the day the carcasses are hauled away to be ground into animal feed. Or so we're told. Catch and release has yet to catch hold in Zihuatenejo, and probably won't until there aren't enough fish left for the local fishermen to make a living.

Turning from the revolting scene, I notice a gringa has come onto the pier and stands looking out across the water. It's hard to determine her age, perhaps a little older than I, no more than mid-forties. Her stance is erect, and her strong, confident bearing is attractive. I stroll towards her for a closer look and perhaps some conversation. She's dressed like a cruiser—Birkenstocks and khaki shorts—and her skin is tanned and weathered, but firm, and radiates vitality. Beside her on a short leash is a medium-sized black and tan german shepherd, who watches me and growls softly at my approach.

"*Hasso*," she says to the dog, "*sei ruhig.*" She's German, the second-most common tourist we've been encountering along the coast of Mexico. Hasso stops growling, but keeps a wary eye on me.

"*Ein schöner Hund,*" I say. Nice dog.

"*Sind Sie deutsch?*" she asks.

"*Nein. Amerikaner.*"

"Where do you learn to speak German?" she asks, in accented English.

"I studied for two semesters at *Universität Freiburg* in the Black Forest. That was twenty years ago. Where did you learn to speak English?"

"I live in Kansas, on a farm."

"What brings you down here?"

"I come to look at the sailing boats."

I introduce myself and say I'm traveling aboard one such boat. Her name is Jana (YAH-nah), and she's a former ocean sailor. "Not for ten years," she says. I tell her I'm about to walk into town for dinner and ask if she'd like to join me.

"Sure," she says, pronouncing it *shoo-er*, "but they may not like that we have the dog."

"We can ask."

We stop at a restaurant called *Victor y Paco*, which offers open-air tables separated from the street by a low painted wall. Strings of bare colored lights and baskets of plastic flowers hang from the roofless rafters. It's too early for the Mexicans to go out to dinner, so the place is nearly deserted. The waiter is happy to have two tourists, even with their dog, and shows us to a corner table where Hasso won't discourage potential diners. We order margaritas, and Hasso lies obediently at Jana's feet. Over dinner and another round of drinks, Jana tells me her story.

She was born on a horse farm in Northern Germany in the decade after World War II. "I learned to ride when I was four years old," she says. "My father was very skilled in training horses. He did not break them, like you Americans do. He was gentle. He told me a horse must learn to trust you and to like you. When the horse has learned, the horse will obey you, because he wants to please you, not because he is afraid."

Jana came of age during the student protest days of the late sixties and early seventies. "It was a very exciting time in Germany," she says. "Everybody is very left, a communist or a radical, and is talking about a revolution, not like the Russians or the East Germans, but how one day everybody will be free. I met a man at university, a leader of the student party, and we lived together for a long time. His friends came over to our flat to talk about solidarity with the people. 'We will go to Chile and throw over Pinochet,' they said, or 'We will fight with the Cubans for the people of Angola and Mozambique.' But they never go anywhere, they never make anything, they only talk, and drink beer, and call each other comrade." As she tells me this, I think of my own generation's heady optimism during those same days: ending the Vietnam war, Nixon's resignation from office, free love, psychedelic drugs, and flower children. From there we somehow fell into the greed and self-centeredness of the Reagan years. How did it all go wrong?

After university, Jana worked as a school teacher near Hamburg until she was thirty, then decided it was time to see the world. She'd heard about a big sailing ship out of Bremerhaven that was taking working passengers to South America and Africa, so she paid her 5,000 Deutsch Marks and joined up with about twenty other people. "We got on the ship and sailed it to the Atlantic. We stopped at Lisbon and the Azore Islands and then went to Brazil. The people owning the ship were not honest. We paid a lot of money, but they gave us bad food and the ship was always breaking. People were very angry."

Disgusted with the ship but enchanted by the sea, Jana got off in Rio and stayed with some German relatives in the area, part of the extensive German community in both Brazil and Argentina dating back to before the Second World War. She bought herself a little eight-meter sailboat she could handle herself, and set out with the dog, Hasso, which her relatives had given her so she wouldn't be alone.

"I sailed to Argentina, to Buenos Aires," she says. "When it was almost winter, I sailed back to Brazil and then to Guyana and Venezuela. In Aruba I met a man, an American, he was also sailing alone. His name is Philip. I like that name, because it means he loves horses. He had a boat like mine. We sailed our boats together, to Colombia, and Nicaragua, and Belize.

"I became pregnant from Philip. We are still sailing and take our two boats through the Panama Canal and to Costa Rica on the Pacific Ocean. We wanted to go to Tahiti but I am pregnant, so we go to Mexico. I am getting really big in Mexico. It was almost time for the baby. We stopped in a bay near a little village named Pechilinquillo. It is very nice, so we stayed there to wait for the baby."

I recall the place. *Atlantean* spent a peaceful night in its sheltered anchorage on our way down the coast from Navidad. We didn't visit the small fishing village at the opposite end of the bay.

"The people are very kind to us," Jana continues. "The women see that I am having a baby, so they take care of me. Philip speaks Spanish, and I learn pretty fast. A young couple, Arturo and Teresa, let us stay with them in their house. No doctor is in the village. When it is time for the baby, a *Hebamme,* a birthing-woman is with me. The baby is a girl, and we name her Teresa, after our friend. The priest baptizes her, and Arturo and Teresa are her god-parents."

Though the people were very poor, everybody had enough to eat. Philip, Jana, and the baby Teresa lived in the village for another six months. Philip fished with the men, while Jana sewed clothing with the women, worked in the gardens, cleaned, and helped with the children. Hasso ran with the other dogs in the village, and barked when strangers came.

"When little Teresa has grown enough, we leave Pechilinquillo. The people have a big *fiesta* for us. I am very sorry to go away and leave these people. They made us feel welcome. We belonged to the village, like we have always lived there. Arturo and Teresa were like my brother and my sister."

They sailed up the coast in separate boats, stopping almost every night. Jana had Teresa aboard her boat, and Hasso went with Philip. They eventually got to Southern California, where they had a difficult time with the immigration authorities until they went through a formal marriage ceremony. Stuck for a way to support themselves, they sold their boats and moved in with Philip's aging parents on the family farm in Kansas, though Philip hated farm life and had run off to L.A. to get away from it. Two more children followed, and Jana bought a few horses, training them in the ways her father had taught her. She was soon highly regarded for her gentle methods and now has a waiting list a year long for horses to train. Unfortunately, Philip resented her success as much as he hated farm work, and refused to help out. After his parents retired to Arizona, he leased out the cropland and demanded that the family move to Los Angeles. Jana refused to go, so they divorced, and a bank loan enabled Jana to buy him out. Philip took their Volkswagen bus and announced he was heading for South America.

"I went with the children to town that day," she says, "because I did not want them to see him drive away. When I came back, I learned he took Hasso with him. It made me very angry, because he only did it to hurt me. He knows how much I love Hasso."

In Mexico, Philip stopped in Pechilinquillo and left the dog with Arturo and Teresa. Jana received a postcard from Philip two weeks ago, postmarked from Guatemala, telling her if she wanted Hasso back, she'd have to pick him up in Pechilinquillo.

"I am so angry with Philip," she says, "but of course I must get Hasso, to bring him home. I leave my work and my children and I fly to Acapulco and go with the bus to Pechilinquillo.

"When I come to the village, everybody is very sad. One day before I come, Arturo is having an argument with a man from another village. Arturo says the man has stolen some of his fishing lines. The other man goes away, but Arturo is very angry. He drinks rum with the other men in the village. When he is very drunk, he takes a pistol from his pocket. He says he will kill this man from the other village. No one knows where he gets this pistol, because it is very hard to buy weapons in Mexico. They are strongly forbidden.

"Two policemen come. Arturo is on the beach with his pistol. He is very drunk, and shouts he will kill this man. The whole village is watching. Teresa cries and calls to Arturo to throw down the pistol and come home. When the police order Arturo to throw down the pistol, he waves it in the air. They shoot him. Eight shots. Arturo falls in the water. When they pick up his pistol, they see it is old and rusty and has no bullets. The police get in their car and drive away. That's all. They drive away.

"Arturo and Teresa have six children. The only money comes from Arturo's fishing. There is no insurance in Mexico, no welfare. I gave Teresa all of my money and stayed with her for four days. She is crying all of the time. I cook for her children and the guests who are coming to the house. Yesterday we buried Arturo. The village priest said a funeral mass. Arturo's brother bought a little cross for the grave, and we decorated it with flowers. The village will take care of the family. It is all the help there is.

"I left Pechilinquillo this morning. Tomorrow Hasso and I go with the bus to Acapulco, and fly to Kansas."

As darkness falls, the restaurant fills with people. Some are *norte americanos* and some are Mexicans, perhaps on holiday themselves. No one seems to notice Hasso lying under our table. A couple of strolling mariachis—a guitar player and a violinist dressed in black jackets, chaps, and sombreros—insists on playing us a song. Tiny white balls jiggle from the seams of their jackets and pants while they sing and sway to the music. I give them a few coins.

"*Gracias, mis amigos.*"

We get up to leave so they won't play us another song.

Jana says she has to go to her hotel because she's catching the early bus to Acapulco. I accompany her to a small but respectable looking place that has a dozen or so rooms overlooking a central courtyard. The desk clerk casts me a suspicious glance, so I say good-bye to her in the street.

I wander back through town, towards the waterfront. Now that it's night, people have come out. They visit in groups on street corners, lean over balconies, buy flowers and comestibles from street vendors. All around is the pleasant buzz of laughter, conversation, and music, vibrant and alive. The streets are narrow and arranged haphazardly, and automobile traffic has been diverted around the central area. The city has a hospitable, human feel. And yet there are the ever-present signs of hardship and sorrow. Impoverished four-foot tall Amerindian women, wearing blankets and braids down to their knees, hurry from one pedestrian to another offering matchbook-size bobble-head toucans and turtles, while their impossibly tiny sad-eyed daughters hold out two-packs of Chiclets gum for me to buy. A grizzled blind man, his back braced against a lamppost, sings a forlorn and endless ballad in a raspy, tuneless tenor, while passers-by drop coins into the woven bag at his feet.

So many stories, so many contrasts. The extravagant villa on the mountainside, the simple village of Pechilinquillo. A city full of life and laughter, a country where death is quick and meaningless. A widow who depends on her village for survival, another who sues to regain her plundered riches. A woman who respects horses as fellow living beings, *norte americanos* who break their horses, who kill for sport.

It's a large world out there, larger than any of us can imagine. What difference does it make in our daily lives that the great pelagic species are being fished to near extinction, that there is corruption among the rich and powerful, that people everywhere suffer from poverty and cruelty? For the vast majority of humankind, the sun will rise in the morning and life will go on. For me, there will be food to eat, clean water to drink, clothes for my body, and a comfortable, dependable boat that provides me with all the home I need. Few of these tragedies affect us directly, and even if they do, how can we possibly combat the rampant injustice around us?

For every such story we hear, there are countless thousands that remain untold, at least to our ears. And yet hearing any one, we can't help but sympathize, we can't help but be saddened, we can't help but believe that the world is a poorer place, for the suffering of so many. Stories such as these are the simple voices of humanity calling to us, resonating within us, and reminding us that we are all part of the great fabric of life on Earth, beautiful in all of its sorrow, and mournful in its joy.

BUNGEES AND BAGPIPES

I'M SITTING ON A WOODEN PLATFORM that's attached to the side of the Skipper's Canyon Bridge, 230 feet above the Shotover River, an hour's jet-boat ride from Queenstown, in the rugged heart of New Zealand's Southland. Four young men in sturdy back-country shoes and shorts, one of them a burly Maori with an amazing jade fish hook hanging from his neck, are safety-harnessed to the bridge supports and watch over me. The fat-free muscles, the sun- and chemical-bleached hair and golden skin, the assorted tattoos and piercings, the screeching low-volume rock on the boom box behind us, their carefree slang-studded banter, all remind me I'm no longer a member of the younger generation. At least they call me "Mate," instead of "Sir."

"Good as gold," one of them says, now that the towel and straps are wrapped around my ankles. "Up you go." They help me to my feet and lead me to the edge of the platform. I have to shuffle and am surprised by the weight of the bungee cord dragging behind me. The woman who took the plunge before me looked plenty scared but didn't hesitate, and the expression on her face when she shot back up to almost bridge level was one of pure elation.

"There you are, toes over the edge, Mate. Spot on." They're still holding me from behind and I'm looking where my feet are, not at

45

the river below. As soon as they let go, I raise my eyes because I don't want to see how far down it is; though my feet are firmly planted on the platform, I'm no longer sure I can stay upright. My stomach is churning and sending its contents both up my throat and down into my bowels, encouraging me to loose both ends. With the other jumpers, the crew counted, "Three, two, one, BUNGEE!" but now when they start their chant, I look down and for the first time actually contemplate how far away the river is. The adrenaline surges and I feel my resolve draining down the toilet I wish I were sitting on. If I wait for "BUNGEE!" I'll never go, so at "one" I flex my knees, throw my arms out like Jesus on the cross, and launch myself into space.

My first thought is, "You stupid idiot," because I've just thrown my life away for nothing. This self-loathing lasts only a fraction of a second, however, because I'm suddenly amazed at the noise—something I hadn't even considered, but which now seems vitally interesting—as the air roars past and peels back my eyelids and hair as if I were standing behind a jet engine. The amazement lasts only another fraction of a second, because my eyes have locked on the water, which I'm racing towards at an impossible rate of speed. My body decides there's no point in saving any adrenaline, now that death is a soon-to-be certainty, and dumps the whole load into my bloodstream.

In the grip of an almost exquisite, fatalistic fear, and with the on-rushing river filling my field of vision, I completely fail to notice at what point I'm no longer falling, but rather am accelerating upwards, away from the river. I'm pleasantly surprised that there was no jerk as the bungee took hold, no noticeable strain on my back or ankles, but that mild, passing pleasure is utterly overwhelmed by the joy I experience at my discovery that I haven't died. I look up to see the bridge coming towards me, realize I forgot to scream, and open my lungs to cut loose with the loudest howl I can muster. Happy, expectant faces are looking over the side of the bridge at happy me looking up at them, and I think to myself, "Do a flip." My body obliges, rather more easily than I had hoped, and off I go again, over the top and back down. This time it's fun, and I'm laughing while I'm screaming—wild, convulsive yelps of joy—and I'm able to pay more attention to reversing direction.

It's over in no time. The crew lets me yo-yo through four or five bounces before slacking the bungee and lowering me towards the water and the jet-boat that has roared into position below. At some point during the last five or ten seconds my body was alerted to the overdose of adrenaline, and counteracted it with a flood of endorphins.

So now I'm hanging upside down from my ankles, ten feet above the water, in love with life, in love with the world, in love with the river and the boat and the bungee cord. A crewman reaches a long pole up to me. "Grab the pole," he shouts, but I'm not interested in the pole. I'm right where I want to be, basking in a rapturous afterglow deeper and more satisfying than the best post-coital warmth I've ever known, happy to stay this way all afternoon if they'll let me. "It's okay," I say, "I'm fine," and swing through a few lazy arcs. But the boatman is insistent, and takes a few stabs at me, like I'm some giant piñata, until I come to my senses and grab hold, at which point the bridge crew lowers me the rest of the way into the boat.

"Good ride?" one of the boatmen asks.

"I love you guys," I say, and sprawl atop a bench seat as they remove my restraints. Together we roar up the river to a rocky beach, where a slew of other happy bungeers waits to greet me.

When I arrive in Auckland, New Zealand, after a two-week passage from Fiji, I almost feel as if I've come home to Seattle. It's the same kind of city: the high-rise central business corridor concentrated around the expansive waterfront, industry and ocean shipping off to the side, tidy residential neighborhoods spreading across the rolling hills, plenty of green trees and parks, and nearby Hauraki Gulf so much like Puget Sound. I take a temporary moorage in the sprawling West Haven Marina, near downtown, and a few days later move to a longer-term slip in the smaller and cheaper Westpark Marina five miles west of the city, on the other side of Waitemata Harbour. There to help me tie up are the New Zealanders Hilton and Melva from the boat *Spindrift*, whom I met in Tonga. They invite me to "tea" that evening, which I find out is dinner, and fill me in on the local knowledge I'll need to get around.

I'm part of the annual mass migration to New Zealand from all over the Pacific. The Harbormaster at Opua in the Bay of Islands, where I went through check-in procedures, told me that the country's various ports of entry expected to process some five hundred cruising sailboats escaping South Pacific typhoon season. Since it's almost the beginning of Southern Hemisphere summer, it's a perfect time to be back in the high-latitudes. Check-in was a lengthy, but unhurried process, partly because the officials, like other Kiwis I've met, were willing to settle in for a long chat, "a good natter," as I've heard them call it. One of the officials was from the Ministry of Agriculture and Forestry, which enforces New Zealand's strict rules against importing anything that might carry pests or diseases. Not only is all fresh produce incinerated, but also canned and packaged goods unless they originate in New Zealand, Australia, or the U.S. "New Zealand is an insignificant little country, but we've one of the world's healthiest agricultural environments," the official explained. "Our reputation is our calling card when we sell our produce abroad. We don't want it crook with the rest of the world's bugs."

Whatever they're doing, it seems to be working: New Zealand is a country to fall in love with. Geographically, it's like slicing a strip of coastal North America from L.A. to Vancouver, B.C., towing it 1,200 miles out to sea, and draining it of all but about four million people. The approaching Christmas season, signaled by the blossoming of the lovely red and green pohutukawas, means the start of summer vacations, and instead of cocooning around hearth and home, Kiwis (which is how the New Zealanders refer to themselves) hit the road. I buy a cheap used car and take a couple of weeks to tour the lower half of North Island, which is a hotbed of geological activity—dormant volcanoes, hot springs, and geysers—and one afternoon find myself engaged in something called "black water rafting," a guided inner-tube tour of underground limestone caves full of glow worms and running streams. South Island, which is accessible via a ferry from Wellington, the nation's capital, offers the Southern Alps and Fjordland National Park, so much like my own Pacific Northwest home. Everywhere I travel are mountains, pine forests (some rather annoyingly planted in straight rows), pristine trout fishing lakes and rivers, and well-maintained hiking trails. I stay in hostels called "Backpackers," where a sheeted mattress (often in a shared room) and common cooking, eating, and "ablution" facilities, cost only around $10/night. In the hostels' television rooms, where *Simpsons* reruns play to a host of scruffy and multi-pierced European vagabonds, I leave signs advertising a crew position for passage to Australia.

Culturally, it's as if New Zealand's clock has been turned back to the 1950s, when people weren't afraid to treat strangers as guests. While we cruisers may not be as free spending as the daily 747s full of Japanese tourists, the Kiwis go out of their way to make me feel welcome. Their country offers practically everything a jaded American could want—fantastic natural scenery, violent crime almost non-existent, progressive environmental policies, racial relations with the growing population of Maoris and South Pacific Islanders simmering but not explosive—but New Zealanders act as if the U.S.A. and Americans have achieved standards the poor Kiwis can only dream about.

When I'm standing in line at a grocery store and the clerk hears my American accent, he or she is sure to start a conversation. "My sister has a boy in Seattle," one will say. "Works for Microsoft, you know. She was there for a visit last month. Loved the place, absolutely loved it." If people are in line behind me, rather than exhibiting annoyance at the clerk's taking time to natter, they're likely to join in, eager to share their own stories about Disney World, the Grand Canyon, or Mt. Rushmore. Once, when four of us Americans are touring in my car, we're held captive by a talkative shop owner in Christchurch. By now we've learned, and one by one we slip away when the man's eye-contact shifts to one of our companions. Finally only poor Catherine is left to listen to the man, and we're laughing when she comes out to the car several minutes later. "Don't *ever* leave me alone with those people again," she says.

But New Zealand's attractions for the weary blue-water sailor go beyond the scenic wonders, the friendly people, and shelter from tropical storms. For the first time in over a year I'm in a modern western country where I speak the language and don't stand out as a stranger. Boat maintenance projects that have been put off too long can be taken care of simply and efficiently. There is access to long-distance telephones, fax machines, and e-mail, the post office is reliable, and electronic bank transfers are quick and inexpensive. Driving on the wrong side of the road takes some getting used to, as do the roundabouts, but those problems are solved more easily than searching for engine parts in Polynesia. And though I live aboard *Atlantean*, and regularly avail myself of the fine coastal sailing the country has to offer, it's as if my stay in New Zealand is an extended vacation away from cruising, a chance to relax and recharge myself for the real work that lies ahead—ushering my thirty-nine foot sailboat the rest of the way around the world.

North Island's Hauraki Gulf is protected from the swells of the Pacific by Coromandel Peninsula and a series of volcanic islands, the largest of which is Great Barrier Island. Great Barrier's rugged humps and shoulders culminate in 2,000-foot Mt. Hobson, known to the Maori as Hirakimata. One afternoon in the midst of Southern Hemisphere summer, I drop anchor in an arm of Port Fitzroy, on the western side of the lightly populated island, where the shoreline is too steep for houses or other development. A dinghy ride to shore and a short walk bring me to the hiking trail through the State Forest and up Hirakimata.

It's an all-day hike, an invigorating trek amidst towering kingferns, pencil-thin pines, and gnarled hardwoods. There are even a few isolated remnants of the island's once mighty kauri forests, enormous conifers that were too well-suited for shipbuilding, and were cut down here and elsewhere in the days before New Zealand's enlightened environmental ethic. The trail is superbly maintained with carpentered staircases and railings on the steep faces worthy of one's home deck, and the view from atop is panoramic, stretching to Auckland and the snow-capped mountains beyond. On the way down, I refresh myself in a waterfall-fed pool of clear mountain water.

It's early evening by the time I return to the boat, another high summer's day drawing to a close. Sun-stoked smells of earth and pine-duff fill the air, along with the sizzle and buzz of countless cicadas. Lengthening shadows creep down Great Barrier's flanks, promising a welcome coolness after the day's heat. The bay has accumulated twenty other boats, sail and power, all flying the New Zealand flag and most rafted together in groups of two or more. Dinghies of gregarious Kiwis crisscross the anchorage, congregating for the evening's beers and barbecues.

Pleasantly weary from my trek, and enjoying a beer of my own, I lounge in the cockpit and follow the sun's descent, until its lower limb grazes the uppermost ridge to the southwest. With surprising swiftness, the hillsides' golden-greens succumb to shadow. When the last sliver of sun disappears, it steals with it the day's whisper of breeze. The cicadas' buzz ceases, and there's a silence on the bay, almost as if the world were holding its breath.

From nowhere, or from everywhere, two faint bass notes resonate in an open octave, as if giving voice to the hum of the Earth itself. Like a sacred summons, ancient but never forgotten, the *basso* warms and builds into the recognizable drone of a bagpipe, the skirl of a lone piper on some unseen perch. The reedy chanter twines into the hollow of the drone, and *Scotland the Brave* commences its solemn procession across the emerald waters. Quavering here, warbling there, the familiar anthem flows freely, yet patiently, like a rill of liquid silver trickling into a pool. My spirit lifts with the tilt of the cadence, then settles peaceably into the satisfying conclusion. The piper repeats the refrain, this time more triumphantly, embellishing the simple melody with flickering mordents and deft grace notes.

We listen, all of us in the anchorage, transfixed. The sunset's gathering color powders the cloudless sky, the island's darkening embrace enfolds us, and the water's luminous mirror suspends all notions of time and space. The piper lingers on the final note, and the drone fades like a long sigh. I cling to the echo as if it were a tender kiss, wanting it to go on forever, yet knowing that its end is part of its perfection.

There follows a moment of reverent silence, then the anchorage erupts into cheers. Boaters clang on ships' bells, blow horns and whistles, clap their hands, shout, and stamp their feet in a spontaneous outpouring of appreciation, in which I enthusiastically join. The piper has given us a rare gift, a gift that transcends our common Anglo-European heritage, our inhabitation of this tiny antipodal outpost so far from the shores of our forebearers, and our shared interest in sailing and socializing. Caught in the warp and the weft of the piper's melody, we are grateful participants in what Joseph Campbell calls "the rapture of life." We've been joined in fellowship to celebrate *this* place, *this* sunset, and *this* moment, a confluence of events that is gone forever but will live on, always, within each of our hearts.

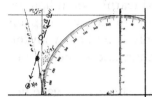

FLORENCE

ONE DAY DURING MY STAY IN BRISBANE, on Australia's eastern seaboard, I decide to visit the Queensland Museum. Admission is free, and the museum's eclectic collection of artifacts ranges from dinosaurs to computers. An exhibit that catches my eye is a small sailboat, *Acrocs Australis*, the name of which I suppose is either a reference to Australian crocodiles, or some kind of play on Acrux, the bright binary star in the constellation the Southern Cross. Only eleven feet in length, this is supposedly the smallest sailboat ever to circumnavigate the globe, manned by an Australian, of course; who else would be brash enough to attempt such an undertaking? While I'm wondering how I would even fit into such a small vessel, a comely young lass strolls over to peruse the display, and I comment aloud that I would never take such a tiny and obviously dangerous little boat out on the ocean, much less sail it around the world. When the woman agrees with me, I add, "The boat I'm sailing around the world is much larger than this." My shameless ploy works, and soon she's asking me all sorts of questions.

Her name is Florence, from Somerset, England, and she's blond, trim and pretty, about 5'3", dressed in white capris, a sleeveless cream pullover, and an adorable straw boater with tiny fresh flowers woven into its band. Her skin is deeply tanned and her face betrays no trace of make-up, but even so it glows pink and smooth with the bloom of youth. Florence's pale gray eyes grow wider when I explain how I got to Brisbane and where I'm going. "As a matter of fact," I add casually, "I'm looking for crew to help me sail the Great Barrier Reef. Do you want to come along?"

"Really?" Florence says, practically jumping out of her flip-flops. "I don' know how to sail. D'ya s'pose I could learn?" Serendipitous good fortune seems to have come my way, and I'm happy to explain how I manage all the technical sailing and only need help with the wheel while I raise the sails or drop the anchor, and somebody to stand occasional watch duty.

"I been workin', savin' up for travelin' 'round," she says. "I gave notice last week. In another week I'm free." Her accent is working-class English with a touch of Eliza Doolittle. Over coffee I find out she's been in Australia for three months working as a maid at a resort on nearby Fraser Island. Her uncle in Sydney arranged her work visa, and she's in Brisbane to attend a co-worker's wedding tomorrow. My only concern about having her aboard *Atlantean* is her age, which I guess to be around twenty-one at the most, perhaps as young as eighteen.

"Twenty-seven in February," she says when I ask. She looks hurt. "Nobody believes me. I got my passport if you want to look."

"No, no," I say. "I believe you. What fooled me is that you're so healthy compared to all these leather-skinned Aussies. Be glad you look so young."

We spend the rest of the afternoon together visiting the Art Gallery next door, where we admire the contemporary art. Florence talks about the colors and shapes she likes and tells me she hopes one day to be a professional photographer. I invite her to dinner, but she says she has plans to meet some of her co-workers from the resort. "If you're thinking about sailing with me," I say, reluctant to let her get away, "you should at least see the boat."

She walks with me back to *Atlantean*, where I take her on the ten-minute tour. "And this would be your stateroom," I say, showing her the forepeak. "We'll move out some of the gear so you'll have more space and, of course, your privacy." She's never been on a sailboat before and is dazzled by *Atlantean's* rich teak interior, as well as the compact utilitarian comfort of the galley and main salon. I make us both strong gin-and-tonics, which we sip in the cockpit in the cooling evening breezes. By the time she has to leave, we've worked out that I'll pick her up in ten days at a train station on the north side of Moreton Bay. She gives me her phone number at the resort to call a day or two before to confirm we're still on.

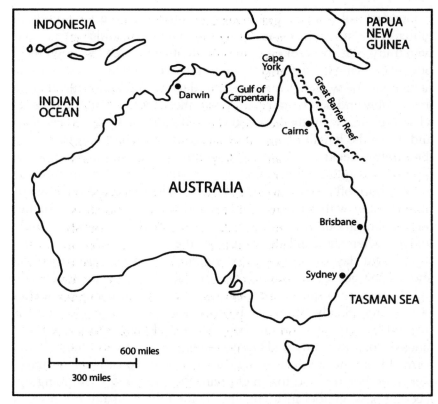

Florence is nearly beside herself with excitement that she's going sailing. "Wait'll they hear 'bout this at Fraser Island!" she says. She's like a child, giggly and giddy, and she prances up the dock, turning several times to wave. I'm smiling myself when I turn back to *Atlantean*.

Craig, the blond half of the gay couple from San Diego aboard *Pandarosa* in the slip next to mine, has been sitting in his cockpit reading a book. He looks up and arches his eyebrows. "Looks like somebody found himself crew," he says.

On the appointed day I meet Florence's train. She doesn't have a lot of baggage, but much of it consists of photographic equipment—a tripod, a collapsible reflector, a couple of carrying cases for the light meters, filters, lenses, film, and her three cameras—which a friendly porter helps her wrestle off the train, along with the single large canvas bag containing her wardrobe and personal effects. I'm surprised by all the hardware. When she told me she wanted to be a professional photographer, I assumed it to be some vague off-in-the-future goal, but she seems well on her way.

Our first sail is an easy one, six hours on the protected waters of Moreton Bay to Tangalooma, where we anchor behind a breakwater with thirty or forty weekend pleasure boats. Florence has been thoroughly enjoying herself all day, squirming with delight whenever I let her handle the wheel. After I've secured us for the night, she changes into a shiny and nearly transparent one-piece leotard that she uses for a bathing suit, swims the hundred yards to shore, and runs barefoot up and down the length of the beach. Though she's firm and fit, hers is the careless sleekness of a child, not of the workout aficionada; nor is fitness the purpose of her exertions, but rather the child's unconscious need to burn off an excess of energy and exuberance. Florence swims like she runs, with reckless abandon and without regard to form, her arms flailing about her and her head thrown back for joy. She's barely winded when she climbs back aboard the boat.

The next day we're in open water, and when Florence discovers she doesn't get seasick (as she'd feared she might), she agrees with my suggestion to sail through the night so we can make the shelter of the Great Sandy Waterway by morning. This part of the coast is marked by long stretches of beaches and elongated near-shore islands—Moreton, Curtis, and Fraser—all of them essentially huge dunes, formed from the sands washing up and down the coast of Australia. Her three hours alone that night with the Aries autopilot doing the steering pass without incident, and by the following afternoon we're anchored at White Cliffs on the inside shore of Fraser Island, the only boat in sight.

The weather turns sour and for three days we're holed up waiting for the high-wind warnings to subside. Florence runs and swims, swims and runs, and after she finds *Tetris* too hectic, I introduce her to the Game Boy's simplest challenge, *Dr. Mario*, which keeps her amused for hours at a time. I suggest we explore Fraser Island, and perhaps visit the resort where she worked, but the mention of it distresses her and she says, "I don' fancy goin' back there, never." She doesn't explain herself, and is only willing to go hiking ashore if we head in the opposite direction. The weather is warm and pleasant, though blustery, and we pass the afternoon searching for brumbies in the grassy dunes and dugongs in the shallows between the island and the mainland.

That night we exchange the sad stories of our love lives: my own too familiar refrain of a fiancée who abandoned me and our planned Bora Bora beach wedding only months before our scheduled departure; hers a tale of infidelity and deception, of a year with an older man in England who, she finally found out, cheated on her nearly the whole time they were together. The ensuing misery has put her off romance and was part of her incentive to come to Australia. "Blokes're always tryin' to get into yer knickers," she says with disgust. But then she adds, "It's not like I'm a prude, you know. A toss with a boy now an' again can be quite good fun."

Florence's lack of prudishness becomes more obvious as we work our way up the coast: to Gladstone, past Cape Capricorn and the start of the tropics, Great Keppel Island, Pearl Bay, Cape Townshend, South Percy, and onwards. She enjoys naked sunbathing, and I enjoy allowing it, though her swimming leotard, particularly when wet, has left little to my imagination. It's only two weeks before we're sharing my bed, but soon afterwards Florence turns sullen and moody and is no longer interested in our love making, and two weeks later I suggest she move back to the forepeak. She does and matters improve between us, though afterwards I'm far more careful with her.

There's more emotional baggage, I find out. On three or four occasions during our time together she calls home to her father, whom she adores, but from the bits I overhear they're one-sided conversations, Florence trying to remain upbeat and getting little or nothing in return. "Just once I wish he'd say he loves me," she tells me one day after hanging up and blinking back the tears. "I don' think he's said it his whole bleedin' life." She has no kind words for her mother, only longing for her father, who she says has always been cold and distant. There may have been a little of the father complex at play when she decided to join me in bed, and equally when she left it.

Florence is a product of the English class system, still prevalent even in these supposedly more progressive times. Her father was a semi-skilled factory worker (now pensioned), and because of her family's station in England's impermeable hierarchy, nothing much was expected of her in school. Though she says, "I got good marks," by age fourteen her teachers as much as told her she'd never amount to anything and had shunted her off to vocational classes, where they trained her to run a cash register. By sixteen she was out of school and working at low-paying jobs, on track towards her prescribed destiny of marriage to a factory worker and producing babies to supply England's demand for lower-class labor. It's highly fortuitous, and a testament to her willfulness, that she made it to age twenty-seven without succumbing to that fate.

Her lack of education is painfully obvious to her, and learning about my own multiple college degrees and various professional accomplishments only depresses her. She's convinced she'll never amount to anything if she doesn't get an education, and for the past year has set about pursuing it on her own. With no guidance how best to proceed, she hit on the idea of reading difficult books, and while we're sailing together she wrestles with Bruce Chatwin's post-modernist account of his travels through Australia, *The Song Lines*. Florence's method consists of reading until she gets to a word she doesn't understand, underlining it, and then looking it up in her small combination dictionary/thesaurus in which the definitions are on the top half of the page and the synonyms are on the bottom. She tells me she's found the dictionary definitions "too hard to suss out," and instead relies on the thesaurus, skimming through the various entries until she finds one or two she understands that seem to fit the sense of what she's reading. It's a slog, and Florence manages only about three pages per session. One day I pick up the book and find she's underlined twelve words on a single page. "Florence," I say, "you don't have to look these up. You can ask me." She's amazed I know them all, and for a few days we proceed with me helping her, but it only contributes to her feelings of inferiority and the tensions between us that sleeping together seem to have generated, and we eventually give it up.

As sweet and unaffected as she is, there's as much that's coarse and uncultivated, which in a less ingenuous soul would be too annoying to tolerate for long. Her table manners are atrocious. She grips the utensils like clubs when she bothers with them at all, shoveling the food into her mouth with slurps and smacks of pleasure, and finishes meals by picking up the plate (leaving behind a plate-shaped ring of crumbs) and licking it and her face clean with her startlingly long tongue. The face gets a final wipe with the back of her hand, which in its turn gets wiped on her shirt or shorts. One day we're eating fried chicken, which Florence calls "chook," and she bites the knobs off the drumsticks and crunches them down. I flinch with each crack of bone and gristle, and when she notices my distress, she says, "What? I've always ate 'em." This happens during her moody period when she sees my implied criticisms in all of our interactions, and soon she's in tears and won't talk to me for the rest of the evening.

Personal hygiene isn't a big part of Florence's routine, and when there's a shower available at a marina, she makes do without either soap or a towel, rinsing herself off to her satisfaction and putting on her clothes over her wet body, which soon dry in the tropical warmth. She self-cuts her straight blond hair with scissors, chopping off bits that annoy her, and it shows. When it's greasy enough for a wash, she uses Joy dishwashing liquid and a swim for a salt water rinse. One day I caution her not to throw her tampons down the marine toilet because they can plug the valve, and she says, "I don' use 'em." When I respond that she shouldn't flush whatever it is that stems her menstrual flows, she replies that she doesn't use anything at all. "I hold it 'til the next time I go to the loo."

Florence's ultimate salvation may come from her interest in photography, if only she can find some way to capitalize on her obvious talent. Her life took a positive turn several years ago when she got a job in a photographer's shop. The proprietor was nearing retirement and treated her kindly, and soon she was helping him with shoots and in the darkroom, where he taught her the fundamentals of the art and encouraged her to experiment on her own. She has a small portfolio of her work with her, and I'm impressed by the quality. Almost all of the photos are in black and white, but many she's hand-painted in watercolor washes and tints, and when I ask her about them, she says, "I dunno, I thought they needed a bit o' color." Her shots of outdoor settings—an ancient farmhouse, a crumbling stone wall in a thin-grassed pasture, a winding leaf-strewn path through a woodland park—are rich in ambience and, to my untrained eye, adroitly composed. When I tell her they are at least as good as "art" greeting cards I've seen for sale, she says, "Go on, you really think so?"

But her forté, by far, is her work with people, whom she seems particularly adept at capturing in their most unselfconscious and natural postures. Her subjects are the working-class English, as common and unrefined as she, and even when they're sitting for the camera, she manages to record unguarded moments when their faces have relaxed, their eyes are bright, and their mouths are transitioning towards spontaneous laughter. In a revealing portrait of a large extended family, the adults are shown in the process of arranging themselves into a set pose—the eldest son directing traffic and the women straightening bows and collars—while the ragamuffin children are still horse-playing in the foreground. I imagine it's Florence's disarmingly cheerful demeanor and her complete lack of pretension that sets her subjects at ease and makes them forget the camera.

The many uninhabited islands inside the Great Barrier Reef provide us with both secluded anchorages and numerous settings for Florence's photos. The continental landmass of Australia has been on its own for millions of years and is said to contain some of the oldest exposed rock on Earth. Whatever the explanation, the rocks and cliffs here look like none I've ever seen, all of them somehow more rounded and weathered, as if they've been shaped by forces that don't follow the usual rules of physics. This is a semi-arid climate, like parts of Southern California, with a wide variety of succulents, salt-scrub conifers, and desert weeds, most of which are only vaguely familiar. Much is far stranger, truly alien in appearance, such as the stands we encounter of some narrow-stalked bottle-brush plant six or eight feet tall, covered with tiny blossoms and surrounded by countless butterflies, clouds of them, black with blue polka-dots on their wings. Sometimes during our explorations Florence insists we return to *Atlantean* for her complete arsenal of photographic paraphernalia in order to capture some interesting manifestation of the local flora or geology. Once when she has her tripod and camera pointed at an unusual rock formation, she says, "What this shot really needs is a nude." Since she doesn't mean my scrawny physique, she doffs her clothes, arranges herself on the rocks, and tells me when to snap the shutter.

North of Cape Capricorn the water is warm and shallow enough for coral growth, and the Great Barrier Reef begins. Though at its southern terminus it lies twenty or more miles offshore, the reef structure effectively blocks the ocean swell, and with steady ten to twenty knot southeasterlies on our tail, we enjoy some of the finest and easiest sailing I've ever known. Our Queensland cruising guide identifies scores of anchorages among the uninhabited islands inside the Reef, and most days I don't bother with the mainsail, letting us run with the wind on a poled-out headsail and the Aires windvane or the electric autopilot doing the steering. As always, I'm struck by how sparsely populated Australia is. It's rare to even see another boat, and on almost every little island where we stop, it's as if we're the first humans to land: no paths, no sheep, no fishermen shacks, no footprints in the sand.

The warmer water means I can start snorkeling again, wearing my tropical-weight wetsuit, and now and then I'm able to spear a nice fish for dinner. Florence has no great love for the taste of fish (boiled potatoes and baked beans are more to her liking, the latter often eaten cold and with much gusto directly from the can), but there's something about pulling free food out of the ocean that captures her imagination. We tow a dragline behind the boat when we're underway, and whenever we stop for the night, it's not long before Florence has baited a hook and dropped a line over the side. Her first strike comes one afternoon at anchor while she's sunbathing on the foredeck, and when I call out to her that the pole is jerking in its holder, she leaps to her feet squealing, "Fishy, fishy, fishy," and reels in as fast as she can. It's only a little four-inch reef fish, but it's the first anything she's ever caught, and she gamely poses for a photo with the prize dangling from the hook, only her sunglasses and visor keeping her from being naked as the day she was born. Her happiest catch is a twenty-five pound wahoo we bring in on the dragline, and one day it hooks a four-foot shark that she begs me to haul aboard. I refuse, but pull the shark next to the boat so she can photograph it before I remove the hook from its nose with a pair of wire cutters.

Although Florence doesn't balk at a long swim to shore, she's terrified of sharks and thinks I'm crazy to snorkel around reefs and coral where they're known to hang out. We're all the way to Airlie, a coastal tourist trap and the jump-off point for the picturesque Whitsunday Islands, before I can convince her that shark attacks are less likely than lightning strikes, and she reluctantly buys herself a mask, snorkel, and fins. A day later we anchor *Atlantean* off a little island and dinghy to nearby Manta Ray Bay, known for its good snorkeling. It's the perfect spot for Florence's introduction to the underwater world. All around us are thousands of brightly colored tropical fish, and in their midst swim two huge groupers, each about four feet long and with broad, heavy bodies. Lining the rock wall are more varieties of soft corals than I've seen in one place, and along the bottom is a tangled mass of blue-gray staghorn coral that looks like an Idaho antler dump during hunting season. Florence wears the women's black, orange, and yellow tropical wet suit I have aboard, which is only a little too large, and it protects her from the small but persistent zebra fish that nip at us whenever they get a chance. My only disappointment is the visibility, which at this time of year is no more than twenty or thirty feet, not nearly as clear as what I came to expect in the South Seas.

We saw numerous signs in Airlie for dive boats out to the Barrier Reef, and rather than pay $140 per person, the next day I decide we'll follow them to where we can dive on our own. Anchoring is prohibited, but we have no trouble finding an open mooring buoy in an area known as Bait Reef, near where three tourist boats have moored. Florence doesn't scuba, so I'm on my own, though with so many divers close by I'm not worried. The Great Barrier Reef is everything I expected it to be, except that the water clarity is again poor, only about forty feet, stirred up by the winter seas. Nevertheless I'm delighted by the mad profusion of coral—every shape and color imaginable—all of which provides habitat for innumerable species of marine life. In places the staghorn coral is like a bramble patch, so thick I can't see through to the bottom, and tiny fish dart in and out of its protective branches. The Reef itself is a maze of twists and turns, and I have to surface frequently to get my bearings. The entire area is shallow, rarely more than thirty or forty feet deep, so scuba gear isn't really necessary, and after my air runs low I swim back to *Atlantean* and persuade Florence to join me. Always on the lookout for sharks, we snorkel another hour and that afternoon go back for more.

The dive boats head back to shore, but I want to spend the night on the Reef; there's a full moon, and as the tide drops, it exposes a foot or so of the reef structure. It's pleasantly eerie being all alone out here, the water flat calm, with the low rumble of the ocean crashing a few hundred yards away. I only wish Florence and I were getting along better. This is exactly the kind of romantic adventure I've been dreaming about for years.

One reason we're not getting along so well is because Florence has been in a funk ever since our argument over a bikini contest she wanted to enter at a booze-hound bar in Airlie. She imagined it was some sort of beauty pageant, the kind that might be sponsored for teen-age girls by the local Rotarians, where she might "pick up a few quid." I tried explaining to her that the modest and frilly pink two-piece she has along (but rarely wears) isn't the bikini style they're looking for, nor could I imagine her playing to the crowd with the bumps and grinds the serious contenders will have to exhibit. Florence thought that I disapproved of her looks and was once again reminding her of her inadequacies. I defended myself by saying I was only trying to save her from what would surely be a humiliating experience, but she didn't want to hear about it. The snorkeling and diving in the following days contributed to an uneasy peace between us, and I'm hoping that our next destination, Magnetic Island, a popular gathering place for young travelers on a budget, will improve her mood.

In the morning we snorkel for another hour, then prepare the boat for the long sail to Magnetic Island, near Townsville, about 150 miles to the north. We're treated to more easy coastal sailing with steady winds, favorable currents, and line-of-sight navigation, orientating ourselves to the numerous coastal beacons that are always in sight, with lights and buoys marking any hazards. It's our second overnight sail together, and all goes well.

We arrive at the anchorage in mid-afternoon and dinghy ashore. Magnetic Island isn't huge, but there are various rustic resorts and campgrounds, hiking trails, and a few tourist amenities, all serviced by a ferry from Townsville on the mainland. Florence spots a sign for horseback rentals and the next day spends the afternoon off by herself riding on the beach. When we meet afterwards at the backpackers' pub, she's in good spirits.

The pub has large communal tables, and we join one with four or five young Europeans. English is the common language, and over dinner and several rounds of beer, everybody swaps stories about Australia and other travels. All is well until Florence leaves the table to call her father from the pub's pay phone. When she comes back, she's down in the mouth and wants to leave. "Robert's in Townsville," she says.

It takes some coaxing, but I get her to explain that Robert was a co-worker on Fraser Island who became obsessed with her. Tonight when Florence called her father in England, he told her that Robert has been trying to locate her and passed on the phone number of the hostel where he's staying, which she called. "He's been in Townsville two bloody weeks askin' after us," she says. "He wanted to come over t'night but thank God the ferry's stopped runnin'." I ask her if they were lovers on Fraser Island, but she's evasive. "I don' think he's barmy, but he was, you know, always starin' at me, followin' me around." She tells me she suspected him of spying on her during her days off when she was nude sunbathing behind some remote sand dune.

"We don't have to stay," I say. "We can up-anchor tonight and sail out of here."

"I promised him I'd meet him tomorrow night. He made me swear I'd be here."

The next night we're at another group table in the pub when Robert appears in the doorway. I've been expecting a lovestruck, sun-bleached, post-adolescent Aussie, but instead Robert is a presentable young man in his late twenties or early thirties, neatly dressed in white cotton slacks and a sports shirt, with a firm chin and carefully trimmed dark hair. If he smiled, he'd remind me of a handsome waiter in a trendy upscale restaurant, but the moment his eyes lock onto Florence, all I can think of is the serial-killer Ted Bundy. She tenses and says, "Don't leave me alone with him."

He strides to the table, never taking his eyes off Florence. "I've been looking all over for you," he says, his tone accusatory. "I need to talk to you."

All conversation at our table abruptly ceases and Florence shifts in her seat. "You just got here, Robert," she says. "Why don't you fetch a glass and sit down?"

"I need to talk to you," he says again, and just when I think he's going to yank her to her feet, he pivots towards the bar, and returns with a glass and a chair that he pulls next to Florence. I pour him a beer from our pitcher and introduce myself, hoping to get a rise out of him and deflect some of the attention away from Florence, but he neither looks at me nor drinks. Some of our tablemates resume their conversations, awkwardly, because the tension between Florence and Robert is obvious. After a few minutes Florence excuses herself to use the restroom and Robert leaps to his feet. "I'll come with you," he says.

"Don't be daft, Robert," she says. "I'm going to the loo. I'll be right back." She's barely gone before Robert leaves the table and stations himself at the door to the women's room.

"What's with him?" one of our tablemates says, a young Swedish woman traveling with her twin sister. "Some kind of *Fatal Attraction?*" Florence comes out and she and Robert have an agitated conversation out of our hearing. I'm about to break it up when they separate, Robert disappearing out the door and Florence returning to our table.

"Robert and I are going outside to talk for a few minutes," she says. I tell her I don't think that's such a good idea and remind her that I'm not supposed to leave her alone with him, but she says, "I'll be all right. He's not going to hurt me." An hour passes before I can't stand it anymore and head outside to look for them. They're not around, and a half-hour later I go outside again. This time they're under a light pole alongside the parking lot. Florence sees me approach and starts to break away.

"Wait!" Robert shouts at me. "Can't you see we're saying good-bye?"

"I think you've had your chance," I say and keep coming, making myself as large as possible, glad that I'm several inches taller than he is. Florence holds up her hand and turns back to Robert, who throws his arms around her. She keeps her palms to his chest and soon pushes him back.

"Good-bye, Robert," she says and walks away. When she gets to me, she says, "Keep moving. Don't look back."

"I love you, Florence," Robert calls behind us. It's not a statement or a plea, it's a command.

That night I sleep with the boat locked and my dive knife and loaded spear gun next to the bed. For weeks afterwards, at every yacht club or marina we visit, we're told Robert has been there looking for us. Sometimes there are letters to Florence that she reads and tears up without showing them to me. Following the daily weather broadcasts, the marine operator announces calls waiting for *Atlantean* from Robert, which we don't return. Stalking is a crime in Australia, and several people recommend notifying the police, but Florence doesn't want any trouble with the law. "It's probably my fault," she says and won't talk about it.

Part of what throws Robert off our track may be our stop in a well-protected and uninhabited little bay called Mourylian Harbour, where we leave *Atlantean* for eight days while we visit some acquaintances of my father's, an American family in Australia for the last ten years. Chip is a trained geologist who makes his living staking out ore claims in the Outback, and he and his wife Diana have four children, ages eleven through twenty. We stay at their house on the beach and also join them for three days in the field at their base of operations far out in the hills, an old assayer's office the family has restored as a second home.

It's my first exposure to the Outback, and though we're only on its margins, I'm fascinated by the desolation. Most of Chip's prospecting is in creek beds, all of them dry, along which are a few scrawny gum trees and eucalyptus. Much of the surrounding countryside is little more than bare dirt and rock, interrupted only by sparse patches of dried-out, windblown spinifex, and thousands of lumpy pink and brown mud piles that I discover are anthills. Ants are Australia's most common animal, by a long chalk, and inspecting any random square foot of ground reveals multiple species headed every which way. We finish our prospecting trip with a visit to a rock hound the family knows, Old Bill, age eighty-four. He takes a shine to Florence and shows her every rock and chunk of petrified wood in his shack while she snaps photos of the gap-toothed grin and sparkling eyes that light up his weatherworn, deeply lined face.

Chip and Diana's youngest child is a girl, Anna, who attends a one-room schoolhouse with nine other children, and with whom Florence bonds instantly. They play games, draw pictures, swing on the outdoor tire swing, and talk with each other for hours about God-knows-what. Florence is in front of the TV whenever it's on, including Anna's morning cartoons before school, and she guffaws with open-mouthed belly laughs during the inane sitcoms. "Twenty-seven going on twelve," Diana says to me after I tell her Florence's age.

Florence's natural ebullience, re-awakened during our week with a loving family in a comfortable, albeit somewhat chaotic home, lasts for about a day after we say good-bye to Chip and Diana and leave Mourylian Harbor. Then homesickness and depression over her father set in, along with uncertainty about her future, her dwindling supply of money, and the problems of being alone with me again. Although we shared the guest bedroom at Chip and Diana's house, we're now back to separate cabins. For the next week up the coast, Florence is listless and spends most of her time with Dr. Mario or cheating on crosswords, and sunburning her butt in the intense tropical sun. She stops bathing altogether and her face breaks out, her hair turns greasy and flat, and she develops a slightly sour smell. When I point out that we have plenty of fresh water aboard for showers, she says, "I kind of enjoy being dirty." A cut on her leg from swimming with the kids shows increasingly ugly signs of infection, and one night I clean it with hydrogen peroxide, warning her she needs to treat it regularly. "I'm not worried about it," she says, by now completely morose. I tell her I won't worry about it either, since we'll be in Cairns soon where there's a good hospital for amputations.

We go hiking at a popular tourist destination, Fitzroy Island, and at the resort a trio of American women we met on the trail invites us to join them for drinks. Florence rudely ignores them and afterwards says, "They were a bunch of bloody dykes. Why should I waste my time?" By now I'm tired of her churlish moods and childish tantrums, and we have another fight, our worst ever. We end it by agreeing to part company in Cairns, now only a couple of days away.

Although I hate fighting, sometimes that's what it takes to get everything out that needs to be said, and the next day both of us make a point of being more polite and considerate with one another. Florence offers to make the lunch and afterwards takes pains to wash the dishes the way I've requested (she generally doesn't bother rinsing off the soapsuds). We can make Cairns that day, but I suggest that we anchor out for her last night aboard, at nearby Turtle Bay. It's a lovely evening, and after Florence swims to shore for a run on the beach, we sit in the cockpit under the stars, surrounded by glowing buckets of Citronella candles to keep the mosquitoes at bay. We reminisce about the many fine places we've visited together, and she tells me a rambling story about a trip to Kenya she once took with her father (despite his other shortcomings, he had a British respect for traveling the Empire's former outposts). She concludes by telling me of an idea she came up with while we were staying with Chip and Diana. "I'd like to buy a horse in Cairns and ride it back to Sydney," she says, "maybe with a little cart for my things." It's typical Florence, sweet and naive.

Although Sydney is some 1,500 miles away, if anybody can hope to inspire goodwill and assistance from the Aussies she meets along the way, it's Florence. After all, God protects small children.

It's a melancholy morning as we motor into Cairns, with me behind the wheel and Florence snoozing in the cockpit, wrapped in her giant orange rain parka. As we're tying up at the commercial dock, I spot two boats I recognize, *Hannah* and *Lazarus*, both of which were with me at the Westhaven Marina in New Zealand. I leave Florence aboard to pack her things and visit *Hannah* to see Ken and Sharon and their new baby. Both boats are about to leave, buddy-boating up the coast for Darwin, then Indonesia, and over a cup of coffee, I tell Ken I'll be right behind them, either with or without new crew. He agrees to stay in touch and I give him the frequencies and times for the little radio net I've been maintaining sporadically with *Pandarosa, Jupiter,* and a few other boats. When I get back to *Atlantean,* I find Florence sitting in the salon with none of her bags packed and looking nervous. "Are you okay?" I ask.

From the deep breath she takes, it's apparent she's been rehearsing a little speech, which she now delivers. "I want to take that trip I told you about," she says, "but I reckon Cairns isn't such a good place to look for a horse. Cooktown is more north, and not so big, and that's where I ought to start. So I thought, 'Well, *Atlantean's* going that way, I'll ask if I can stay on 'til there.' Then I got thinking, with me on board, you prob'ly won' find anybody to help you here in Cairns. An' I thought, 'I can't leave him out there alone sailin' all the way to Darwin by himself.' So anyway, what I want to ask, that is, if it's all right by you, I'll stay on 'til Darwin."

I'm not positive it's all right by me, but I'm already worried about Florence in the big city, short on cash, with Robert on the loose, and her carrying all of her valuable camera equipment. On the other hand, Cairns is full of tourists and intrepid travelers, and I wouldn't mind trying my luck at finding new crew to Darwin or beyond. But it's not a choice, really, between Florence and somebody else. "Thanks, Florence," I say. "I'd love to have you along."

A serious purchase keeps us in Cairns for a couple of days. My Metzler inflatable dinghy has finally given up its wandering Teutonic ghost. Scratched and patched too many times and baked by the relentless tropical sun, it won't hold air for more than an hour or two. Another sailboat at the commercial dock offers me ten dollars for the carcass, which I'm happy to take. My cruising budget can't absorb the US $1,500-$2,000 a good replacement inflatable would cost, so for about

US $250 I buy a used hard-shell dinghy, an ugly little rowboat made out of molded orange plastic. It's lightweight, unsinkable and can be lashed onto the foredeck.

We stock up on provisions for the three weeks I estimate it will take us to get to Darwin (Florence loads the shopping cart with twenty-six cans of baked beans) and I pick up my mail at the Cairns American Express office. In addition to letters from family and a few friends, there's a letter for Florence from Robert, c/o *Atlantean*, which begs her to see him and gives her the address and phone number of the Cairns hostel where he's staying. Florence spends a long afternoon composing a one-page response, explaining how she's staying on with me to Darwin, that she doesn't love him, and suggesting he get on with his life, then asks me to deliver it so she won't chance running into him. Since we have a 1,200-mile sail ahead of us with practically no towns or outposts along the way, there's not much point in his trying to follow, though I have my suspicions that he'll be waiting for us on the dock when we make Darwin.

A few days later we're in Port Douglas where I have to perform an emergency repair job. Florence is distracted and moody throughout the day, so I keep up a cheerful monologue in case she's having second thoughts about coming along. Knowing that she's always concerned about money, I offer to buy her mask, snorkel, and fins when we get to Darwin, and to pay for her bus ticket back to Cooktown. That perks her up some, and finally over a fish and chips dinner at a nearby pub, she explains she's been fretting about her upcoming trek from Cooktown to Sydney. The solution she's come up with is to buy a donkey, because a horse would overly strain her limited budget. "Just a little donkey," she says. "I could lead him and he'd carry my things. He'd be my friend." She talks through her idea until she's cheered herself up, and the next morning, at my suggestion, she calls the Cooktown newspaper to place a classified ad that includes Chip and Diana's phone number for responses. When it's time to cast off that afternoon, she's reverted back to her silly, giggly twelve-year-old alter ego.

We're sailing the route explored by Captain Cook over two hundred years ago, and it's amazing to think the first European to chart these waters had come so far up the coast with no clear idea of the Great Barrier Reef's existence. Sailing the shoreline during the day, Cook was troubled by the persistence of shallow water and the abundance of coral, and when a suitable anchorage wasn't readily available, he deemed it prudent at night to sail slowly seaward. This worked so long as the Reef lay far offshore, but in this area it's much closer. One night while heading away from land, to Cook's and his shipmates' horror, *Endeavor* struck that section of the Great Barrier Reef that today bears his vessel's name. The hull was breached, and it was only through the crew's heroic efforts and the lucky chance of a wind shift that they were able to beach the ship near present-day Cooktown. After months ashore in a strange land, with no prospect of outside help, Cook and his men patched *Endeavor* and set sail again, this time probing the Reef more carefully. Lizard Island, *Atlantean's* next destination, has a thousand-foot peak, Cook's Look, from where Cook searched for a safe passage through the Reef to the east. Unable to find one, he had no choice but to proceed northwards and hope that the channel between shore and the Reef would eventually bring them clear.

We make Lizard Island after a sometimes tense twenty-hour sail through some tricky narrows, and drop anchor in Watson's Bay near *Jupiter*, whom I hail on the radio. Brad, the boat's gay cook, tells me *Lazarus, Hannah,* and eight other boats left this morning, all bound for Darwin, but that *Jupiter* will be staying three more days. "Join us over here for dinner tonight," he says. "Serena's niece from England is with us until Darwin. She and Florence can gossip about the Royals."

Serena is *Jupiter's* owner, a semi-retired architect from land-locked Sun Valley, nearly blind in one eye, and a chain-smoker with little previous sailing experience, but something has motivated her to travel the seas. She's put together a first-class boat, a Little Harbor 65. There's no shortage of space for the six of us around the salon table, opposite a full-keyboard digital piano bolted to the cabin sole and safely under wraps ("I thought I'd have time to learn to play the damn thing," Serena says). I don't know the source of Brad's connection with Serena, but he's probably the only member of Lincoln, Nebraska's gay community to ever sign on as a cook on an around-the-world voyage. Ron is Serena's professional captain, a New Zealander in his fifties whom she hired in Auckland, and her sixth captain since *Jupiter* began its voyage in the Caribbean a couple of years ago. The niece, Constance, is in her late twenties and has only been aboard since Cairns. Serena, Brad, and Constance are witty, urbane, and glib, and for me the evening is a riotous affair of alcohol, cigarettes, and sarcasm. Most of the humor being dashed about seems lost on Florence and Ron, and after Brad has cleared the dishes and we sophisticates crack into yet another fine bottle of Australian Shiraz, the two of them depart for the cockpit.

After three days of hiking the rocky hills, relaxing in the sun, and snorkeling (Brad calls the nearby patch of coral the Clam Club for all of its giant clams), we decide to buddy-boat with *Jupiter* the rest of the way to Darwin. The winds are brisk as ever, always on our tail, and though *Jupiter's* waterline would allow for a greater hullspeed than *Atlantean's*, it's a much heavier boat and they're lazy sailors, so most days we lead the way. We anchor every night, and while away our evenings aboard *Jupiter*, not only because we're invited and there's no point in all six of us cramming onto *Atlantean*, but also because Florence has attached herself to Ron. He's another father figure for her, ruddy complected, kindly and non-judgmental in the way of so many New Zealanders. She's at her ease with him, partly because the two of them together have about as much formal schooling as any one of the rest of us.

We're approaching the Cape York Peninsula, as inhospitable as any stretch of coastline in Australia. Most of our stopping places are in the lee of some barren, sun-blasted piece of rock, as if a chunk of Utah or Arizona were plucked out of the American Southwest and dropped into the ocean. One night we anchor in a crook of the mainland called Portland Roads, along a flat expanse of beach beyond which are miles of steamy mangrove swamps teaming with snakes and crocodiles. We're one of about twenty cruising sailboats here, all headed for Darwin (Brad dubs us the Portland Roads Parade), along with eight or ten shrimp boats. The big shrimpers lie at anchor all day while their crews sleep and their noisy generators power the freezers, and at night they drag the shallows for prawns and whatever else their nets haul in. It's mid-afternoon when we arrive, and I radio Brad. "What do you say we see about buying ourselves a mess of shrimp?"

"I have some *fabulous* recipes for shrimp," he says, and proceeds to tell me about them until I cut him off. Brad takes his cooking seriously; even the barbecued burgers we had last night came on buns he'd freshly baked, complete with onion flakes and sesame seeds. Florence wants to join us and grabs a camera when Brad picks us up in *Jupiter's* dinghy.

We pull alongside the first shrimper we come to, *Ocean Harvester*, and shout over the roar of the generators until the mate comes on deck. He's a shirtless, squint-eyed Aussie, with naked women tattoos, a cue-ball-smooth head, and a smear of mustard on his lip. "Smile," Florence says as he leans across the rail, and she snaps his picture. His face brightens when he sees the little blond pixie behind the camera, and he invites us aboard.

"Now whatcha goin' doin' that for, takin' me picture?" he says when he offers Florence a hand up, but she's grinning and so is he.

In a moment they're introducing themselves—the mate's name is Bob—leaving Brad and me to climb aboard on our own.

"Is this all yers, Bob?" Florence asks. "I never been on a boat like this." The next thing, Bob has whisked Florence away for a tour below. Brad and I stay close by the companionway door on the hot, odoriferous deck, cautious not to explore the mass of hoists, cables, and nets on the boat's stern lest we upset something. After a few minutes Bob and Florence are back, both chattering away while Florence clicks more pictures.

"So you'll be wantin' some prawns," Bob says to Florence, a filterless cigarette dangling from the corner of his mouth. He breaks open a freezer and heaps twenty or thirty huge frozen shrimp into a plastic bag. "These are Kings. They're the best eatin' prawn, to my way o'thinkin'." He opens another locker. "'Course, some likes the Tiger Prawns. Good on the barbie, they are." Another twenty or thirty prawns go into the bag.

We brought our money along, and I'm getting a little nervous about how much this is going to cost. I interrupt Bob mid-handful. "We'd like about $25 worth, however many that is."

Bob gapes at me. "Whaddya think, I wuz gonna charge ya?" he says. "There's more prawns out 'ere than me 'n my mates know what to do with." He tosses another handful in the bag. "Now y'oughter try the bitty Endeavor Prawns, I s'pose." Another locker produces handfuls of these. "How 'bout lobster? You need some lobster?" Florence shrugs and looks at us. Well sure, yes, Brad and I stammer, unable to believe our good fortune. "We keep 'em below," Bob says. "Wait right here, back in a jiffy."

While he's gone, Brad hefts the bag. "There must be fifteen pounds in here," he says. "Do you have any idea how much these are worth?"

We hear raised voices from inside the cabin and Bob comes back empty handed; it seems the captain or crew has chastened him about giving away too much of the catch and has drawn the limit on the precious lobster. While Florence snaps a few more pictures, we thank Bob for his generosity and again offer him money, which he waves off. He gives Florence a sweaty hug before we climb back in the dinghy and roar our treasure back to *Jupiter* for a shucking and de-veining party.

A couple of hours later we've stuffed ourselves on garlic-and-butter prawns over a bed of seasoned rice, sliced olives, and sun-dried tomatoes, and there's still half more left over. All compliments go to the chef, but Brad won't hear of them. "Thank Florence," he says.

"Bob would have thrown Greg and me to the crocodiles. I thought he was going to give her the keys to the boat."

That night the shrimpers work the shallows with their big spotlights blazing and are back again before we're up in the morning. Though there are high wind warnings, the Roads are a rolly anchorage and we agree with *Jupiter* to move on. We sail hard for a couple of days, the winds at times up to thirty knots apparent, but we're still protected from rough seas by the Reef. The Equator isn't far away—we're about 11° south latitude—and the sun is a constant, unforgiving glare. Florence rarely wears anything at all, and won't believe me when I tell her loose clothing will keep her cooler by keeping the sun off her skin. She's young and likes her tan and doesn't care how she'll look at age forty.

On our run to Mt. Adolphus Island, the last stopping place before rounding Cape York, the northern tip of Australia, there's an accident aboard *Jupiter*. Both boats have been using spinnaker poles on the headsails for downwind sailing, and while Ron and Brad are lowering theirs for the night, it gets loose and strikes Brad on the head. He's knocked unconscious for a few minutes, and there's a nasty cut that will require stitches. In spite of the accident, Serena insists we join them for dinner, a big leg of lamb they've defrosted. We dinghy over and watch Serena scamper around the galley while nauseous Brad lies on the settee with an ice bag on his head, issuing instructions and heaping abuse on her. The lamb turns out beautifully, though Brad complains the mint sauce is too thin.

Jupiter diverts to Thursday Island, a tiny outpost at the entrance to Torres Strait where Brad can get medical attention. We debate whether to wait for them so we can buddy-boat the five-day passage across the Gulf of Carpentaria, past desolate Arnhem Land and onwards to Darwin, but conditions are favorable for negotiating tricky Endeavor Passage and I decide we'll proceed on our own. It's a little unusual to be starting an open-water voyage without a well-stocked boat and a careful dockside inspection of the mast and rigging, but it's been over two weeks since we've been in a town, and our fresh water is down to below half. At least we won't starve; there are plenty of baked beans aboard.

"What is it yer always writin' down there?" Florence asks from the cockpit. I'm sitting at the chart table with a child's school theme-book, half of its pages filled with my illegible scribblings. We're about to enter the flat pale-green expanse of the Gulf of Carpentaria, a relatively shallow body of tepid water the size of the State of

Oregon, and Australia's spawning grounds for summer typhoons. I explain to her how I keep a journal, a more complete record than the official log that only shows dates, destinations, weather conditions, engine usage, and the like. "I'll read you what I've just written," I say.

Sunday, July 10. It looks like it's going to be a long way across the Gulf of Carpentaria. Fortunately, the first leg of the trip, through notorious Torres Strait, was easy. Twenty to twenty-five knot winds pushed us from Mt. Adolphus Island, and by the time we got to Cape York at 0920, the current was in our favor. Florence celebrated turning the corner by drawing a sign that said, "Over the top down under," with the word "under" written upside-down. It was decorated with little fish and very cute. We held it in front of us and posed for pictures.

With the favorable wind and current, we smoked through Endeavor Passage. The knotmeter registered 5.5 knots and the GPS said we made 9.5 knots over the ground. We flew past the rocks and shoals and unmarked hazards, and now there is only one more set of banks at the western end of the Passage. The wind has all but died; it's about five knots, barely enough to keep the main inflated. The electric autopilot does the driving, no Aries, no headsail. The westward current should last another hour and by then we'll be out in the Gulf.

I checked the fishing line we're dragging behind the boat. Twice I've seen a tuna hit it—once it came completely out of the water with the lure in its mouth. He bit through all of the rusty hooks I had on it and got free. I switched lures; we're now using "Mario," as Florence calls the squid she bought in Cairns. Maybe we'll have fresh fish for dinner tonight.

Florence giggles. "I like the bit about Mario," she says. "So it's kinda like a diary."

"You should keep one," I say. "You know, this donkey trek you're making, if you wrote down what happened to you each day, you could turn it into a book, especially if you have good photos. I'll bet a lot of people back in England would be interested in how a young woman from Somerset walked the entire east coast of Australia."

"Go on, I could never write a book, not a proper one."

"You wouldn't have to. They have ghostwriters who do the actual writing. You tell them the story and they put it on paper, all right and proper." I show her a copy of *Maiden Voyage* that I have aboard. "See," I say, *"Tanya Aebi with Bernadette Brennan."*

Florence finds this concept amazing, that she'd be listed as the author of a book she didn't actually write, and says she's willing to have a go at a journal. I give her a spare themebook, and a few days later I spot her sitting at the salon table, chewing on the end of her pencil. After quite a long time she comes up to the cockpit. "I got down something I quite like," she says, and reads the single sentence she's written. "'Three days isn't enough to appreciate the sizeativity of the ocean.'"

"That's good, Florence," I say, "but what do you mean by sizeativity?"

"You know. How big it is."

"I don't think sizeativity is a word," I say.

She frowns at the page. "Well it ought to be," she says. "It's a good word."

After a week in Darwin it's time for Florence to leave. We're staying in the over-priced Cullen Bay Marina, the only marina I know of with its own set of locks, installed to cope with Darwin's five-meter tides. Our alternative was to anchor far out from the yacht club, which most of the hundred or so cruising boats have chosen to do, though it means either dinghying to shore at high tide or dragging it across the mud flats. They're all gathered here for the start of the Darwin-Ambon Race, officially a competitive regatta, but also a convenient way to obtain the required Indonesian cruising permits and visas, along with nominal protection against pirates from the Indonesian Navy. Paperwork and fees for the race have to be filed a month in advance, including a crew list and passport numbers. Since Florence wouldn't commit to going with me, I couldn't apply, and have therefore decided to wipe Indonesia off of my list of destinations, a minor disappointment because Bali and possibly Komodo were the only places I planned to visit. I don't really know enough about Asia to want to go there.

Jupiter arrives a few days after us—Brad looking quite dashing with his new stitches—and takes a slip near us in the marina, along with a few other boats I recognize, generally the better-financed cruisers than those I normally hang with. Serena's niece flies home to England and Serena departs for a 1.8 million acre sheep station in the Kimberlies owned by a man she met in Sun Valley. That leaves Brad and Ron aboard, and soon Florence, though she doesn't sleep in Ron's bunk as he might have liked, but rather in a little hammock he rigs for her on deck, as if he were a kindly grandfather indulging a favorite grandchild. Brad complains that their jejune conversations are driving him mad.

Saying good-bye to Florence is more poignant than I expected. I've already given her $150 for her snorkeling gear and the beans she's leaving behind, and bought her bus ticket, and now I hug her and thank her for sticking with me through all those months and miles. We're both a little misty. "I want to hear how the donkey trek goes," I say. "Write to me. Don't make me wait for the book." I don't mention my regrets that our short-term and ill-advised bed sharing didn't turn out better.

"I'll never forget you, Greg Smith," she says when she breaks off our hug. Ron is standing by a discreet distance down the dock to accompany Florence to the bus depot. She pats the bow of the boat as she walks away. "Good-bye *Atlantean*."

Epilogue

Six months later, I collect my accumulated mail from the American Express office in Cape Town, South Africa. There are letters waiting for me from all over the globe, mostly from friends and family back in the States, but also from people I've met along the way. The post office provides the blue-water cruiser with a lifeline, one of the few means of countering the loneliness and weariness brought about by time, distance, and unfamiliar surroundings.

The letter that charms me the most comes from Florence, postmarked New Zealand and forwarded by my mother. Through Florence's childish scrawl and appalling spelling and syntax, I'm able to decipher that she successfully completed her 4,000 kilometer trek from Cooktown to the Blue Mountains south of Sydney, in the company of her donkey, Zac. She sends along a photo of the two of them, Zac wearing Florence's straw boater with flowers woven into the band, the same one she was wearing when I met her in the Queensland Museum. On the letter's two pages of flimsy airmail paper, she laboriously describes her first day underway, paying detailed attention to the arrangement of Zac's load. After that, she apparently tires of the task. "Anyhow, people were auffly sweet," is all she says in summary of the rest of the trip. She mentions that she's touring New Zealand with Ron, the now former captain of *Jupiter*, and she wishes me well.

There's no address for a response, but that evening, as the first star graces the South African twilight, I return the wish to her, half a world away.

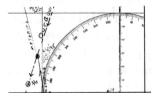

A TOURIST IN MAURITIUS

EXTENDED TRAVEL BY SAILBOAT, what is typically referred to as cruising, is a unique way to see the world. Cruisers face the same problems as tourists and travelers of other stripes—incomprehensible languages and customs, corrupt officials, isolation amid a sea of strangers, never enough money—but cruisers enjoys the advantage of bringing their homes along wherever they go. Every night I sleep on my own pillow in my own bed, surrounded by the possessions and comforts that define who I am: the shelves of books I've read and will read again, the CDs and tapes I listen to, my clothing stored in lockers or lying scattered about the cabin, the pots and pans I use for cooking, and the assorted mementos and decorations that have special significance only to me. *Atlantean* may offer no more living space than somebody else's hallway, but it's my home, and that can be a huge comfort when it's time to bar the door against the outside world. On the other hand, it's equally important to avoid isolating oneself aboard the boat, and it's sometimes a challenge to create a worthwhile *travel* experience after arriving somewhere. There's always plenty of boat work to be done, food and fuel to buy, and uninterrupted sleep to catch up on after the rigors of an ocean passage, but at some point the cruiser can and should become a tourist.

We arrive in Port Louis on the island nation of Mauritius after eighteen days crossing the Indian Ocean. Check-in procedures are accomplished by a barrage of Indian officials, whose reams of paperwork I wade through in due course. The only glitch comes when I admit to owning a spear gun, and it takes the *functionnaires* an hour of consternation and confusion to finally decide it must be confiscated. I'm issued a receipt that they assure me will result in the spear gun's prompt return when we're ready to leave the country. Afterwards, we motor out of the smelly, crowded harbor with its dozens of Asian fishing boats rafted together like floating housing projects. I don't know why the fishing fleet has congregated here—maybe it's the off-season for whatever they're catching—but the boats are all similar, about a hundred feet long and painted white, with Chinese characters on their steel hulls. The crews are aboard, sometimes working on deck or jumping into the foul waters for a questionable swim, and though mostly male, there are plenty of females and even children, as if the boats are run by extended families or small villages; they, too, are carrying their homes with them to strange lands.

We move to an anchorage off Mauritius' Grand Baie Yacht Club, and the next day my crew, Ioan and Jelle, shoulder their backpacks for a week of fending for themselves. I can't blame them. We've been on the ocean thirty-seven of the past forty-six days and have covered almost 6,000 miles since leaving Australia. *Atlantean* may be my home—even if it's halfway around the planet from where I've spent most of my life—but it's not theirs, and we could all use a little time apart.

I'm not anti-social, however, and enjoy spending a daily hour or two over a beer with the other cruisers anchored off the yacht club. There are the club's members about as well, but they're French for the most part and keep their distance, though they don't seem to mind us cruisers hanging around using the showers, toilets, and lawn chairs, so long as we buy beers, coffees, and the occasional meal. Among other boats that I recognize from my travels (we are, after all, part of a moveable community in which we eventually become familiar with each other), there are two cruising couples about my age or a little younger: Clive and Lila aboard *Isa Lei*, and Spider and Kim aboard *Skerryvore*. They're a mixed lot, Clive from England, Lila from Denmark, Spider from Australia, and Kim from the East Coast of the U.S. They've been here a month and talk about moving on, but like cruisers everywhere, inertia takes over and the moss is growing on their anchor chains. They pass on news of other mutual acquaintances, give me the low-down for getting around Mauritius, and are good for a chat whenever I pass through the Club after touring around or buying my daily loaf of french bread from the bakery down the road.

Mauritius has become a minor European vacation destination, and the Grand Baie end of the island is where most of the beaches and tourist hotels are. It's too commercial for my tastes, though not nearly as glitzy or brazenly carnal as the Aussie Gold Coast or the college student party-grounds in Mexico. There's probably as much sex happening among the vacationers who meet in the bars and discos, and there's more topless sunbathing on the beach, but no bikini contests or dancing on the tables. Europeans are in general less inhibited about matters of the flesh, while Americans, and perhaps the Aussies as well, seem to need the spur of alcohol to release themselves from their puritanical heritage.

After I shower and shave off my six-week growth of beard, I'm ready for the bus ride into Port Louis to take care of business and have a look around. Madagascar, our next destination, will require a visa before entering the country, and I want to buy Maloprim or Lariam as prophylaxis against Madagascar's Chloroquine-resistant malaria (the official word is that malaria has been eradicated in Mauritius). It's also time to pick up mail and check in with my sister, to let her know not to alert the authorities that we're lost at sea.

Mauritius is a fairly large island of volcanic origins, resembling for the most part one of the Society Islands of French Polynesia. Its latitude is higher, however—about 20° south—and the vegetation is not so lush. But precipitous razor ridges with their dramatic spires and jagged pinnacles are much the same as on Tahiti or Bora Bora, and are equally impressive. The island's location in the west-central Indian Ocean at one time made it a crossroads for sailors from everywhere, from the original Arab and Malay traders, to the Portuguese, Dutch, French, and English in later years, though its importance has waned considerably. Mauritius was also known as the sole abode of the dodo, a large, slow, and meaty flightless bird that was wiped out hundreds of years ago by sailors looking for an easy meal. The solitaire, a similar, but not so large bird on nearby Réunion Island, suffered the same fate. The colonials' importation of slave labor, and the eventual immigration of large numbers of Indians to work the sugarcane fields, has resulted in a dynamic polyglot of diverse cultures and languages, a diversity that has probably contributed to the island's economic success.

The forty-minute bus ride into Port Louis costs ten rupees (seventeen rupees to the dollar), and takes me through the cane fields. Everywhere there are huge slave-stacked piles of volcanic rock, sometimes arranged in walls or fences, cleared from the land to make room for the cane. Most of the farm labor is still by hand, which at least keeps unemployment numbers low. The journey reminds me of the wild bus rides in Mexico: foot to the floor followed by slamming on the brakes, passing in the face of oncoming traffic, and speeding through the narrow streets in the little towns and villages along the way.

Port Louis is a major city and a microcosm of the mishmash of cultures on the island. Indians are the most prevalent, but there are also plenty of Asians, Africans, and Europeans, the last being definitely in the minority. French is the language everybody speaks to some extent, and almost the only language I see in print. English, however, is the official language, though it appears it's only used in the schools and by the government—laws, official notices, that sort of thing—the result of the settlement of some squabble rather late in the colonial cycle of carving up the world, when the English took over from the French who had been here longer.

There are a few high-rise office buildings on the central business district's wide boulevards, sprinkled in among the solemn government edifices, but for the most part the city consists of narrow streets and endless small shops selling absolutely everything, from washing machines to live animals to countless dodo-inspired tourist mementos. Traffic is in the French style: pedestrians taking their lives in their hands, trucks forcing their way through the crowds, everybody driving as fast as possible and using their horns constantly.

My first stop is American Express, where I find the usual disappointingly small cache of accumulated correspondence—my Mother's early birthday card and a few notes from friends. The helpful woman in charge of the office says she can arrange my Madagascar visa for a nominal charge (fifty rupees) above what it would cost if I deal directly with the Madagascar diplomatic office in Curepipe (three hundred rupees). The only catch is that we're not to let them know we'll be arriving by yacht, which would involve more time and expense, since the paperwork would have to be sent to Madagascar. I'm always hesitant to fool with official procedures, but I can't spare the time if I'm going to stick to our schedule (we're meeting another boat in Diego Suarez), and the woman assures me nobody in Madagascar will know the difference. When I sign the visa application, I notice she's written in fictional flight numbers, dates, destinations, and hotel names.

After convincing me to take a minibus tour of the island ($15, leaving in the morning, they'll pick me up at the Veranda Hotel next to the yacht club), the American Express woman directs me to the telephone exchange, where a credit card call causes more consternation among the attendants. The twelve-hour time difference means it's late back home, so I keep it short. Next stop is the pharmacy, where the white-coated Indian behind the counter lectures me on the superiority of Lariam (which is more expensive and he has in stock) over Maloprim (which he's out of and can't get for another week).

It's around noon when I've finished my business, and I take an extensive walking tour of the town. Rather than eating in a tourist restaurant where I know I'll pay too much, I try out various street vendors I encounter along the way, most of whom offer fried doughy concoctions with mystery fillings ("fried garbage," is how I've taken to calling street food the world over, though I love it). My favorite is a kind of soft flour pancake with a glob of chili or curry sauce folded into it, two rupees each. Soon I've worked up a thirst and decide to take a chance on the milky fruit drink I've seen offered from numerous carts. It comes in a tall glass with lots of ice, and though I have my doubts about its hygienic properties, I slurp it down, cold and fruity and delicious. When I'm through with the glass, the vendor swirls it in a bucket of highly questionable water and puts it back on his cart, ready for the next thirsty customer.

The city is busy, noisy, and crowded. An open sewer runs through a poorer residential section and into the harbor, but otherwise the place is not unpleasant. I discover the large central market near the waterfront that can provide us with our fresh produce needs (as well as meat, if the fly-caked carcasses hanging in the sun don't put us off) when we return to Port Louis to check out. By late afternoon I'm hot and tired and feeling dirty, so I find the central bus terminal, where dozens of crowded busses wait to transport workers to their homes all over the island.

Next morning I'm sitting in the front seat of a minibus, the only unaccompanied person among the six others taking the tour with me—diverse ethnicity, origins unknown at this time, though French is the spoken language. Our driver is a young Indian or Pakistani, like most other aggressively ambitious people on this island, and I don't quite catch his name when he introduces himself and responds to my offer of a handshake with a light brush of his long, slender fingers. He tells us we're going to visit the city of Curepipe up in the hills, which wasn't what the booking agent said but is where I want to go, so perhaps he modifies the itinerary to suit his mood.

As we motor through the fields, our guide talks about the cane, which is being harvested now, September through November. They don't burn the fields, since there's plenty of cheap labor: dark-skinned men and women in straw hats and loose white clothing wade through the fields, hacking with their machetes and loading stalks of cane on carts. We hear it's not a good year—yields are off twenty percent, and prices are down in the European markets where the sugar goes—but what's agriculture if not a perpetual disappointment?

Around the outskirts of Port Louis we pass numerous clothing manufacturers, mostly knitwear makers, another way to use up the supply of cheap workers. There's also a lot of manual labor on the roads and construction sites, reminding me of roadside scenes in Mexico, but here more of the crew is performing useful work, probably because there are tools to go around, and more heavy machinery. Mauritius is prosperous enough that it can afford to maintain good roads and create jobs.

South of Port Louis we merge onto a four-lane highway full of cars, trucks, motor scooters, and bicycles. We pass through an area of light manufacturing, warehouses, and auto showrooms, resembling any typical "strip" on the margins of a U.S. city. I also note several signs in Arabic and a few mosques, but all of these exurban developments soon give way to more cane fields. The red volcanic earth and whatever happens to be grown or built on it butt up close to the raw rock of the mountainous backbone to the island, which approaches the sea at Port Louis. We work our way over the ridge, around slow moving "crawlers" (as the warning sign calls the heavy trucks), and down to the coastal plain again, where a more residential town lies in the distance.

We pass a winery—I wasn't expecting this—and I decide I should sample Mauritius wine, maybe tonight. The local brewery soon goes by as well—Phoenix, a pilsner, which they serve at the yacht club and I've found to be quite drinkable. Next comes a suburban shopping mall with its main store, "Continental" (the large French retailer I've seen in Tahiti and Paris), and the twin fast-food scourges of the developing world, Kentucky Fried Chicken and Pizza Hut. A golf course is flat and short, with grass like a mown cow pasture, then comes a more manicured estate with gates and gardens, which a sign identifies as "Clarisse House." Interspersed among these attractions are small truck farms where straw-hatted workers with watering cans and hoes tend to their crops.

Our first stop is in an area called Floreal in the foothills near Curepipe, at a row of boutiques: two sweater shops and two model ship makers. The ship models are of old-style sailing ships, ornate, highly detailed, and only a little tacky, about $1,000 for the big ones (all price tags are in Mauritius rupees and U.S. dollars, though I've seen almost no American tourists). The Indian salesman assures me the models can be well packed and would make an excellent souvenir of Mauritius. One hundred percent teak, he says (no doubt coming from the rapidly dwindling tropical hardwood forests that once covered this or some other island), and built right on the premises; a quick glance in the back reveals four men around a table full of miniature planks and spars, gluing the models together. I like the half-hull plaques better, and yes, they can make one of *Atlantean* if I'd like, very reasonably priced. I'm carrying my daypack and nearly have to buy a ship model I don't want when a loose strap hooks a bowsprit and tips it on its pedestal. For my wallet's sake I move on to the clothing outlets.

While we browse, more minibuses show up; this is obviously a regular stop on the tourist circuit, pursuant to some sort of deal between the merchants and the drivers. My fellow captives dutifully file into the shops and shift into shopping mode, pulling out tee shirts and sweaters, trying them on, some even buying them. They talk quietly among themselves and scrutinize the shelves of tourist junk, much of it kitschy variations on the dodo bird motif.

We coast down the road to our next stop, a diamond showroom. There's beautiful stuff here; it's hard not to like diamonds. Prices in U.S. dollars are a little harder to like, however, though I have no clue as to whether the prices or the quality are good. I briefly consider a diamond ear stud, and then dismiss the notion—maybe in South Africa, where the diamonds actually come from. Next door is yet another sweater shop, offering nice heavy ones with good patterns for only about $16, but our group isn't very acquisitive. The guide doesn't care; perhaps he works on head count rather than commission.

Our next stop is non-commercial, Trou aux Cerfs, the old volcanic crater, which isn't particularly large. According to our guide, it's been asleep "one million years," but could blow anytime. From the parking lot there's a panorama view of the island, from the rugged mountain peaks behind us and out toward Port Louis and the coastal plains, where several jagged pinnacles stand like sentinels facing the sea. It's cool up here, maybe four or five hundred feet above sea level, but hardly the highest point on the island, not by a long shot, so I wonder about our guide claiming this is *the* volcano crater—how'd those other peaks get there? A few intrepid hawkers display collections of little brass dodos and souvenir key chains with clear plastic tubes full of the "Seven Sands of Chamarel," which I understand will be featured later on our tour. The breeze picks up and I think about those sweaters.

The town of Curepipe is visible along the other side of the volcano; it's surely a more pleasant place than Port Louis, with clean, cool air from the steady trade winds blowing over, sweeping vistas, and probably some refreshing rain from the windward mountains wringing out the clouds. Our drive to the crater passed several elegant villas, at least elegant by Mauritius standards, one of which had a sign "Residence, The European Community," probably the EC diplomatic mission. Gates and hedges surrounded the grounds of these places, and expensive Peugeots and Mercedes were parked everywhere. Diplomats and rich people the world over enjoy the highlands, while the vast majority of the population stays close to where they work for a living, or where public transportation stops now and then.

I've determined this is the normal tourist route; the same crowd of European tourists follows or precedes us everywhere we go. Not only the minibuses, also the car and driver people, an option offered to me by the American Express agent. For $100 per day or thereabouts, I could hire a car and "go anywhere," as the woman said, as if I or these other tourists have a clue about where to go. The tourists are equipped with video gear and expensive cameras, designer handbags and fancy sunglasses. I hear Spanish, French, German, and Italian, and something that might be Greek or Serbo-Croatian spoken by a swarthy family, and observe an eclectic assortment of tee shirts on almost everybody, even the old folks, from *Save the Whales* to punk surfer themes.

Soon we're driving again, now on a high plateau, and I realize Mauritius is flatter than it appears from Port Louis and Grand Baie. The most rugged mountains run just behind Port Louis and cut off the view of the rest of the island. There are gardens up here, lots of flowers, and a cemetery with mostly Christian crosses, probably for the French. Where do they put the dead Indians and Pakistanis? Maybe all the trees on the island were burned for funeral pyres. An extensive array of radio aerials behind a chain link fence has a sign that says "Indian Space Research Center, Mauritius" a reminder that India has a space program to complement its nuclear weapons aspirations, a disheartening combination.

We pass a tea plantation, then a forest of the straight, skinny pines found in oceanic climates, none more than thirty feet tall. There's a lake in the middle of the trees that our guide reports is the main drinking water reservoir on the island. Who knows if they treat it? At least it's fenced off, and the manager of the yacht club has assured me the tap water is "potable"—I've been poting it for several days with no ill effects. Someone in our group asks if there's a river running into the lake, but our guide says the reservoir is full of rainwater, which in my mind doesn't really answer the question. We see wild monkeys with long curled tails by the side of the road that our guide says are indigenous.

Our next stop, Grand Bassin, is a small volcanic lake that the local Hindus have proclaimed a major religious site. The story we're told is the lake is connected by an underground river to the sacred waters of the Ganges thousands of miles away, never mind the distance or the fact that the Indian Ocean is 12,000 feet deep between here and there. Faith is a wonderful thing, even in this jaded and secular era.

I wander the grounds perusing the fading pastels on the various shrines and temples around the lake, until a guide/caretaker/priest spots me and invites me into one of the buildings. "Shoes off please," he says and sits me down on a pillow next to the altar of Shiva the Destroyer. A cup of tea would be nice, I think, but he's not offering. My host is wearing a white bedsheet draped toga-style over his sports shirt and slacks, and speaks the irritating sing-song English Indians throughout the world have mastered for convincing you you're getting the best possible deal. He tells me in February there's a huge religious festival here, with tens of thousands of people splashing in the lake and making offerings of coconuts, camphor, flowers, and other valuable commodities. It explains the acres and acres of empty parking lots we passed on the way in.

He asks me about the notebook in which I jot the occasional observation, so I tell him I'm a journalist traveling around the world by yacht, the type of not-so-outlandish lie I make up now and then to avoid having to relate the same story over and over. The yacht part gets his attention, and he calls a colleague over to join us. They want to know about sharks out in the ocean—very scary, yes, how big? Also, will I go to the Bermuda Triangle? Very, very scary, yes indeed. The second fellow starts going on about the Tee-tah-neek (which I gather is the *Titanic*, though he talks about it as if it went down last week) and the vast quantity of gold at the bottom of the sea in shipwrecks. "With your sailboat, all you have to do is go get it," he says. "You'll be rich."

A mentally retarded or perhaps Down Syndrome man with a big push-broom is working the floor, and whenever he gets near us he waves his arms and shouts slurry words at me in a friendly, non-threatening manner. I don't understand what he wants, and each time he demands my attention I smile and nod sagely, which seems to satisfy him and sends him on his way. As I stand to leave, my hosts assure me that photographs are allowed in the temple, and donations are graciously accepted. I smile and nod sagely, and neither take pictures nor leave an offering.

Back in the minibus, we cruise on to Curepipe, where a cathedral—St. Theresa's—makes it look like a provincial French town, and the big Prisunic (another French chainstore) across the street raises a snicker of familiarity from my traveling companions. Our driver pulls over and tells us we have an hour and a quarter to feed ourselves and see the sights. "You can buy tee shirts and souvenirs in the shops," he suggests as he locks up the van. We discreetly go our separate ways since we haven't as yet introduced ourselves to each other.

Feeding myself may not be so easy, I soon discover. There are plenty of restaurants and maybe they're open, since the doors are, but nobody's eating in them. I hate being the only one in a place, as if everybody else knows something I don't. Instead, I search out more fried garbage from the few street vendors set up in the shade, and top it off with a mysterious pink drink that's probably giardia infested. It's delicious, of course, with what I hope are globs of tapioca floating around in it.

Other European tourists wander the streets aimlessly, their drivers having disappeared and stranding them helpless, probably holed up in a good restaurant only the locals know about where they don't allow roundeyes. Prowling taxis honk at us letting us know they're available for a ride to the airport, and if not today, maybe tomorrow? "Lowest rates," the Indian drivers assure us. A large warehouse market a few blocks off the main road has the usual produce offerings and food stalls, and here is where I finally find a public toilet—very hygienic, for sure. Our guide is waiting at the minibus when I return.

The main road to Chamarel washed out in a cyclone earlier this year, which necessitates a long trip down the west side of the island, and then backtracking along the same route, rather than enjoying the proverbial scenic loop. We're in cane country again, with lots of open fields, and the going is slow behind more crawlers. I realize I've seen no grazing animals on the island, but the moment I record this observation in my journal, the minibus stops while a dozen long-horned oxen are herded across the road. I recall yesterday seeing a couple of ox-carts with two huge wheels, maybe six feet in diameter, hauling sugar cane. The Hindus probably don't eat these animals.

The coast road is beautiful. We drive between tall rock promontories that look like something out of the American southwest, and catch glimpses of coral reefs and lagoons beyond the beaches. I understand the Black River area on the southwest side of the island is a lovely anchorage, but offers no amenities or services, as if being without services weren't itself an amenity. *Atlantean* won't be going there; Madagascar beckons. We drive by an extensive area of shallow rock-bordered evaporation pools where salt is dried from seawater. Wicker baskets are stacked up everywhere—do they really collect the stuff manually?

In the lee of the mountains the countryside has become more like the African savannah; trees are dry and twisted, in isolated clumps and thickets amid fields of brown grasses and blowzy volcanic rocks. Fences for small farms and animal pens are made of thin vertical wooden poles lashed closely together. Even the people look African, dusky dark skin and kinky black hair, walking along the road in the middle of nowhere, some of the women carrying black umbrellas as sunshades.

We climb and climb the hairpin turns on the road to Chamarel, honking our horn on every narrow bend, until we come to a scenic overlook above the lagoon of the Black River. Our guide announces a photo-op, and we pile out of the minibus onto the side of the road, watchful for the occasional traffic honking past us. A huge tour bus lumbers by with a single Japanese tourist in the front seat, a young woman; I guess they run no matter what. Fancy charter fishing boats lay at anchor in the Black River Lagoon, and our guide tells us about the "world famous" Blue Marlin Big Game Fishing Contest held there each year. Is it catch and release? I ask. "No, you can keep your fish," he says, as if that's one of the main attractions.

The village of Chamarel is hot and dusty, set amid cane fields baking in the sun. There are wild flowers growing by the side of the road, but they're tired and dry. Men sit on their haunches either in the sun or the shade, it doesn't matter, many inexplicably wearing tall rubber boots. It's mid-afternoon and nobody's too active. The minibus turns onto a deeply rutted dirt road that leads through some very marginal cane fields backed against the low hills, where it looks as if they've recently burned off the forests to clear the land. We go past a small waterfall pouring into a sinkhole, and our guide assures us we'll have another photo-op here on the way back.

At the gate a bored attendant collects twenty rupees from each of us (the guide gets in free) and we drive to a parking lot beneath a sign touting the mysteries of the "Seven Sands of Chamarel." We file out into the hot afternoon sun to view the attraction itself, a patch of bare earth about the size of a football field that gradually slopes upwards in a series of small humps. Nothing grows on this patch, which consists of various red, ocher, mauve, and other pastel soils, apparently volcanic in origin. Our guide claims the colors are self sorting, due to different densities; if you mix them up and shake them, they'll separate, so you needn't worry about spoiling the key chain tubes that for some reason don't seem to be offered for sale here. Chamarel is not what I'd call one of the major wonders of the world, but there are, nevertheless, several distinct colors; I can't say there are precisely seven, since they're not exactly lined up. While I'm drinking in the spectacle, a mosquito tickles the back of my calf. My slap leaves a bloody mess, so I know it got me first, and malaria crosses my mind.

Our by now familiar caravan of tourists and a few new ones are showing up. I hear the usual mix of languages, and spot a clone of my former fiancée, blond and beautiful, but she's speaking French when I maneuver close, wasted on some sallow dweeb who's got his arm around her, reminding me that I still miss my ex from time to time, now almost three years after we split up. All the tourists mill around and kick at the dirt. "Seven?" everybody seems to be asking.

Back on the road again, I seize the initiative and draw my companions into conversation. They're an interesting lot, at least on the totally superficial level of French I can speak. First, we have a mother/daughter combination, the mother fortysomething, the daughter maybe late teens, early twenties, on holiday together. They're from-France-French, both under five feet tall, cute little munchkins. The mother is by far the racier: short-short cut-off jeans, ruffled white peasant blouse, braless, hair loose over her shoulders and bleached a tawdry blonde. The daughter is conservatively dressed and baby-fat chubby, mousy brown hair, but with the obligatory nose stud and Doc Martens black army boots. She doesn't talk much and is probably embarrassed that her mother refuses to act her age.

The second couple is a European French woman with a dark-skinned man, probably Algerian/Arab, both in their twenties and speaking French. They're very affectionate, holding hands and scrunching into one another, and I conclude they're newlyweds on their honeymoon. She has a bandaged foot, from a coral cut, and walks with a slight limp. For her sake I hope he's not taking her to a traditional Islamic home, wherever his home happens to be, and where she might have trouble adjusting.

the corner of the cockpit under the dodger, puling softly with closed eyes, until the next rumble of nausea. Then she hauls herself together, snatches gasps of fresh air, and lurches for the wheel in a desperate attempt to keep a grip on her gorge.

The day also exacts its toll on me. Unable to leave Kym alone in the cockpit for more than a few minutes, there's little I can do to relax. The howling of the wind, the pounding, the spray ripping through the cockpit, all keep me at attention, ready to spring into action should something go awry. We're taking a real beating, as heavy as any I've known, but I can't heave to (a defensive maneuver in storm seas) because we'd eventually be driven back into Cook Strait and the lee shore behind us. Every few minutes the wind gauge leaps to forty knots, heeling us hard over. I cling to a cockpit cleat, every muscle in my body tensioned against the heel, until the gust subsides to a manageable thirty. Meals consist of what snacks I can grab during dashes to the galley. Kym and Mark refuse to either eat or drink.

I keep a careful weather eye to the west, where the front should have emerged by now to dish out a final hammering before giving way to better conditions, but the skies remain stubbornly clear. Sunset approaches and with it comes a measure of relief, the winds easing to twenty-five knots and gusts becoming rarer. Majestic Mt. Egmont looms to the northeast, afire in the blaze of the setting sun.

Kym is done in. "The worst is over," I tell her, hoping she'll take heart. "You need some rest. Please try to drink something." I offer her my water bottle, but she shakes her head and slumps down the companionway ladder to her bunk.

The seas are still rough, but not nearly so steep, and *Atlantean* is riding better in the lighter, steadier wind. After a few minutes, I engage the Aries windvane (autopilot) and retreat to shelter under the dodger. I watch for the green flash as the sun goes down, and as usual, fail to see it, then make a wish on the first star I spy twinkling in the darkening sky. I wish for better weather, and as if in answer to my prayers, the winds continue to ease, settling down to a pleasant fifteen knots a point west of northwest. In a burst of optimism, I furl the staysail and let out the larger yankee, and its extra power drives us more smoothly through the sloppy seas. I'm in no hurry to shake a reef out of the main, a chore to re-tie should the wind spring back up.

I'm dog-tired, and for the first time today I can let down my guard. I make myself a sandwich and a cup of hot tea, and rinse my face with the remaining hot water. It's a beautiful, clear night, sparkling with the constellations of the Southern Hemisphere. I stretch out in the cockpit, accustoming myself to the idea of a couple of weeks at sea after my four-month stay in New Zealand. The waves foam past in bursts of glittering bioluminescence, and I fight to stay awake.

The evening weather forecast was a repeat of the last several days'. The weather front remains stalled offshore, but when it finally moves, it will be followed by strong southwesterlies. That's fine with me. Our course to Sydney calls for us to sail north of west, and a southwest wind means a fast close-reach or beam-reach, even if it knocks us around a bit. It's far better than beating into gale force northerlies. Maybe then we can finally establish the routine of a long passage: the pleasant monotony of alternating watches, the satisfying tracing of our daily progress, the rituals of meal preparation and personal ablutions at sea, the challenges of dealing with the wear and tear on the equipment.

At midnight *Atlantean* approaches the garish blue-white glitter of the Maui offshore drilling platform to the west of North Island's Cape Egmont. It's my mark to switch to starboard tack, and time to wake Mark or Kym to handle watch duties until dawn. My body aches with fatigue. I turn on the nav station light and peer into the dark cabin. The sounds of the waves gurgling past the hull and the creaking of the rigging are peaceful, comforting. Both Kym and Mark are breathing deeply, sound asleep. It's the best thing for them, and I wish I could leave them in peace, but I can't, because I have to get some sleep of my own. I shake Mark's shoulder gently.

"What? Huh?" he grunts, grappling his way back to consciousness.

"I need you to stand watch," I say in a hushed voice. "Can you handle it?"

"Oh. Sure. Watch. Right." He sits up uncertainly.

"Are you feeling better?" I ask.

"I guess so. Fine really."

After he climbs into the cockpit, I rouse Kym on the low-side bunk. She snaps awake with a startled gasp, as if emerging from a frightening dream. "Sorry, Kym," I say, laying a comforting hand on her arm. "We're about to tack. You'll want to switch to the other bunk, or get down on the cabin sole."

She blinks a few times in the dim light, refusing to accept the realization she's still a prisoner on *Atlantean*. "All right," she mewls.

With Mark's assistance, I switch us to starboard tack and reset the Aries when I'm satisfied we're running smoothly. "Stay on as long as you can, then wake up Kym," I tell him. "There's not much to do but watch our course and make sure we don't run into a ship. If the wind picks up again, we'll have to take in the yankee. Call me the moment a gust touches twenty. Got it?" He nods, and off I go to bed, too tired to remove my sticky clothes.

Sleep during the first few days of a passage is always difficult, partly because of the unfamiliar motion, and partly because of the discomfort of sliding around in my bunk. Tonight is worse, with my nerves frayed from the constant attention to *Atlantean's* every move, and I sleep only fitfully. Whenever I hear an unusual sound or feel an abrupt shift in the boat's trim, I awaken instantly and lie still, waiting until I'm certain all is well. But after a few hours of this, my need for sleep gets the best of me and I drift into oblivion. As I sleep, it's as if I'm in a sealed room, shut off against the onslaught of pounding seas and flying spray. Aware of impending danger, I struggle to wake up, but can't. Whenever I rise to half-consciousness, a gentle voice reminds me the watch will call if there's any trouble. "Go back to sleep," the voice says. "Don't worry."

Day Three

Somewhere in the night, outside the walls of my dreams, there is the sound of sails flapping violently in the wind. I swim up through the depths once again, and the flapping grows louder, and now I feel myself sliding as the world around me shudders and rolls me awake. It's no dream. I'm back aboard *Atlantean*, and in the darkness, I can hear the howling wind and the hull crashing through the waves. The digital readout on my watch says 0426.

I climb on deck to find Kym behind the wheel, battling winds gusting to over thirty knots. The larger headsail is still up and the boat is badly overpowered, even with the shortened main. "Thank God you're here," she cries. "It's been like this for over an hour."

"Didn't Mark tell you to get me up if this happened?"

"I'm really, really frightened," she says.

"It's okay, Kym," I say. "It seems worse in the dark. I'm sorry you didn't call me sooner." I wrestle in the yankee and put out the staysail, easing the sheets to take us a little farther off the wind. It improves matters considerably, and after a few minutes I engage the Aries. "It should be all right now," I say to Kym, who's quivering under the dodger in the corner of the cockpit. "Do you think you can handle it?" My head is spinning from lack of sleep and I want to get back to bed.

She gives me the frightened stare of a New Zealand possum caught in the headlights. "Please, could I go lie down?" she whimpers. "I'm feeling ill."

"I'd really appreciate it if you could stand watch for at least another hour or two. I won't go back down until you feel more comfortable. You'll get used to it, Kym, I promise."

"I want to go to bed," she says, so I dismiss her with a weary nod. She's no use to me in this state.

The clear skies have disappeared and dawn is little more than a gradual lightening behind the ashen overcast. Winds stabilize at around twenty-five knots, and I doze off and on in the cockpit between gusts. Once it's light I make my breakfast and wash up in the head, resigned to standing long watches until my crew gets it together.

At about 1030 I spot an ominous wall of black cloud approaching from the southwest. It's the weather front, and I think to myself, as soon as it passes we'll have good sailing. The front races towards us, curtains of rain pouring out of its leading edge. "Mark!" I call below. "I need your help. On the double!"

"Check out what's coming," I say when he joins me in the cockpit. "Better fasten your safety harness." Winds are up to thirty, rising rapidly, and the front is only a few hundred yards away. "Bring in the mainsheet, tight as it'll go," I order while I winch in the staysail. "We're heaving to." I put the helm hard over, forcing *Atlantean's* nose through the eye of the wind. "Kym, we're tacking!" I shout below, so she can brace herself. The sails flap loudly as they spill the wind, then fill with a snap when *Atlantean's* momentum carries her through the turn. Instead of releasing the staysail sheet and setting the sail to starboard, I leave the port sheet tensioned and backwind the staysail. When the turn is complete, I spin the wheel back to windward. The boat noses back toward the wind, but without more speed, it can't complete the turn.

No sooner have I lashed down the wheel than we're engulfed in darkness. The wind gauge jumps to fifty knots and the first blast explodes around us. A huge wave strikes us broadside, driving a floundering *Atlantean* hard over to starboard. I watch helplessly as solid water submerges the rail all the way to the coach house and spills over the cockpit coaming. We hang suspended for a moment, motionless, until the 7,000 lbs. of ballast in *Atlantean's* keel takes hold and the boat hauls herself upright. The scuppers gush like waterfalls.

A shriek cuts through the cabin. "We're sinking!" Kym screams, terror driving her voice into unexplored octaves. I race down the companionway stairs, and curse myself. Gallons of seawater have poured out of the head sink and now slosh about the cabin, the result of opening the sink drain to wash my face a few hours ago when the head was on the high side, then forgetting to close it before we tacked. I close the through-hull fitting to keep more water from backing up the drain, and then fetch towels and a bucket. Kym stopped shrieking when I came down, and now clings to a grab rail, staring at me in fright. "It's okay, Kym, it's okay!" I shout over the noise. "It's my fault. I fixed it."

"Are we going to die?" she asks, her voice quavering.

"No, Kym," I say, still angry at myself, "we're not going to die. We're hove to. The boat will be calmer now. Don't worry. It's built to take weather a lot worse than this." The sound of heavy rain reverberates through the cabin. "I've got to get back out. Here are some towels. Mop up the water if you can and dump it down the galley sink." I can't be more reassuring with other urgent matters to attend to.

I wedge the companionway hatch in place behind me as I climb into the cockpit. The rain is unbelievably heavy, coming from the sides, not falling out of the sky, but rather shooting from unseen water cannons trained on *Atlantean*. I squint into the gloom as the wind whips stinging blades of spray and rain into my eyes, but visibility ends fifty meters away in solid gray walls. I've never seen so much rain, and even under the meager shelter of the dodger, it pours off our rain parkas, runs into our eyes and down our legs. After a few minutes, the torrents become more vertical and the drops larger, flooding the sea around us. Although the wind still howls, the force of the rain knocks down the waves, rounding their crests and drowning the white caps. With the passing of the front, we'll not only have calmer seas, but also a thorough rinsing of the salt we've accumulated over the last two days.

Heaving to has us in a holding pattern. The backwinded staysail pushes *Atlantean's* nose off the wind, while the mainsail and rudder try to round us up. We end up facing about forty-five degrees to weather, sliding slowly backwards, with the wake from our backward movement smoothing the oncoming waves. The constant angle minimizes rolling. I've always found heaving to vastly superior to lying ahull, which simply means taking down all of the canvas and leaving the boat to the mercy of the elements, where it might turn sideways to the waves and roll uncontrollably.

Within a half-hour the rains stop and the winds ease as the front moves on. "The wind's down to twenty knots," I call to Kym, to give her some encouragement. In the turbulence following the front, the wind swirls around us from several directions, unable to make up its mind. I expect it to gradually shift to the west and south, as predicted, but instead each gust seems to pull it a little farther to the north. Not only that, it's again gaining strength. When I check the barometer, it's fallen another millibar since the front hit.

Two hours later we're back in the teeth of a full gale, with steady forty-knot northerlies, worse than anything we've had yet, and with no idea when it might pass. Faced with uncertainty, it's generally my policy to press on—we could stay hove to, but for how long? Eventually we'd be driven all the way back to Cook Strait, and I don't want to be anywhere near land in this kind of weather. It's better, I decide, to resume our course and put New Zealand as far behind us as possible.

The staysail and the short main snap taut when I bring the stern through the wind and continue the turn until we're on a close reach. The pounding resumes and *Atlantean* surges ahead. Not having to sail hard to weather, we fly along at over six knots, sometimes touching seven or eight, all the while getting battered by side-breaking waves. When I'm convinced we can hold our own, I set the Aries and tell Mark I'm going below for a few minutes.

While we were hove to, I mopped up the water in the cabin as best I could, doing my best to ignore Kym whimpering in her bunk. Now that we've shifted back to starboard tack, the water that accumulated in nooks and crannies on what was the low side comes spilling out, and I want to clean it up. In addition to the seawater we took through the drain, there are plenty of other leaks—from the solar vents, around the stove chimney, and through the hatches—it's impossible to keep water out of a boat in heavy weather. This time it's so bad that water has gotten inside the headliners and streamed down the inner hull, taking years of accumulated dust and grit with it. As usual, chaos reigns in the cabin, and the war sounds of bombs and cannons boom around us.

"Can't we turn back?" Kym asks from her bunk while I wring out towels in the bucket.

Lack of sleep and food over the past two days have exhausted my patience. "No, Kym," I snap. "Turning back will put us in Cook Strait, where it's probably even worse. If you don't want to die, we'll do better staying out here. Come up to the cockpit. You'll feel better."

"I can't," she groans. "I'm far too ill." I give up on her and return topsides. Though Mark is clearly worried, he keeps his concerns to himself. Unlike Kym, I feel I can count on him in a pinch, and am glad to have him along. The worst would be to endure this alone.

Wave after wave crashes into the boat, and blasts of spray lash at the dodger. There's little to do but hang on. The sails are well balanced and the Aries windvane takes it all in stride, steering the boat better than I could—tireless, uncomplaining and efficient. I long for this to be over. The cruel thing about a storm at sea is that there's no respite, no moment's peace. There's only the relentless noise and the constant violence to the boat and crew, sapping your strength, your will, your ability to think clearly. Yet, in spite of my fatigue, I have to stay alert. Under these conditions something bad could happen at any moment.

Something does.

Atlantean crashes down off a wave and lurches awkwardly to one side. I feel, more than hear, the pop and sudden release of tension that signals an equipment failure, and leap to my feet in time to see the staysail collapse and tumble to the deck. The next wave strikes us solidly and washes the sail over the side. "What the—?" I exclaim, my mind refusing to register the event. The foot of the staysail lies draped over the port rail, thankfully still attached to the boat by the clew sheets and the tack.

The sight of the staysail coming down breaks the tenuous hold Mark has been keeping on his fear. "Kym!" he screams. In a flash, she's at the companionway ladder. "We've lost the sail!"

She bursts into tears. "Oh God, oh God, oh God!" she wails. "We're going to die!"

I have to see what happened and can't waste time on them, so I clip the tether of my safety harness to the jack line running the length of the deck and hurry forward. All I can think of is that the staysail's come apart, the head's torn out, and the sail's ruined. Powered only by the main, *Atlantean* rounds up in the wind and stalls. Waves slam into the hull, rocking us violently, while the leach on the luffing main stutters and slats. Seconds later, the bow falls away from the wind and the main fills, heeling us over again. With the wind tearing at my rain gear and waves washing over me, I kneel on the foredeck and haul the staysail back onto the boat, praying it will be intact. If not, I have only the tiny storm jib to replace it.

The dripping mass of white polyester comes over the rail, stained with streaks of blue bottom paint. A quick inspection of luff and leach lifts my spirits; the sail is undamaged! Looking closer, I discover that the furling car shackle at the head of the sail has failed, a mangled piece of it somehow still hanging from the head cringle. I spot the rest of the broken shackle lying against the bulwark. No problem, I think, I have plenty of spare shackles. But then the realization hits me like a punch to the stomach—to attach the new shackle, I need the furling car. I look up and spy the furling car on the stay, held aloft by the staysail halyard, forty-five feet above the deck.

Frantic, I lash the staysail to the safety lines and scramble to the mast. "Please come down, please come down, please come down," I pray aloud while I uncleat the staysail halyard and shake it free. Nothing happens. I shake it again and again. The furling car remains aloft, stuck fast, and my heart sinks.

I'll have to climb the mast.

The very thought chills me to the marrow. There's no other way to lower the halyard, nor is there a spare or separate halyard already rigged for the storm jib. I stare up at the mast, gyrating crazily against the gray sky. How can I possibly do it? I return to the cockpit to give Mark and Kym the grim news.

"Somebody's got to rescue us!" Kym cries. "You're going to kill us out here!" She's approaching hysteria. Mark stands by mutely while I struggle with the wheel to find a position that will hold us hove to, but with only the main it's no use and we either round up and stall, or fall off too far and heel hard over. While I'm working, I consider our choices and afterwards explain them as carefully as possible, more to clear my own thoughts than to ask for advice.

"Our first option is to run before the wind, back to New Zealand," I say.

"Yes!" Kym rasps, as if her most fervent prayer has just been answered.

I look her in the eye. "I've ruled that out unless all else fails," I say. "The only shelter is all the way back in Tasman Bay, and that means dealing with the entrance to Cook Strait. We're far safer holding well off a lee shore, even if it is a hundred miles out.

"We can't use the other headsail, the yankee, to stabilize the boat," I continue. "In this wind, it would overpower us, possibly blowing out the yankee or even threatening the mast.

"We can sit here like this and wait for better weather, but the weather forecasts have been calling for better weather for three days, and it's only gotten worse. The barometer is low. Way low. I don't know how long the mainsail will hold up. If we lose the main, we're cooked." To accentuate my point, the boat rounds up and the sail flaps angrily. I'm glad I had a new main built in Auckland; the old sail would have shredded by now.

"Lying ahull is an option, but we'd get tossed around like marbles in a can. We might even get knocked down. It would be rougher than anything we've experienced yet, but it's my first choice if my plan doesn't work."

"What's your plan?" Kym asks, her voice shaky.

"I'm climbing the mast to bring down the halyard. After that, we'll raise the staysail and heave to again."

"You can't go up there," she shouts.

"I'm going to give it my best shot."

Kym bursts into tears and disappears into the cabin.

I'll need Mark's assistance and explain to him what I want. It's not a difficult job, but it means leaving the relative security of the cockpit. "You'll stay at the bottom of the mast and tend the halyard. When I grab the furling car, play out the line so it doesn't foul. Once I'm down, hang onto the furling car for all you're worth so it doesn't go back up the stay. I'm not going up there twice." Mark listens carefully and nods; I knew I could depend on him. We make our way forward, the tethers to our safety harnesses dragging along the jack lines, the wind beating on us, the waves soaking us. Kym appears in the companionway to watch, looking despondent.

We position ourselves at the base of the mast. *Don't think about it*, I tell myself. *Just get up there and get the job done. Don't look down. DON'T THINK ABOUT IT.*

There's no good way to hook another halyard to my harness for Mark to winch me up. Knowing I wouldn't be flying the spinnaker with my inexperienced crew, I foolishly removed the spinnaker halyard in New Zealand to eliminate some of the clutter at the base of the mast. The yankee halyard is a poor possibility, since using it requires lowering the furled headsail, then dismantling the yankee's furling gear—difficult work on the bow of the pitching boat, and which risks losing valuable equipment over the side. The mainsail halyard would work well, but it's holding up the main, and the main is our only source of stability in these raging seas. I decide the best approach is to clip my tether to the vertical rise of the taut mainsail halyard, so it will slide along the halyard as I climb. That way if I fall, I'll stay on the boat and at best only be seriously injured when I hit the deck. It sounds better than sure death in the water, since Kym and Mark would never figure out how to rescue me.

The last I checked, the wind was blowing a steady forty knots, with gusts over forty-five, the roughest sustained weather I've ever sailed. The first time I climbed the mast, other than tied to a dock, was in Juneau, Alaska, on flat calm water. When a boat went by, the wake nearly shook me loose. Now I'm going to try it in breaking five-meter seas.

It's a small consolation that I don't have to go up all fifty-six feet. From just beyond the spreaders, about thirty-eight feet high, the staysail furling car should be reachable.

DO IT NOW! I tell myself.

I hook my harness to the main halyard. Mark crouches at the base of the mast. The wind howls around us, as loud as I've heard at sea, maybe as loud as falling off the Skipper's Canyon Bridge with a bungee cord tied to my ankles. Only this time I have to keep my fear in check, because I'm not in good hands, there's no assurance that every precaution for my safety has been taken. The mainsail leach snaps furiously adding to the din—how much more can it take?

I pull on my spare dry sailing gloves, grab the mast steps, and jam the rubber toe of my boot into the bottommost rung as far as it will go. I'm off the deck. Hand over hand, step by step, I climb aloft. The shrouds, the halyards, the spinnaker pole and its lines—everything conspires to be in my way. The hollow aluminum mast magnifies the impact of each wave, each vibration of the off-balance boat, and transmits them directly to my body. Staring at the mast and nothing else, I keep my mind a blank, and maintain the three-point stance, with only a single hand or foot probing for the next step.

One hand reaches the spreaders, a crossbar over halfway up. The wind screams through the rigging, louder than it was on deck, and is now a rocket roaring in my ears. *Atlantean's* bow crashes off a wave, swinging the mast like a pendulum, arcing it through the air and flinging me forward, forcing me to hang on for dear life. At the end of the arc, the boat rolls and the mast lurches sharply to port. Another wave raises the bow and the whole scenario repeats itself, except this time the boat lurches to starboard. I keep my eyes riveted to the mast, and wait for the rolling to subside, but it doesn't.

The lower shrouds join the mast a foot below the spreaders, which means there was no room to install a mast step. Instead I have a long threaded bolt extending five inches through the tang holding the shrouds in place. This provides plenty of foothold when the boat is dockside, but now it's little more than a place to rest a toe until my foot reaches the spreaders.

I place my boot on the bolt and will myself to shift my weight to it. My gloves are soaked, and when I grip the step above the spreader, water squeezes out and runs down my arm. The wind seems even stronger, ripping at my rain parka and stinging my eyes. The mainsail leach chatters like a machine gun a few feet from my head.

I can feel my nerve giving out. The boat careens off another wave, thrusting my perch over the water. I hug the mast to my chest, the sharp edges of the steps cutting into my arms. The fear builds rapidly now, and against my better judgment, I look down at the boat crashing through the foaming, angry seas. It's a very long way down.

My resolve breaks completely, and I give in to terror. It surges through my body in ugly spasms, sends my stomach into my throat and chokes me. I can't get a breath. My hands and feet clutch the mast in a death grip. I have never been so frightened in my life. It's a mindless, timeless fear. There are no specific thoughts, no visions of myself crashing to my death, only this visceral, paralyzing helplessness. The wild motion of the sea flings me left and right, forward and back. The noise is deafening, the world chaos. I am consumed by the fear.

Then, as if somebody has spoken it to me, an idea crystallizes in my mind, clear and bright. *"GET DOWN,"* it says, *"NOW. FALL IF YOU HAVE TO. GET DOWN!"*

Without thinking, my toe comes free and finds the first lower step. Then a hand grabs the spreader, then the other hand. Now another foot frantically seeks the next lower step. I no longer care if I miss a foothold. The fall would be welcome, bliss, a release from this torture, but somehow my hands and feet find their marks. I untangle myself from the rigging and fight my way back down. Another step and another. I miss the last one and crumple to the deck, collapsing at the base of the mast.

Unable to believe the boat's solidity beneath me, I wrap my arms around the mast boot and curl into a fetal tuck, indifferent to the lashing spray. My body shakes uncontrollably, I can't catch my breath, and my eyes open and close blankly. Mark stands to one side, staring, not moving or saying anything. I don't know how long I lie there, maybe a minute, more likely five. "I can't do it," I finally manage to gasp. I unhook my harness, re-attach it to the jack line, and half-crawl back to the cockpit.

Kym stares at me with complete despair. "I thought you were going to die," she mumbles hoarsely. "What would happen to us then?" I lie down in the cockpit, utterly drained, still shaking. Withdrawn into myself, hugging my knees to my chest and silent, I feel nothing but hopeless anguish.

During the next hour, life slowly returns to my body. Concern for the boat is probably what brings me around, because I realize if I don't do something soon, something else will fail. It's only a matter of time. The trembling stops and I'm able to sit up and pull myself together.

There must be a way, I think. I rack my overtaxed brain for ideas and come up with one: if I can handle the boat hook, a long pole with a hook on the end, I won't have to climb so high. I can stand on the spreaders, hook the furling car, and pull it back down.

With Mark trailing behind, I return to the mast. Up I go again, but the boat hook is a terrible distraction. Maintaining a hold on it impedes my progress to the point I'm ready to let it loose, but somehow it stays in my hand. I arrive at the point I reached before, to the threaded bolt below the spreaders, and again the winds seem to grow stronger, the motion of the boat more violent. I cling to the mast while the waves toss me around the sky. In the grip of the same fear, I clamber back down.

It takes another hour before my third attempt, and this time I leave the unwieldy boat hook behind. While I'm glued to the shaky mast, *Atlantean* bucks and rolls in the churning seas. At the spreaders, I look up at the black clouds speeding through the gunmetal sky. The furling car is simply too far away, too high. Four more impossible steps loom between me and any chance of reaching it. Paralyzed by the fear, I can go no farther. Again I retreat and crawl back to the safety of the cockpit.

The wind gauge is stuck on forty, except when it bounces even higher. How long can it continue like this? What little stamina I have after more than two days of battling the gale is now depleted. Each time I climb down, I feel weaker than before, and wonder whether I'll be able to attempt it again.

It's late in the day and time for my radio contacts. I drag myself below and turn on the radio, but after ten minutes of hailing my cruising friends and getting only static in response, I turn the dial to Kerikeri's frequency. John signs on, and asks if there are any emergencies. I wait a moment to see if somebody has a more urgent problem, then press the transmit button. "Kerikeri Radio, Kerikeri Radio, this is *Atlantean*, repeat, *Atlantean*, whiskey bravo bravo niner seven four one. We are experiencing difficulties and request that you respond." I'm not one of their paying customers, but I need to talk with somebody, anybody. John acknowledges my call and I explain our predicament. From the safety and comfort of his land-based transmitter, there is little he can do except sympathize. He agrees with me it's better not to run towards Cook Strait, where they are predicting a full gale.

"What about the full gale I've got out here?" I shout into the microphone. "You've been promising better weather for three days."

"Well, yes," John answers with typical Kiwi aplomb. "We thought it would improve after the front passed, but it appears there was a low parked behind the front nobody knew about. It's on the weather chart now."

"I don't think I can go up the mast again today," I say. "It's getting dark."

"It should calm down a little over night," John says. "Can you hang on until morning?"

"I don't know," I say. "I guess we haven't got a choice." There's nothing more they can do for us. We're in danger, but not so much that we need the Coast Guard to come out and get us. Not yet, at least. I sign off.

In desperation, I unfurl the yankee a few turns, to see if I can use it to heave to. It unrolls too far, and threatens to swamp us, and it takes us several tries to get it refurled. I start the engine briefly, thinking it might provide some stability, but the boat hobbyhorses badly and the propeller cavitates. Afraid of sucking water through the exhaust pipe when the stern plunges beneath the waves, I shut it down. It's nearly full dark when I decide to climb the mast one more time.

This time, I make it.

Perhaps I've burned all of the fear out of me. Perhaps I no longer care whether I live or die. Perhaps I can no longer stand watching *Atlantean* tear herself to pieces. After I climb the first few steps, Mark hands me the fully extended boat hook, which I hang from my harness. It's too difficult to hold in my hand during the climb and I'm indifferent to its fate. Upward I go, one step at a time. Like before, when I reach the spreaders the wind seems to accelerate, grabbing at my clothing, clawing at my fingers. The boat pitches again and again, and I tighten my hold. This time, for the first time, my feet make it all the way to the spreaders. I lock my left arm around the mast with the intermediate shroud carving at the crook of my elbow. I scarcely feel the pain. My mind is a blank, not because I consciously keep it so, but because it's lost the ability of cogent thought.

I strain upward with the pole, forcing it steady against the wind. It's six inches too short, and I have to go up one more step. Leaving the relative stability of the spreaders and forcing my foot into the next stirrup, I rewrap my left arm around the mast and swing the boat hook towards the furling car. The eight-foot pole levers as the boat jerks back and forth, and I miss several times. "Come on, you bastard!" I scream. The leverage is too great, and I can't control the pole's wild oscillations. I find the next step and swing the pole. I miss, and swing again, and miss again. My elbow throbs, the mast batters my knee and thigh every time the boat hits another jarring wave. My wrist aches with the strain of holding the pole and my hand grows numb, extended as far above my head as I can reach.

I swing one more time. The tip of the boat hook catches the furling car and pulls it six inches down the stay before slipping off. Encouraged, I swing again and succeed in getting the whole hook looped around the cable. I pull down, but nothing happens. I pull harder. The car refuses to budge. I curse Mark and shout to him to loosen the halyard. To do so, I have to look down, and the sight of the boat pounding through the black, storm-tossed sea nearly freezes my blood. "SLACK, DAMN IT, GIVE ME SOME SLACK!" I roar. In agony, I watch Mark work furiously with the coiled halyard at the base of the mast. He gestures upwards and shouts something, but his words are ripped away by the wind.

Still tugging at the boat hook, I trace the run of the halyard in the gathering darkness until I find the problem. The slack halyard has fouled under my boot—I'm standing on it! I release one of my two precious toeholds and shake my foot, until another oscillation of the mast forces me to ram my toe, and the tangled halyard, back into the step. On my third attempt, I kick it free. I pull again, and the furling car slides a foot down the stay. Not letting go of the pole, I search with my toe and find a step down. When it's firmly in place, I pull the car another foot lower. My feet reach the spreaders and I pull the car down farther.

Getting around the spreaders is the trickiest part. I jam the pole under my arm as I grope for the next step. Twice I lose the pole and watch it swing out into space. Miraculously it doesn't slide off the halyard, and both times I'm able to reach out and snatch it as it flies back towards me on the next wave. I work my way down, one precious step at a time. With six or seven steps to go, I long to jump, to take the express elevator down to the deck, but some rapidly fraying thread of sanity keeps me at my business. My arms and legs are numb, my chest constricted, and spasms of fear course through my intestines. I've been having them for so long, I've stopped noticing them.

And then, Mark is there. He reaches up from the deck and grabs the pole, takes it from the bloodless claw that was my hand. I clatter down the last two steps and fall in a heap at the base of the mast. As before, I wrap my arms around it and suck solace out of the solidity of the deck. "You got it!" Mark shouts. "You got it!"

"Don't let go," I gasp. With a trembling hand, I fumble in my pocket for the replacement shackle I brought with me, but my fingers won't grip the metal. "Tie it to something," I stammer. "I've got to..., I've got to get back..." I can't finish my thought, what little there is of it. I crawl on my hands and knees to the cockpit and curl up under the dodger, shaking.

"What happens now?" Kym's worried voice reaches me from somewhere off in space. I ignore her and recede into myself, huddling, willing my lungs to take deeper breaths, my heart to slow its pounding, my muscles to unclench.

All day, I've kept tucked in the back of my mind a vague notion about how I would feel when I finally recovered the halyard. If not exactly triumph, I believed there would be at least some satisfaction that I'd risen to the occasion and gotten the job done. Instead, there's nothing. Only emptiness, exhaustion, and a fading memory of the fear that had held me in its grasp. There is a tiny sense of relief, relief that it's over, but that relief is lost in the yawning void of insignificance.

I've been humbled. I set out on this trip to test the limits of my endurance, and now I've found those limits, even pushed them beyond what I dreamed imaginable. Yet there's no satisfaction in the accomplishment. Nature has demonstrated her absolute indifference to my puny efforts to meet and match her. The sea, the wind, the rain—they care not one wit about the three humans on this fragile concatenation of fiberglass, wood, and wire, alone on a vast expanse of ocean. Why do we humans think we can challenge the might of the sea? Nature could squash us dead at any moment and it would signify nothing.

A single piece of metal failed, a spring-loaded piston inside a molded stainless steel fitting. For years it held up against incredible strains and stresses, until one day the elements decreed its limits had been reached. It was impossible to predict it would happen. Who can know how many parts on *Atlantean* are destined to fail at any moment? When something does fail, there's nothing to do but struggle against whatever hardships present themselves and fix the damage as best I can. Where's the glory, where's the triumph in that? We weren't sinking, nobody was in imminent danger of dying. I risked my life for nothing more than keeping a bad situation from getting worse. A more knowledgeable sailor might have found a better solution, a braver man might have quelled his fear and scampered up the mast on his first try. For me, I only did what I thought I had to do, and, this time, I succeeded. To what end? Nature always wins. At best, we can only delay the inevitable, put off the end for another day.

And yet: I climbed the mast, I recovered the furling car, I found a solution to a serious problem. Why? Because I'm human, and we humans can't help but soldier on, in spite of the ultimate futility. It isn't our arrogance over Nature that we're asserting, it's our refusal to give in to the inevitable, our compulsion to take control of our own destinies. It's the life force that drives us, that inexplicable urge that is Nature's answer to the cold laws of entropy. Wind and waves, the physical processes of corrosion, friction, and stress, are constantly reducing the world to chaos and disorder, while the life force within us—within every living organism—resists the pull into nothingness, insists that we create order, that we strive towards increasing complexity. It leans over our shoulders, imploring us, *"Create! Grow! LIVE!"* My ordeal on the mast was a small, mostly insignificant victory over the forces that would tear my boat asunder and send us to our deaths, but it was a victory nevertheless.

Our problems are far from over, though thankfully it appears the worst have past. When I finally rally, it's full dark. The wind still rages at forty knots around us, the mainsail is still slatting and flapping and stalling us, and the seas still pound the boat, crashing waves over us, but it's time to do what we can. Mark and I edge our way onto the foredeck, and while he holds a flashlight, I install the new shackle. We winch the staysail up as far as we can, then scurry back to the cockpit. I trim the thrashing lee sheet, and *Atlantean* resumes her push through the waves. When she's up to five knots, I put the helm over, turning the boat through the wind and backwinding the staysail. The wheel spins back to windward and we're hove to. The relief is unbelievable.

We remain that way for fourteen hours.

Mark and I split watches during the night. At first I'm too worn out to sleep, and later can only sleep in fitful snatches. I don't have the energy to get out of my wet clothes, the clothes I've been wearing for three days. I lie semi-comatose in my bunk, until from somewhere my strength gradually returns. I nibble on a few crackers and some cheese, and drink hot tea, and eventually find sleep.

Day Four

Morning of the fourth day dawns with no improvement in sight. I check in with Kerikeri Radio and give them the news about my successful trip up the mast. "Conditions should be improving anytime now," John says. "Look for winds to ease and clock around west to southwest."

I'm not so sure. The barometer has dropped another five points during the night, to 997 millibars (or hectopascals, as the Kiwis say), and the wind remains in the north at a steady forty knots. I've been using the GPS in the rough weather, instead of the sextant, and my morning fix reveals we slid thirty miles to the east since heaving to. By noon the winds have eased a fraction and shifted to northeast, yet again proving John's prediction wrong, but lying hove to has given me a chance to recover and rebuild my confidence. I heat up a couple of cans of stew, the first hot food I've eaten in two days.

A dilemma faces me. It's sorely tempting to stay put until the weather breaks, then limp back to New Zealand, but if we return, my crew will surely bolt the moment we get to the dock. How long will it take me to find replacement crew? Furthermore, what effect will this experience have on me? Turning back is like an admission of defeat. Will I be able to summon the courage to take to sea again, let alone battle the Tasman?

On the other hand, there's no reason we can't continue. The damage is repaired, and *Atlantean* is built for these seas. Conditions are tolerable for a fast, albeit rough beam reach. It's only my crew I'm worried about. They're worn out and surely yearn to turn back, but that can't matter. Kym and Mark signed on for the passage, and they'll have to live with it.

My decision is to proceed to Sydney. Without telling Mark or Kym, I bring the boat around and fill the sails. *Atlantean* takes the bit in her teeth, leans hard over, and is soon plowing through the heavy seas. Kym staggers out to the companionway and clutches at the ladder. "Are we going back?" she asks. She's a pathetic sight, with deep rings around her eyes and her greasy hair hanging in her face. When I tell her no, she flings herself back into her bunk, in tears.

We're again tearing across the Tasman, at times over eight knots. Waves rip across the deck and through the cockpit, and more water leaks into the boat. Whenever I go below, Kym refuses to look at me. More alarming, Mark appears worse each time I see him in his bunk. Neither he nor Kym ate any of my stew, although Mark has at least kept up his fluid intake. By early afternoon I need some rest, and call for him to take my place. To my surprise a bedraggled Kym appears in the companionway, wearing her rain gear and safety harness.

"Mark's running a fever," she says. "He can't get out of bed. I'll take his turn."

I clip her harness in place and tell her to hang on. "The Aries is doing all the work," I say. "For God's sake, Kym, call me at the first sign of trouble. You don't need to deal with it alone. We'll get through this. Trust me. Trust *Atlantean*. She won't let us down."

I go below to check on Mark. "I'll be all right," he says with admirable pluck. "I must have got a bit of a chill last night." He's been going barefoot in the cockpit so he won't get his expensive trainers wet. I give him two aspirin and a full glass of water and tell him to sleep as best he can.

After four hours, Kym's terror gets the better of her and she calls me from the cockpit. "When's it going to stop?" she wails. It's her favorite refrain, along with, "We're going to die!" What can I do? I send her back to her bunk and stay in the cockpit as long as I can. As the night wears on, the wind clocks through the east and, amazingly, goes into the south. The barometer climbs five millibars, signaling the passing of the low. We're now running fast on a rolling broad reach, battling turbulent four-meter seas. The wind gauge registers twenty-five knots apparent, which means winds are still around thirty, coming in from the port quarter. Earlier, Kerikeri Radio reported severe gales with winds over fifty knots lashing Cook Strait and its approaches.

Before I can wake Kym, Mark climbs into the cockpit, saying he's slept hard and broken the fever. He eats some hot food I make him before I go to bed. I envy him his hard sleep, since I can't sleep for more than about a half-hour before some crash or roll jerks me back to consciousness. Later that night, Mark calls me after his endurance gives out and he can't pry Kym out of her bunk. Dead tired, I flop back into the cockpit.

Day Five

We finally see some improvement as the night turns to day. The barometer continues its climb, indicating the lows are gone, and the wind goes into the southwest as Kerikeri Radio has been predicting for nearly a week, bringing us onto a beam reach. Yet the wind refuses to drop below twenty-five knots, and the seas are a confused mess. Kym resumes drinking, and chokes down some chicken broth I prepare for her. Mark and I both feel much better, though the ride is still uncomfortable. Even with the improved conditions, I can never relax. I keep a careful eye and ear on the boat, and make regular trips to the foredeck, battling the soaking spray, to inspect the mast and rigging. The broken shackle has shaken my confidence. What will go next?

It's been an awful five days, not only the worst sailing I've ever known, but also the worst five consecutive days of my life. We've logged only an unimpressive four hundred miles since Nelson. It's not over yet, but it can't continue, can it?

That afternoon, when Kerikeri Radio calls *Atlantean's* name on the roll, I respond with a poem.

> *Our position's latitude three-eight degrees*
> *Minutes, twenty-seven*
> *One-six-eight degrees, eight minutes east,*
> *I'd hardly call it heaven*
>
> *Our course is good for Sydney,*
> *About two-six-five magnetic*
> *But beam reaching at about five knots*
> *Is really quite pathetic*
>
> *We're reading one-zero-one-three*
> *Hectopascals on the bar,*
> *Visibility's very good*
> *You can see really far*
>
> *Winds are from the southwest*
> *Two-five, three-oh, three-five,*
> *When we finally get to Sydney,*
> *I'll thank God we're still alive*
>
> *Waves are also southwest,*
> *A four or five meter swell*
> *But the way the boat is crashing*
> *I'd say it's rough as hell*
>
> *Cloud cover is all over,*
> *I'd venture one hundred percent*
> *But fortunately for us, all day*
> *Not a drop of rain it's sent*
>
> *We're tired and sick and hungry*
> *We've been five days in this poop,*
> *None of us can stand the galley*
> *Long enough to cook the soup*

So now the watch is in the cockpit
Hanging from his tether
Screaming, "John, for God's sake, tell us, please,
Where the hell's the good weather?"

My bit of doggerel merits several microphone clicks of appreciation and John's on-the-air chuckles. Even Kym offers me a grudging
smile.

After sunset the winds ease steadily, the clouds break, and the stars
reveal their diamond brilliance. Kym stands watch, but gives up around
midnight after only two hours. "Pleeze," she whines, "I've got to go
lay down. I'm really ill." I relieve her and discover us laboring along
under less than ten knots of breeze. The boat rocks uncomfortably in
the lumpy seas, an awkward, disorienting motion, especially without
much wind to fill the sails, but it's a blessing not to have to listen to
the constant howling.

Rather than shake out more sail, I start the engine. The batteries need
recharging since we haven't used the engine over the last several days.
The always-dependable Perkins diesel fires right up, and with its added
power, the boat stabilizes considerably. I set the electric autopilot on a
direct course for Sydney and go below to inspect the bilges.

They're nearly overflowing because the automatic bilge pump blew its
fuse after the filter jammed with debris from all the water we've taken. I
spend the next two hours hand-pumping the bilges, cleaning the filter,
and mopping up, until everything is in good order. By then there's no
wind at all, so I wrestle the sails down and straighten the mess that's
accumulated in the cockpit and under the dodger. Satisfied there's nothing urgent to do for *Atlantean*, I turn my attention to myself.

There's no question about it. I stink. For five days, I've worn the
same saltwater-soaked clothes. With the engine running, there's a good
supply of hot water, and I treat myself to one of the finest, most well
deserved showers of my life, disappointingly brief though it is, followed
by shaving off five days of beard. Fresh clothing feels like heaven. Mark
relieves me later that night. In the warm comfort of my cabin, our gentle
rocking passage through the calming seas and the steady drone of the
diesel lull me into my first deep sleep since we left Torrant Bay.

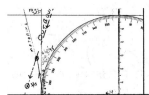

TONGUE LOOSENERS

TONGA'S VAVA'U GROUP: it's hard to imagine finer cruising grounds. Scores of small islands lay sprinkled over an area ten miles square, protected from the ocean swells by a reef system to the east. A foreign-based charter company operating out of Neiafu supplies its paying customers with a chart book of the local waters. Some cruiser got hold of it, and now all the cruisers in Tonga, including me, have photocopies of each other's photocopies, obtained for about $0.20 each at the post office's coin operated machine. The chart book numbers the best anchorages, and when cruisers contact each other on their radios, they'll say, "We're at Sixteen," or "Meet us at Seven." A sign scrawled on the notice board at the Bounty Bar, where cruisers congregate, will announce, "Bonfire and potluck at Twenty-Four Tuesday night."

The individual pages display the particular anchorages in detail, safely tucked behind reefs or sheltered in the lee of small islands, sometimes nestled in a protected lagoon. The water in these anchorages is so clear that standing on the bow I can make out the individual links of the anchor chain, all the way to where the shank buries itself in the sand. We don masks and flippers, fall over the side, and paddle around gawking at the brightly colored fishes and corals. Once, when we return to the boat from a wall dive, I spot a half-dozen squid,

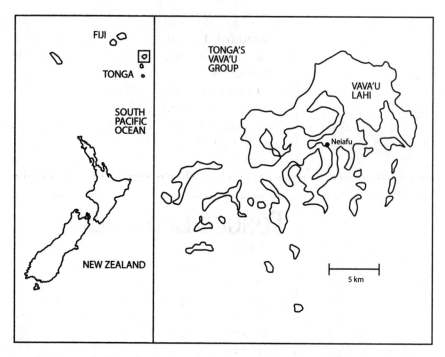

each about eighteen inches long, hovering in *Atlantean's* shadow. Their iridescent purple bodies and green eyes glow eerily, while their tentacles wave and point in the swell as if they were conducting underwater symphonies.

One of the many highlights of our scuba diving is a visit to Mariner's Cave, the unmarked entrance to which is four or five feet below the water's surface. Local legends say a beautiful princess (is there any other kind?) was led to the cave by the dolphins, to escape an attack from the islanders' enemies, and there she hid out until she could rally her people to defeat the invaders. Once we find the cave's entrance, we swim through a short passage, emerging in an open cavern, the roof of which is about thirty feet high. Light filtering through the underwater opening provides the only illumination, but it's enough to make the damp walls glisten and shine. As the water level rises and falls with the swell, the air pressure in the cave changes substantially. On the up-swell, our ears pop and fog forms around us. On the down-swell, our ears pop again from the pressure drop, and the fog instantly disappears. After a few minutes we swim down the rock face and find a second outlet thirty feet below the surface. We exit through the lower passage and enjoy the wall dive along the side of the island, ending up in another underwater entrance to a grotto a few hundred yards away. The roof here is open to the sky, and thousands of sardine-sized fish flash by, in and out of the shaft of brilliant sunlight light that streams down the walls and turns the water an opalescent blue-green.

The numerical nomenclature for these jeweled anchorages is more practical than the actual names printed on the charts, but it's the Tongan names I love. They're as soft, round, and tender as warm breezes whispering through the palms, as gentle as the rustlings of waves lapping at the white sands, and evoke the allure of the South Seas as they do throughout Polynesia. They're moans of pleasure, the innocent burblings and cooings of infants.

Taula. Lua Loli. Mu'omu'a.

Some are daunting in their length and seeming complexity.

Luaafuleheu. Fotuaikamamaha.

The sounds don't come easily to western tongues accustomed to nasal vowels, hard consonants, and abrupt glottal stops. They're not so much tongue-twisters as tongue-looseners. Arising deep in the chest, between the heart and the stomach, they slur and slide up the throat and around the tongue, then spill out of a smiling, toothless mouth.

Olo'ua. Nukulahanga. Malafakalava.

Perhaps I'll save these cheap photocopies of the charts I accumulate on my travels, to help explain the shapes of land and water. The world atlas is useless for the scale of a small boat and a coral atoll, and our atrophied imaginations want pictures and diagrams. *Where might these places be,* we ask ourselves, *in relation to me?* For now the impressions of islands, of coral, of winds, waves, and warmth, remain vivid, but can I really convey to others what sailing the South Seas is all about? And even if nobody hears my stories, someday I may want the charts for myself. Someday when these images and impressions have turned to memories, and the memories have grown dim. Someday when I again want to feel these tongue-looseners lolling around in my head, and spilling out of my smiling, toothless mouth.

A WEEKEND IN NEIAFU

Saturday

I'm standing at the window of the Tonga Co-Op watching the locals crossing the muddy streets and crowding the slippery wooden sidewalks. It's Saturday morning, market day in Neiafu, the largest town in these northern Tongan islands known collectively as the Vava'u Group. Every family from miles around has come here for the shopping and socializing, unfazed by the steady, soaking drizzle. They go about their business under umbrellas, or in rain slickers and parkas emblazoned with corporate logos: "Northern Idaho Telecom" or "Dominion Construction, Ltd." or the Pacific Islanders' favorite, "Chicago Bulls."

"Sorry, sir, but with no receipt, we cannot replace this item." I stir from my reverie and turn to the Tongan employee of the Co-Op. He holds two cellophane packages of rolled oats ("Suitable For Hot Porridge" they say on their labels). "Are you sure your wife bought it yesterday?"

When I came in, I said my wife had purchased the bag of oats the day before so the clerk wouldn't think it had somehow become contaminated in my possession. Of course there is no wife, and it's actually been three or four days since I bought the oats myself and

145

tossed the receipt on my way out the door. But it should have been a simple matter to show them the unopened package crawling with weevils and exchange it for an untainted one. After all, this is the only place in town that sells them. At first all went well. The clerk at the counter told me to leave the offensive package behind and get another off the shelf. By the time I got back, this other fellow had shown up, insisting on proof of purchase.

I make a few half-hearted arguments and excuses, trying to appeal to the man's sense of simplicity, not to mention justice. Can't he just take the bad package and give me a new one? He stares at me, uncomprehending. Some genius got the very un-Tongan idea of computerizing the inventory in the store, and unless this purchase goes back through the computer, nothing is going to happen. Computers clearly have no place in Tongan society or in my present predicament.

I pick up both bags and say, "Look, this one is full of bugs. It's obviously bad and of course we bought it here..." Glancing down, I realize I no longer know which bag I brought in because both are alive with weevils. Any enthusiasm I had for the subject evaporates. "Forget about it," I say. "Maybe you can sell them to somebody else."

As I turn to go, he says, "If you come back Monday, I will discuss it with my manager." He's trying to be helpful, but he can't buck the computer.

I leave through the open double doors and step onto the Co-Op's covered porch where Tongan men wearing calf-length skirts and translucent rubbery sandals wait for their wives to finish their rounds. They smoke skinny hand-rolled cigarettes and blabber away in vowely Tongan, sounding like a gathering of monstrous toddlers with unformed palates. The hoods on their rain parkas are pulled back to reveal ball caps: "John Deere," "Steinlager Beer," and the ubiquitous "Chicago Bulls." I suppose yachties and tourists trade hats and jackets for the local tapa cloth, fruits, and fish. Tonga doesn't seem to be the sort of country where brand name counterfeiting could possibly pay off.

Clusters of young girls engage in universal young girl behavior, standing in tight circles under the awnings and chomping gum. They shriek hysterically and talk too loudly, and pretend to ignore the teenage boys who are pretending to ignore them. The boys prefer to stand in the rain, the better to show off their indifference. They sport their best tee shirts and baggy knee-length shorts, and shove and splash each other, no doubt hoping someone will suffer the ultimate humiliation of falling in the mud. A few of their shirts are done up in macho Polynesian motifs, such as a magnificently muscled South Seas warrior cocked to heave a spear (historically, the Polynesians were more into clubs, but no matter). Surfboard marquees, Harley-Davidson motorcycles, and of course the Chicago Bulls are also popular. Many of the boys are trying to grow mustaches, and tattoos are becoming more common, though tattooing is not part of the Tongan cultural tradition. Most of the tattoos I see are the geometric designs found in the Marquesas Islands and in Western Samoa. Johanna, the Dutch woman who's been crewing for me since Bora Bora, got a sporty Marquesan anklet inscribed for her in the Cook Islands, and more than one young Tongan male has shyly asked me about it. None of them would dare address a direct question to a woman.

Across the street is the Bounty, the local cruiser hangout that must have had a late night because it isn't open yet. Now and then a drenched yachtie—a "palangie" as the Tongans call white people, though not to our faces—scurries up and tugs at the door. When it won't open, he looks around irritably, wondering where he's supposed to wait for his wife now that he's laden with her purchases, the agreed upon place is locked up, and there's no other shelter from the rain. After a while a palangie woman in a worn parka and drab full-length skirt strolls across the muddy street, produces a key, and to the relief of a now small knot of impatient yachties, opens the door to let them drip all over her floor.

I start for the Bounty, and then change my mind when I realize hot coffee is still fifteen or twenty minutes away. Instead, I head for the marketplace, up the street past the fire station, where the Saturday market is in full soggy swing. At the entrance to the square the same Tongan evangelist I saw last week flings hellfire through a tiny and badly distorted loudspeaker. It's all in Tongan, though the tools of his trade—the wooden cross around his neck, the clutched well-worn Bible, the accusatory finger—supply ample clues as to content. Behind him a ragged chorus of six women and two men—one with a guitar, all sopping wet—belts out some song so loudly and shrilly I can hardly follow the tune. They never seem to finish, nor change songs for that matter, on and on, now and forever without end, amen. No shoppers pay any attention or pause to ponder the fates of their immortal souls.

The marketplace is like a corral into which enormous people have been herded, though none match the reputed stature of His Royal Largeness—Tonga's King—at 6'7" and 400+ lbs. Practically everybody here carries a significant amount of weight, but I wouldn't describe them as obese, not in the way some Americans back home are enveloped in great rolls of fat, stuffed like bulbous sausages into gargantuan double-knit pants and tops. Here it's as if people pack a lot of well-marbled meat on their substantial bone structures. Black umbrellas add more bulk to the long-skirted women who shop or tend the basketted offerings, and I bob out of the way whenever an umbrella slides by at an eye-threatening height.

In the outer section of the market, semi-permanent plywood stalls offer stacks of unrefrigerated chicken eggs, various prepared foods, and suspicious looking meats. I've taken a shine to some kind of local dumpling, probably only coconut flour deep fried in coconut oil, but it's chewy and sweet and costs a trifling 10 centiti (100 centiti make up a pa'anga, denominated by the symbol $ and worth about US $0.80). I buy a few at a stand operated by three hefty ladies hovering over a bubbling cauldron of hot oil, and they wrap my purchase in a page torn from a month-old Australian newspaper. The paper is soon soaked through by the grease and rain, leaving a newsprint stencil on my warm dumplings.

Munching my breakfast, I run into a sodden Tristen and her husband Mike from the boat *Stormy Weather*. Tristen's frizzled blond hair, plastered to her head and face, makes her look like a wet cat who would prefer to be elsewhere. Soon she will be, Mike tells me after Tristen goes off to buy tomatoes. "On Monday Tristen's flying back home for awhile," he says, "to take care of some personal business."

Such as not cruising, I think to myself. Tristen recently circulated a survey among the women on the yachts in the harbor, consisting of her self-composed questions designed to address that thorny issue, "Can cruising really satisfy a woman's needs?" I hear she's getting lukewarm responses; most women who have made it this far across the Pacific have a fairly serious commitment to the lifestyle. Perhaps Tristen is out to demonstrate to Mike that where they really ought to be is holed up in a house in Santa Fe or Taos.

Mike, in contrast, loves everything about cruising, is unmoved by Tristen's distress, and has told me on a number of occasions that he'd like to explore the challenge of single-handed sailing. He'll say, "T, you let me sail this next passage alone, and then fly over and join me when you're ready." Tristen hates the idea of Mike not needing her more than she hates cruising, so in the end she sticks with him. The trip home is likely a chance for her to decompress—some of us would consider it "recompressing"—and maybe help them keep their marriage together. Mike says they're sailing around the world, but I doubt they'll get that far.

Tristen returns with her tomatoes and tugs at Mike's sleeve. "Let's go, Michael," she whines. Mike and I agree to look for each other next week, perhaps buddy-boating together out to the anchorages, after which I say goodbye to Tristen and wish her well back home.

I wander through the market, finishing my dumplings. It's amazing, the quantities of roots and tubers offered for sale, sold by the basket load. The baskets are made of hastily yet expertly woven palm fronds, each about two feet long and holding twenty pounds or so. Into these are piled dirt-encrusted purple or white or brown tubers, each three or four inches in diameter, sometimes larger, selling for $6-$8 a load. I'm not buying, after eating my fill of taro and other starchy staples in French Polynesia and the Cooks. Baskets of coconuts and huge stalks of bananas are also on display, along with the normal third-world-market fare of tomatoes, cucumbers, and unidentifiable indigenous delectables. Last week I bought ten pounds of some kind of tiny clam for $5, and split them with another boat. They tasted like Pacific Northwest steamers, and we didn't get sick, as a few less adventuresome cruisers suggested we might.

After leaving the market, I stop at the bread shack on main street and buy a fresh-baked loaf for $0.60. Like everything else, the bread is wrapped in a torn section of newspaper, this one the June 16 edition of *Kalonikali Tonga*. I stuff the bread inside my green rain parka and begin the trek to the dinghy dock for the return ride to *Atlantean*.

Town is like a scene out of the Old West, with dirt streets and wooden storefronts, perhaps because Tonga was never a western possession and lacks the capital improvements colonials typically leave behind. The few cars move by slowly and courteously, so as not to splash me while I pick my way through the mud and chuckholes of main street. I yield the covered sidewalks to the groups of locals chatting amiably among themselves, oblivious to those of us forced to detour around them. As always, I'm struck by how many pigs are on the loose, whose numbers likely exceed the resident human population. Everywhere I look is a sixty or seventy pound sow nose down in the bushes, or in a garden, or in the garbage, with six or eight puppy-sized piglets in tow. The pigs are various piebald combinations of gray, black, and white, and mud-covered, impossible to tell apart if in fact anybody bothers. Tongans love their feasts, and we hear just about any occasion is a good excuse for a pig roast.

What do the locals think of us palangies with our fancy and not so fancy sailboats, invading their island home? It's a question I've pondered for a year now, throughout Mexico and the South Pacific, and have never reached a satisfactory conclusion. As elsewhere, there is little meaningful interaction between the cultures, as if both sides recognize the impossibility of either being able to fathom the other. Notions of universal brotherhood are pragmatically reduced to simple acceptance, without any real understanding of each other's lives. There is mutual envy: the yachties yearn for the paradisiacal setting and stress-free lifestyle; the locals covet the abundance of unattainable consumer goods. The yachties think they can have it both ways, and the Tongans never stop to consider what they'd be giving up.

Modern medicine and a religious and cultural aversion to birth control have resulted in a rapidly growing population of Tongans, while at the same time the fragile reef ecosystems that have supported these islanders for generations are dying. One formerly popular dive site was called the Coral Garden, and now it's an expanse of gray, lifeless coral, with only the occasional gray, uninteresting fish swimming about, as if it got the wrong address to the party. Part of the desolation is attributable to the crown of thorns starfish, which feeds on live coral and has recently begun showing up in Tongan waters, but the main cause of the destruction is people. The government finally prohibited the use of dynamite for fishing, but we hear it's still commonly used. Big feast coming up? Tossing a quarter-stick in the water is an easy way to harvest a lot of fish in a hurry, though it kills the reef and renders the area dead for years to come.

It's overly facile to blame Tonga's problems on stereotypes of short-term third-world thinking (as in "What's for lunch?" along with the more practical, long-term approach, "What's for dinner?"). Yes, these once technologically primitive societies want the affluence we've attained, and yes, they are unwittingly destroying the environments that have long sustained them in the process. What's more difficult is coming up with workable solutions that treat the desires of the people with dignity and respect, and address the long-term environmental concerns as well. In this regard, Western man has little to say for himself.

An organization that's doing something positive is Earthwatch, and last week I attended their presentation at the Paradise Hotel, to which all of the cruisers were invited. The evening started with a depressing Cousteau documentary about the worldwide destruction of coral reefs, precisely the kind of film that makes me wonder if Environmentalism would be more popular if there were some way to address our collective plight with a trifle more humor. At least it was followed by a more optimistic piece about saving Tonga's giant clams, which are disappearing rapidly and are in acute danger of extinction. We've seen the empty shells on our dives, some nearly a meter across, but no live ones. The reason they're disappearing is obvious—a large clam can feed an entire Tongan family—but the clams don't even begin reproducing until they're twenty-five years old, and most make their way to the supper table long before that. The Tongan government has banned their harvest, but people need to eat and poaching is rampant. The Earthwatch people are sponsoring a program for villages to seed and protect colonies of clams, and by making it a point of civic pride, the program is showing some early successes. At the end of the evening many of the cruisers asked what they could do to help, but other than giving money, which we're all short of, and being careful not to anchor in fragile coral, which is sometimes impossible to know about, and using our holding tanks, which nobody does because there are no pump-out stations, there's not much direct action we can take. At least we're not causing as much of an impact on the environment as we would if we were living full-fledged American-consumer lifestyles.

Still protecting my loaf of newspaper bread from the rain, I reach the dinghy dock, where I climb into my inflatable Metzler and cast off. The dinghy has an inch of rainwater in it, but I proceed without bailing, figuring it will get wetter anyway. The wind has raised a chop and the going is slow, past the many boats whose owners have elected to stay put in the harbor rather than venture out to the anchorages.

We haven't had a sunny day for over a week. Yesterday started off tolerably well, 100% overcast, but warm, dry, and bright under a thin cloud cover. In a burst of optimism I delivered my laundry, including my precious and oh-so-comfortable triple-ply cotton bed sheets, to the Vava'u Guest House up on the hill, to be washed and dried for the reasonable price of $1.50/kilo (including soap, for which other places charge extra, as if I'd mind having my laundry done without it). All was well with the weather until about 1500, and I looked forward to sleeping that night between clean sheets. However, minutes before heading to shore to recover my laundry, the skies darkened and opened to torrents of rain; about an inch fell in the ten minutes it took for the squall to move on. Though I was certain of the outcome, I nevertheless made the trek to the Guest House in the hopes my laundry had beaten the downpour. Alas, from the road I recognized the familiar patterns of my sheets, towels, and underwear dripping drearily from the lines behind the place. The proprietors and I agreed they would leave my clothes on the line until they were dry, but as soon as I got back to the boat the rain resumed and hasn't stopped since.

Now instead of cavorting in this tropical island paradise—swimming, sailing, exploring the anchorages—I sit glumly aboard *Atlantean*, stuck in crowded Neiafu harbor, waiting for better weather and the return of my laundry. Except for the temperature, around 72°, this may as well be December in Seattle. Or June in Seattle, if the truth be told.

I'm alone for the time being. Johanna has taken the week to sail off with another single-hander, Keith aboard *Sophia,* and may jump ship if she decides he's offering a better deal. No matter; every day I grow more comfortable with the idea of solo sailing. The wind drones through the rigging, the anchor chain scrapes across the dead coral, and the rain runs off the canvas "sun" cover into the rain catcher, now superfluous with my water tanks filled to overflowing. It will be another afternoon of reading, writing, eating, practicing my guitar, and playing too much Nintendo. It's a slow life, but not unsatisfying. I ought to find something that needs fixing or cleaning, but it's hard to get motivated in this gray gloom.

Sunday

The roosters' crowing awakens me the next morning, an hour before the sun is up. Throughout Mexico and Polynesia, wherever I've anchored near humans and their habitations, it's the roosters that announce each day, well before we sleeping travelers want to hear about it. Usually I check the condition of my bladder and either roll over and go back to sleep, or stumble to the head, careful not to wipe the sleep from my eyes so I can finish getting my nightly ten hours. This much sleep, I tell myself, is necessary to make up for those days and nights of little sleep at sea. But this morning I'm up early because I've been invited to church by my young Tongan acquaintance, Willy. He's the sixteen year old assistant at the boatwright's shop where I had *Atlantean's* bow roller and pulpit straightened after an anchoring mishap in Niue, and I recently loaned him a Bob Marley tape he liked.

Willy's employer, Don, is an expatriated American who has become an essential resource for cruisers in these waters whose boats are in need of repair. Don has a graying beard and thinning hair, and is a small man, but woven of the kind of tight gristle you'd find in a wind-ravaged mountain fir. His left eye wanders a bit, contributing to the wary look I've seen on other expats, a hard-bitten cynicism that says, "I may not fit in all that well around here, but it's a damn sight better than putting up with the bullshit back home." His accent is out of the West, arid and sparse, and while his manner is not overtly hostile, it discourages further questions. From the appearance of his workshop, which is crowded with tools, equipment, and disorderly stacks of salvaged metal, wood, and parts, he's been here for years. I imagine filterless cigarettes, a sometimes-excessive fondness for alcohol, and a local woman of long standing are elements of Don's no doubt fascinating history.

The rain finally stopped late yesterday afternoon, and the clouds parted to reveal a spectacular sunset. I bailed out the dinghy before dark and enjoyed a lukewarm beer under a clear starry sky. It's sunny this morning, clement and pure, and I breakfast in the cockpit on banana, papaya, fresh bread, and fried eggs, all washed down by several cups of rainwater. Afterwards, I shave to look more presentable for Willy's congregation, though I usually only shave every other day and already shaved yesterday. I decide long pants would be appropriate for this conservative, religious society, and retrieve my lightweight khakis from their hanging locker. My jeans are in deep storage, and shorts are out of the question, because all except the most tattered are held hostage at the laundry, probably still on the line waiting for the sun and wind to dry them. The plain short-sleeved cotton shirt I planned on wearing is missing two buttons, so I choose my Hawaiian print—suitable only for casual wear back home, but rather dressy in this part of the world. At least it's clean, since I never wear it.

I climb into the dinghy and start the outboard, pleased to find the seats still dry. During my half-mile ride to the dinghy dock, I pass other cruisers busying themselves with sunny-weather boat projects, contrary to Tonga's legally mandated "no work" policy for Sundays, which can land native Tongans in jail or subject them to stiff fines, including for such egregious and immodest activities as Sunday swimming. Only the bakeries are exempted; Tongans aren't willing to forego fresh bread. Those cruisers whom I know and greet along the way laugh when I suggest they join me for church, and some ask me to put in a good word for them with the Almighty. We cruisers tend to be a secular lot when we're safely at anchor, though a storm at sea might call for a revised outlook.

Near the dinghy dock, I catch up with Betty and John, also dressed in their Sunday best, rowing ashore from their fine old wooden ketch, *Integrity II*. They're a Canadian couple, though Betty is English by birth, married when they were each about forty, and are now in their early sixties. John used to work in the timber industry, mowing down forests around the Great Lakes. Betty was with BOAC in the fifties and sixties as an airline "stewardess" (as they were then called) before she met John, and later became a nurse. Though John is a man of thoughtful mien and few words, Betty has plenty of words at her disposal and is not shy to spend them on any subject you care to mention. Childless, she possesses a surfeit of motherly generosity and is forever offering me cakes and cookies, or inviting me to dinner on their boat. Two glasses of wine will wind up Betty for hours of stories. She loves to talk about her wild life as a fly-girl ("A different boyfriend in every town") and claims to have married John in order to settle down. Some years ago she and John served as volunteers for a Canadian organization similar to the Peace Corps, and lived in the western Pacific island nation of Vanu'atu for two years. Their current trip will bring them back to Vanu'atu, where they intend to spend several months with old friends and colleagues, after the customary sojourn in New Zealand to await the passage of typhoon season.

At the dock I help Betty climb out of the dinghy (lumberjack John declines my offer of a hand), and tell them of my invitation to attend Willy's church. Betty and John say they visited the Methodist Church the week before and are willing to try out Willy's church, whatever it may be. We set out walking for the Bounty Bar, where Willy and I agreed to meet.

Yesterday the streets swarmed with people, but today you could shoot a cannon down main street and not hit a soul, not even a pig. Everything is closed, including the Bounty. We arrive a little late, since I've had to slow my usual pace to match Betty and John's measured gait, but there's no sign of Willy. We wait for a few minutes, discussing which of the town's several churches we should visit if Willy doesn't show, and at 0945 set out in the direction of church bells coming from beyond the post office.

After we've gone a block, a young boy approaches us and asks where we're going. We smile and say, "To church."

He seems puzzled and asks, "Are you going to the wharf?"

"No," we repeat, "we're going to church."

Still troubled, he thinks for a moment, trying to piece together his English (which they learn in school), then asks, "What church?"

I tell him we don't know, and point toward the bells.

He brightens. "Ah," he says, "that is our church."

His English is pretty weak, but careful questioning reveals he's Willy's brother, sent here to meet us. He says his name, and it sounds like "John-Donna," which is what we parrot back at him. He nods at our efforts, though he doesn't appear completely satisfied we've got it right. He's probably around twelve years old. Betty flatters him shamelessly about what a big, handsome fellow he is, and compliments him on his fancy Sunday clothes: a flowered shirt that looks a lot like mine, a black polyester ankle-length skirt, a very new-looking woven mat folded in half and belted around his waist (we understand the folded mats are passed down through the families, and the really old, ratty ones are highly venerated).

Near the church, Willy joins us. "Thank you Mr. Greg for coming to our church," he says formally, with a little bow, before I introduce him to Betty and John, who recognize him from the boat shop. He wears a pinstriped long-sleeved white shirt (open collar) with his blue skirt and belted mat. I can tell language is going to be a problem, because even Betty runs out of things to say in the brief time it takes us to get to the church.

Tongans are milling around on the lawn and church steps when we arrive. "Do you want to go in now?" Willy asks. It's about two minutes before starting time, so we say yes. He seems surprised, then nods, and shows us to some seats near the back right side of the church. About twenty people are already seated on the left side, women toward the front, men in the middle. Willy goes back out, but John-Donna sits on the left to the rear of the men's section. I get the idea the almost empty right side of the church is reserved for special cases. One aging couple, perhaps guests, sits alone near the front, and behind them are women with young babies. Back right must be the palangie section.

The church is plain, with twenty rows of hard wooden pews on either side of the center aisle. The walls are bare except for several louvered and glassless windows that let in plenty of light and air. The business end of the church is sectioned off by a rather crudely wrought ornamental iron railing, behind which are the VIP pews, set against the walls atop woven mats bordered with bright red and yellow tassels. A table draped with a white cloth occupies the middle ground between these high-backed benches, and on it are two lit candles framing a head-and-shoulders poster print of Jesus, eyes and hands heavenward, laminated or shellacked onto a varnished plywood board. "God Bless Our Church" is written on the board in an arc of billowy sparkle-paint letters, which suggests to me the assemblage might have been a gift to the poor savages from well-meaning church ladies back in Kansas. Behind the table is what I suppose passes for the altar, a wooden dais about six feet high and twenty feet wide. Around a cross painted on its face are various texts written in Tongan, one of which contains the number 1929, perhaps the date of the church's founding. Faded red draperies adorn the upper portion of the altar, atop of which sits the further-raised lectern.

The people are turned out in all of their Tongan finery. To the traditional costume of skirts and belted mats, some of the men have added dark suit coats. The women wear light colored dresses over long dark or white inner skirts that reach below their dresses. Unlike in the rest of Polynesia, the women aren't wearing fancy hats, probably to avoid the sins of pride or vanity.

At 1000, the bells toll a more urgent message, and there's a rush of activity as the minister and elders parade through an open door next to the altar. Twenty more people scurry through the main and side entrances, and find their seats on the left, men and women completely separated. Our host, Willy, is a doorkeeper, and stations himself next to the right hand side door, facing another young Tongan on the opposite door.

The minister and elders wear black coats and skirts, and clerics' black shirts with stiff white collars. Not all of them have woven mats, though those we see are frayed and no doubt indicate great stature. The senior is a bespectacled, white-haired patriarch, and the lines of his face are etched in a perpetual scowl. Even with his age-diminished physique, he's a commanding presence. Leaning across the lectern and thumbing through his Bible, he begins droning a mechanical litany before the people have settled into their seats.

This initial address calls for responses at predetermined intervals, all of which are in Tongan, so we can't understand a word. A fellow with a big voice, perhaps a deacon, or a retired Oakland Raiders defensive end, is seated strategically in the very middle of the back of the church, and gets the crowd started with the correct responses. Much of the congregation is still flipping through their prayer books and jostling one another to find their spots on the benches. In the midst of the preacher's litany, everybody jumps to their feet, and the fellow in the back begins a loud song that drowns out the minister's voice. "Maybe that's why he looks so unhappy," Betty whispers to me, referring to the preacher. "They never let him finish." We snicker to ourselves.

The first song is brief and is followed by a more elaborate number. The singing is typical of the four or five church services I've attended throughout Polynesia: what the congregation lacks in pitch, it certainly makes up for in power. All four voices—bass, tenor, alto, and soprano—have separate parts, not only notes, but rhythm and text as well. At times it sounds totally cacophonous, and the melody lines are nearly impossible to ascertain, but after a while (and we listen to it for quite a while), the ear grows accustomed to it. As Christianity has done wherever it converts the heathens, I suppose the missionaries merely added religious text to the traditional Polynesian vocal forms. The congregation sings from memory, which is impressive given the length and complexity of the pieces, and suggests the singing I've heard two or three evenings this week was choir practice.

When the song ends, everybody abruptly turns their backs and drops to their knees on the linoleum floor, heads down on the pews. This catches us a little off guard, though Betty instantly follows suit and hits the deck like an impassioned pilgrim. It's apparently prayer time, so John and I sort of rotate in our seats and bow our heads as low as possible.

The preacher begins a rhythmic delivery, almost like a chant. After each stanza, the congregation groans or mutters something in Tongan. At first the preacher delivers his lines in a sort of monotone, but as he goes on, he turns up the volume and pitch. When his voice gets too high, to almost a shriek, he drops back down into the lower register, but by no means diminishes the volume. Although there's no artificial amplification, my ears start to ring. The crowd is similarly aroused, judging by the fervency of their responses, but they can't out-bellow the minister. After a good five minutes, the minister is so caught up in his delivery, he practically sobs out his imprecations. I consider sneaking a peak to see if he's gotten to real tears, but I'm afraid if I so much as raise my head, lightning will strike me dead. I stare at the wood grain on the pew and wonder how long this can go.

It finally does end, and we resume our previous postures. Willy and his fellow doorman open the side entrances, and another fifteen or twenty people stream in to take seats, either embarrassed about being late or happy to have avoided several minutes of kneeling on the hard floor while thunderbolts were being hurled about.

We listen to a few more songs and a responsive reading or two, while the babies cry and the big fellow in the back sneaks up on misbehaving boys to swat them before they start having too much fun. Little girls are dressed in frilly finery completely unlike the modest attire worn by their elder sisters and mothers, and, if under the age of three or four, they enjoy license to roam at will. One repeatedly comes into our row, staring at us silently. I smile and wink at her, but get no response before she toddles off.

It's difficult to stay interested in the proceedings, not understanding a word of them. The church doesn't have the usual religious orna- ments upon which to cast a dreamy eye. Instead, I look out the open door beyond the VIP section where the omnipresent Tongan pigs with their bevies of piglets root through the churchyard. They don't come into the church, though there's apparently nothing to stop them if they were so inclined. I conjure an amusing image of the elders pushing their way through a mob of snorting porkers, en route to tending their human flock.

We're about halfway through the hour when it's time to learn our lesson. A song ends and the preacher leans across the pulpit, glowering at us, stony disapproval of our malignant lives streaming darkly from his furrowed brow. All whispering and shuffling immediately cease. When we're sufficiently cowed, he closes his Bible and begins.

His first utterances are growled more than spoken, his voice thick with contempt. We are beyond hope, he tells us (or so I imagine), wretched beings utterly unfit to lick the dust off the steps to God's Holy Kingdom. He enumerates our sins, and they are legion. With each charge levied against us, his rage grows, as does the volume. The people hang their heads in shame. And the sins of our fathers will be visited upon us, we learn, even unto the tenth generation. He calls for the wrath of God to rain down upon us, for fire to pour from the sky, for pestilence to plague us and locusts to eat our eyes. On and on he rails, berating us for our hopeless condition. Many people in the audience weep audibly. Betty is near tears, rocking in her seat with her eyes closed, and even John flinches guiltily.

The unremitting onslaught continues for twenty minutes, during which the preacher's voice thunders over the congregation. He slaps his hand on the lectern, thrusts his arm in the air, points, shouts, practically foams at the mouth. The rafters reverberate with his roar. He builds to an impossible crescendo, culminating in a final terrifying shout that echoes into silence. No one in the church moves a muscle.

An anguished howl escapes from the preacher's throat. His eyes are shut, his lips drawn back from his teeth in a rictus of agony. Oh, how he suffers for us, our preacher. Only Christ on the cross suffered more than he does. How can we possibly comprehend the terrible trials he must endure, pleading with the Lord to take mercy upon our wretched and undeserving souls? To be our preacher, our intercessor before a jealous and vengeful God, is a burden no man should have to bear. His voice trails off in a hoarse whisper, and he slumps away from the lectern. He pauses for a moment, and then wearily straightens himself and walks rigidly back to his seat.

It would be interesting to know what he really said.

Fortunately the congregation has prepared a rousing song to cheer us up. That ends, and again it's time to rotate and drop, while another of the elders delivers what sounds like a much nicer, friendlier prayer. The bells ring and everybody pops out of their seats, smiling and chatting happily. It's time to go. The fellow with the big voice walks over and wordlessly shakes our hands. We shuffle along with the crowd out the back door. "They never passed the collection plate," John notes as we leave.

Willy and John-Donna meet us in the street, and offer to arrange a car to take us back to our dinghies, which, to their visible disappointment, we decline. Betty, however, can't resist the temptation to feed somebody fresh cookies, and invites us all to *Integrity II*. I beg off, wanting to get over to the Guest House to see how my laundry is doing, but Betty won't be denied. We walk together back to the dock, and when I have the boys in my dinghy on the way to *Integrity II*, Willy asks if he and John-Donna can visit *Atlantean* afterward. An hour and too many cookies later, we escape Betty's hospitality. On our way to *Atlantean*, I let Willy drive the dinghy. He promptly accelerates into a wave and soaks his poor brother, riding in front.

After drying off John-Donna, I seat the boys in the main salon aboard *Atlantean*, where we struggle with conversation. Most of the topics we can think of were exhausted on *Integrity II*, and they're not hungry for the lunch I offer. They sit stiffly on the settees and stare in open-mouthed wonder at *Atlantean's* teak interior, as if they can't believe anybody could live in such splendor. I play a CD for them, a technology they're unfamiliar with, and we smile at one another, tapping our feet and nodding our heads to the music.

I'm curious about the sermon, but when I ask Willy about the anger, the vehemence, he looks confused and uncomfortable, as if I might be suggesting some sort of sacrilege. "God is great," he says meekly when I press him to explain the preacher's message. "Love Jesus." It's no use; we lack the means of deeper discourse. Yet I don't understand the preacher's motivation. Is there an epidemic of sin raging through Neiafu, rampant commandment-bashing that merits across the board condemnation? The Tongans seem such a peaceful, contented people, as evidenced by the devotion and joy they pour into their singing; as some sage once said, evil does not easily abide where the residents regularly lift up their voices in song. Perhaps the explanation is something as base as keeping the populace docile and under control through fear of divine retribution, a tactic that works elsewhere, including in my own country. But how could I ever know without staying longer and making a determined effort to understand Tongan culture? Socio-religious analyses are not part of my self-interested travel plans. After a few weeks of play, I'll be gone, blown by the balmy breezes to the next island nation of coco palms, sandy beaches, and blue lagoons.

But what if I did stay on? Could I be like Don with his boatyard, or the palangie woman who runs the Bounty, expatriates who have settled in Tonga and more or less call the place home? Not hardly. After a short while, I'd miss the aspects of my own culture that I value, the arts, the conveniences that make life easy and comfortable, and the companionship of friends and acquaintances with whom I share a common background and values. I'd feel the pull of the land where I grew up, with its fir forests, fresh mountain snows, and vast open spaces. I'd chafe at the no-work edict on Sundays and the dietary staples to which my body is not accustomed. But most of all, I would find it difficult, probably intolerable, to always be the "Other," identified for my skin color and cultural heritage, for my passport and supposed access to unimaginable riches. This would be the case even if I made a determined effort to "go native," if I learned the language, attended the churches, worked side by side with the locals, or married a Tongan woman and had mixed-race children. Under such circumstances I eventually might get to the point of appreciating, perhaps even understanding, the Tongan's traditional culture, but there's no way that I would ever, or could ever, become part of it. We Americans are regularly accused of objectifying the various peoples of the world (including our own resident minority populations), but our country is far more integrated than Tonga will ever be, or at least for the foreseeable future.

Finally there's simply no more strained conversation to make. As it is whenever native visitors stay too long, I'd like Willy and John-Donna to leave so I can go about my business, whatever it might be, and they're content merely to hang around watching me go about my business. It's part of the impossibility of mixing the cultures. When I tell them it's time to go, they're disappointed. Willy asks if he can borrow a tape, and I say yes, as soon as he returns Bob Marley. I dinghy them back to the dock, where Willy promises he'll bring me a stalk of bananas on Monday, along with the tape. Maybe I'll take him sailing, if Don will let him off work. But for now all I want is my laundry, and that's where I'm headed, Sunday or not.

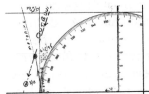

PLEASURES OF PASSAGE

IN THE GLORY DAYS OF SAILING, the Indian Ocean was known as "the sailor's reward" for its consistent and ample trade winds and rare stormy weather, ideal conditions for clipper ships that liked nothing better than thirty knots on the stern quarter. The westward passage is still a pleasure; some cruisers boast of sailing for days or weeks without once changing the sail set. On the downside for a small boat are the long and deep cross-swells originating in the storm-lashed Southern Ocean, which make for a somewhat rolly ride. Another difficulty is the distance between stopping places; unlike the South Pacific with its thousands of islands, the Indian Ocean below the Equator is largely empty. My first destination after leaving Darwin, in Australia's Northern Territory, is Christmas Island, fifteen hundred miles distant (an Australian phosphate mining and casino gambling outpost, not to be confused with the recently renamed Kirimati in the Pacific); the Cocos Keeling atoll (also an Australian possession) is another five hundred miles. From there, many cruisers travel twenty-five hundred miles to Madagascar, a sizeable land mass that millions of years ago drifted free of Africa's east coast, or to tiny volcanic Mauritius, once home to the extinct dodo bird. My ultimate goal is to round the tip of South Africa, and I expect to be on the Indian Ocean a total of sixty days before getting there, not counting stops along the way.

Crewing for me on the passage is a young Welshman, Ioan (YOahn), whom I picked up in Darwin. He's been bumming around the world for two years working where he can, and qualified for a charter captain's license in Australia's Whitsunday Islands. "It's not ocean sailing," he told me, "running the punters out and back, making sure nobody falls over the side, holding their seasick bags. I can get the sails up and down." He lobbied hard for the position because he wants to be in South Africa in time for the upcoming World Rugby Championship, and readily agreed to sharing expenses. At the last minute, and against Ioan's wishes, I added a hulking Dutchman to our company, Jelle (YELL-ah), a recent university grad who's been backpacking around Australia. Jelle has a sister in South Africa, and he says she can show us around when we arrive. Three's a crowd, but it's the end of the passage I'm most worried about, approaching South Africa with its legendary storms and seventy-five foot ship-breaking waves. It might be good to have a third hand aboard.

Land is where friction develops—money disappearing at an alarming rate, frustration and a lack of understanding with officials and the locals, and the feeling of being cooped up on a boat that's not going anywhere. The more I sail, the more it's the ocean passages I look forward to—settling into the rhythm of the shifting watch schedule, the satisfaction of charting the daily progress, the routines of caring for the boat and oneself, and simply beholding the world as it slides past at the pace of an easy jog.

The Green Flash

We're a week out of Cocos and it's approaching sunset, my favorite time of the day. Although the skies are generally fair, the trade wind belts are characterized by the constant daytime presence of small, widely scattered cumulus clouds, technically *cumulus humilis*, which I call "trade wind puffies." For reasons I've never fully understood, the clouds disappear within an hour after sundown and reappear an hour after sunrise. Towards the horizon they stack up to look like more than they really are, and that can produce wonderful sunsets.

During the past two and a half years of ocean sailing I've seen hundreds of sunsets, and it's safe to say no two were alike. Though sundown on the ocean doesn't often blaze with the kaleidoscopic dazzle I saw along the east coast of Australia, the cloud formations can be dramatic. Sometimes the setting sun disappears behind a band of clouds, and then re-emerges low in the sky, its golden eye peeking through a narrow slit above the horizon. Often there are different varieties of clouds—lumpy, wispy, cottony, billowing, or herringbone—and they take on fantastic shapes and shadings from the fading light. The most breathtaking cloud displays were near the Equator in the Pacific, where at times as many as nine thunderstorms towered around us, though the sky directly above was clear.

My preferred sunsets are those where I can follow the sun's descent all the way into the sea. The solar disk flattens and distorts as it touches the horizon and is soon a blazing red orb twice its normal diameter, seeming to linger a moment before completing its departure. Watching the sun disappear behind the long, slow curve of ocean, it's easy to picture the Earth as a sphere. I visualize the foreign shores lying to the west that are still enjoying the full light of day. Pushing my mind's eye farther, I look down on the distant lands of home where dawn begins to glow in the eastern skies.

I dearly want to see the green flash, and no sunset is complete without concentrating on the setting sun until it completely vanishes. I'm not even sure what the green flash is supposed to look like, but I know what I want it to be: a once-in-a-lifetime explosion of brilliant green fireworks sweeping across the horizon. The lore among sailors says it's only visible at sea the instant before the sun sets. One cruiser I know claims the green flash is the momentary greenish-white glow that I've sometimes seen on the sun's upper limb, but for now I'll go on believing there's more to it than that.

There is much I want to witness before I die: the northern lights, a total eclipse of the sun, the green flash, the birth of a baby. As frustrating as sailing can be, at times it helps to recall the sage's shopworn but oft ignored advice, that life is a quest for an ever-elusive goal, that what's more important is the meaning we derive from the search itself rather than its fulfillment. I take comfort from the ritual of pausing at the end of each day, to lay my work and worries aside, to reflect on the slow uncoiling of my life, to contemplate the significance of the day's events, and to pay homage to the sun, the source of all. In my endless pursuit of the green flash I've experienced more beautiful and spectacular sunsets than I can remember. How can I complain?

While the light slowly softens and warms this evening, I seat myself at the base of the mast facing to the west. Ioan and Jelle know not to disturb me with unnecessary conversation, that this is my private time for peaceful meditation. The gentle wind spills off the sails and laves me in its velvet caress. *Atlantean* sways in the shifting steps of her ceaseless dance to the irregular rhythms of waves and swells, soothing me with foamy whispers and bubbly splashes.

Tonight there's no kaleidoscopic display. The hinted colors fade when the sun slips behind the massed clouds on the horizon and fails to reappear. No matter. I linger another moment at the shrouds, breathing deeply of the warm air, refreshed and relaxed. I've shifted gears. Day is done and night can begin.

Celestial Navigation

I'm fascinated by celestial navigation. Armed with a reliable watch, the nautical almanac, a precision sextant, and simple arithmetic, I can determine *Atlantean's* location on the planet to within a few miles. Celestial navigation is the perfect marriage of scientific ingenuity and the romance of the sea.

I calculate three or four fixes a day, depending on weather conditions and how precisely I want to know our position. Each fix requires at least two sextant sightings or "shots," measuring the exact angle above the horizon of various celestial bodies, including the sun, the moon, the four navigational planets (Jupiter, Saturn, Mars, and Venus), and/or numerous bright stars. For the stars and planets, I take sights at dawn and dusk, when it's dark enough for them to be visible but light enough for a clear demarcation between horizon and sky.

This evening I seat myself on the cockpit coaming with a sturdy winch wedged between my knees, and remove the black sextant from its velvet-lined case, careful to shelter the precious instrument with my body against any salt spray. *Atlantean* rocks, sways, and lurches even in the calmest of seas, so remaining as still as possible during the two-handed manipulation of the sextant gives my stomach muscles a workout. Tonight's targets are a waxing half-moon, the planet Jupiter, the southern sky's Fomalhaut, and Scorpio's red Antares. Ioan stands ready with pad, paper, and the digital wristwatch that I've checked against the short-wave radio's time-tick. When I've located Fomalhaut's pin-prick of light in the sextant's view finder, I squeeze the trigger on the adjustment arm and slide it back and forth until the split-image optics superimpose the star on the ocean. When the solitary bright speck is just skimming the horizon, I call "Mark," and Ioan notes the exact time and sextant angle. After a second sight for confirmation, I repeat the process for Jupiter and Antares, and then move on to the moon. It always amuses me to watch the lunar dance atop the wave crests.

I'm the only cruiser I know who uses celestial navigation. The Global Positioning System (GPS) with its array of navigation satellites and inexpensive receivers may spell the end of navigating by the heavenly bodies; I've heard the U.S. Naval Academy no longer requires sextant training. But so long as there aren't rocks and reefs to run into, I enjoy the personal challenge of old-fashioned navigation, the way voyagers have traversed oceans for the last two hundred years—never mind how the Vikings or the Polynesians or even Columbus, for that matter, found their ways around. I tease my fellow cruisers that I'll know where I am when some hacker shuts down the Pentagon computers and their GPSs suddenly aren't working.

But perhaps a deeper reason for preferring celestial navigation is because for once in my life, the moon and the stars *matter;* they're not just pretty lights up in the sky. I learn to identify the stars and their constellations, and familiarize myself with their movements the same way I acquaint myself with all my surroundings: the boat, the sea, the wind. The celestial bodies have always been meaningful to humans—the vernal equinox, the solstices, comets, eclipses, and shooting stars, all heralded important events—and navigating by them connects me with traditions that stretch beyond recorded history. The Polynesians began their New Year with the appearance of the Pleiades, and for the ancient Greeks, Arcturus's orange twinkle in the morning sky signaled the end of summer. Celestial navigation is a small good thing, at worst only a harmless diversion, but these days when most people live in cities and so much of the sensory data we receive is mediated by human artifacts, how many of us can say that what happens in Nature makes a difference in our lives?

Night Moves

Night watch is one of the great pleasures of passage making in the tropics. If the day has been hot, it's now comfortably cool, though in the Indian Ocean it often cools enough to require a sweater before the night's over, on top of the usual shorts and tee shirt. My practice is to downsize the rig before dark to avoid having to shorten sail if the wind picks up, so maintaining a lookout for ships, monitoring the compass, and adjusting the Aries windvane (autopilot) are often the only duties. The crew is in bed and I'm alone, with four hours to spend in peaceful contemplation of life and the world around me.

One might suppose the most commanding aspect from the deck of a sailboat is the vast expanse of water on all sides, but it's only about four miles in any direction to the visible horizon (the last wave crest you see before the Earth has curved away from your line of sight), which is not even as far away as the other side of the Grand Canyon. Rather, it's the immensity of sky one is aware of, and never more so than at night when the starry canopy is unbounded in all directions. During the day I may be occupied with the business of sailing, or repairing equipment, or reading a book, but at night, alone in the cockpit, I'm free to contemplate the endless wilderness above.

I've tracked the moon through all of its phases many times. Moonrise and moonset come rapidly, and more than once the rising moon has been cause for concern until I realized that bright silver glow wasn't a freighter steaming over the horizon. The full moon bathes the sea and skies in ethereal light, and at such times the night feels safe and comforting. Occasionally the moon shines so brightly I can read or see the horizon clearly enough to take sextant sights. But even when there's no moon, the stars provide surprising illumination; I can think of no night I could describe as "pitch black," even under 100% cloud cover, far from any city's glow.

Familiarity with the constellations and four hours on watch make apparent the sky's rotation around its poles. The southern constellations aren't as recognizable to me as our more familiar northern ones, with the exception of the Southern Cross, the pride of the Aussie and Kiwi flags. It's easy to pick out, with its two bright pointer stars, Alpha and Beta Centauri, the former being the sun's nearest stellar neighbor in the galaxy. The Southern Cross looks more like a kite, with a dim fifth star along one side, but it's an elegant arrangement nevertheless, and it wheels around the southern celestial axis, where there's no counterpart to Polaris of the northern skies. The two Magellanic Clouds are also clearly visible from the Southern Hemisphere, mini-galaxies of a few million stars each, only 150,000 light years away and orbiting around our own Milky Way. Most of the northern constellations are present, with the exception of those near the pole such as the Little Dipper, and the rest are often upside-down; Orion pursues the Seven Sisters while standing on his head. When you look at the sky over successive days or weeks, you realize that about eighty percent of the celestial canopy is visible at some time or another on any single night. The horizons shortly before the sun's rising or shortly after its setting reveal most of those stars that are otherwise obscured by the light of day.

Even the heavens are getting crowded. I've counted as many as fifteen satellites going overhead on one night watch and sometimes wonder if one of those is the space shuttle or the international space station. On the other hand, sailboats rarely follow the most direct lines between countries, so we almost never see airplanes.

Leaving from Darwin on August 3rd meant we had the entire Christmas Island passage to enjoy the Perseid meteor showers. I would often see forty or fifty shooting stars an hour, some of them merely a faint flicker, others blazing lights that would streak almost completely across the sky. Three or four times I saw fireballs that lit up the boat as bright as signal flares. I always use falling stars as opportunities to make wishes of well-being for the people I care about back home, friends and family, or to make a silent appeal for a safe passage. Some nights everybody I know is doubly or triply blessed.

Making wishes for people leads me to thinking about them, and one recollection leads to another. At times these trains of thought leave me almost entranced, like daydreaming but more intense in the night with so few other distractions. I find myself calling to mind people I haven't thought about in years, from high school or even earlier, whom I knew better and spent more time with than most people I've known since or will meet in the future. As a child my heightened sensory awareness was unencumbered by my underdeveloped powers of reflection, but nowadays reflection overpowers awareness and I disappear down long corridors of memory, recalling past events in vivid detail. What are my old childhood friends and schoolmates doing today? Do they ever think about me? Does anyone care?

I often listen to my tape player on night watch, the first forty-five minute side of a tape after I've been on for an hour, then the other side after another quiet hour. I've heard my tapes so many times that I've taken to mixing them up in their box and pulling them out at random, not looking at the label and surprising myself when the first strains come through the headphones. Sometimes it's pulse-pounding rock and roll, and I'm dancing around the cockpit, but tonight I switch off the tape after Bob Seger's anthem to the passage of youth, *Night Moves,* is over. Seger is one of those popular songwriters whose gift it is to capture the mood of an entire generation—my fellow baby-boomers, all of us once so young, so strong, so idealistic—with deceptively simple lyrics. I'm already feeling nostalgic, and when I hear him sing of waking to the sound of distant thunder, and how the music we grew up with and loved in the springtime of our lives comes back to us, now that autumn is closing in, a wave of melancholy washes over me like the Indian Ocean's following seas.

It's time for the blues, and when the blues come down, the cruising life is almost too much to bear. This isn't some idyllic jaunt around Lake Washington, folks, it's hard work, harder work than I've ever done. The elements are brutal on the equipment, and it's a full time job just to keep the boat sailing. But keeping the boat sailing is the easy part. Keeping the skipper sailing is another story.

The dreary facts of how my trip ended up being a solo affair are never far from my mind: the mutual dreams, the inevitable break-up, the decision to set out alone. I realize now that I spent my first year of cruising nursing my resentment about having no partner, no soulmate, no special person with whom to share the journey. I may have finally gotten beyond that, finally accustomed myself to being on my own, and I hope that by now I'm fully appreciating what's going on around me even if it's necessarily a personal affair. But that doesn't mean it doesn't get lonely out here. Sometimes when the frustrations stack up, when it seems that nothing is going right, when I'm tired of doing all the work and shouldering all of the responsibility alone, I long for somebody to share my burdens, to pick me up, to give me a squeeze and tell me it's going to be all right. Other times it's the pain of witnessing beauty and wonder that I can't share in a meaningful way, when I feel my appreciation is cheapened because I have nobody to be my mirror, nobody who can reflect the event back to me, to reaffirm my sensations, to legitimize that sense of wonder and joy I want to feel and provide what author Richard Ford calls *sanction,* perhaps the most nurturing and bonding aspect of love between two people.

I know other cruising couples; they may have their ups and downs, but they're partners, they help each other, they're out here together. They're the ones I envy most often—Willi and Lou on *Whirlwind*, Brian and Mary Alice on *Shibui*, Ken and Cheryl on *Hannah*—and I think about how easily I'd fit into their circle if I were part of a couple rather than always the odd man out. Instead we remain at arm's length. They find it difficult to relate to me and what I'm doing because they're not alone, and I'm not part of what they're doing because I'm not half of a couple. I have companionship but few close friends, and this peregrinate life never affords me enough time to develop close relationships before moving on. Crew is transitory and there's always a distance created by our respective roles, owner/captain vs. crew. I share more in common with other cruisers, but they too are bound up in their own full-time concerns.

Sometimes it's not the loneliness, it's a sense that all of this has no purpose, no meaning, that I'm throwing my life away for naught. Even when I step back and tell myself, "Yes, you really are accomplishing something noteworthy, something very few people will ever do, something that others only dream about," it has a hollow ring to it. "So what, that I'm out here?" I ask myself. "What will it mean for me when I'm too broke and too lonely to continue and have to go back to the real world?"

Perhaps the poet Auden was right:

> ... But the really reckless were fetched
> By an older, colder voice, the oceanic whisper:
> "I am the solitude that asks nothing and promises nothing;
> That is how I shall set you free. There is no love;
> There are only the various envies, all of them sad."

The blues, they come and they go. In the end, the fact is I'm out here, sailing around the world, and I know I can keep at it—for a while longer anyway, always for a while longer. Completing each leg of the trip brings me closer to realizing my goal, and closer to home.

Bioluminescence

However melancholy I may feel for a time, night watch is more than a silent reverie, and my nightly routines help keep the blues at bay, or put them behind me. I reserve a portion of each watch for calculating and plotting my last star sight, for a cup of chamomile tea and a cookie, for checking the compass and scanning the horizon for freighters, and for admiring the glitter of bioluminescence in our wake.

I've never understood the process of bioluminescence, though the hull's passage through the waves produces it in amazing quantities, especially on a moon-dark night. Ioan says it's caused by the rupturing of millions of microscopic plant and animal bodies—smashed by the turbulence, their life force is extinguished in a final flicker of light—but as darkly romantic as that notion may be, that the passage into death produces life's most incandescent moment, I don't think he's right. Whatever the cause, the soft green glow stretches fifty feet or more behind us, from where it has flared from the stern quarters or boiled off the rudder, sometimes punctuated with basketball-sized explosions, other times with bright sparks, singly or in bursting sprays.

The light show is even more apparent in the cold waters of the higher latitudes, and "sparkin'" is what a friend used to call paddling the dinghy to shore at night when we were exploring British Columbia's Inside Passage.

I've twice experienced an especially mysterious and dazzling display of luminescence at sea that I've heard other sailors talk about but never explain. It occurred both times after the moon had just gone down, once during our passage through the Timor Sea and once in the Indian Ocean. Normally the night sky is lighter than the water, even if it's cloudy, but on these two occasions I realized all at once that the entire sea was lit up far brighter than the sky, though there were no clouds and the stars were as clear as ever. *Atlantean* traversed the waves as if upon a shimmering carpet of sparkling stardust. If it hadn't been for the splash of the water and the rocking of the boat, the illusion of flying atop clouds of light would have been complete. Perhaps the sea had been soaking up the moonglow and was giving it back all at once. Both times the phenomenon went on for about five minutes and was so mesmerizing that I was tempted to get Ioan out of bed to confirm my eyes. But just as quickly as it had appeared, it was gone; I blinked and everything was back to normal, leaving we wondering if I'd seen anything at all, or if for a long moment the curtains had parted and I'd been granted a view of mythic Avalon.

Visitors

I always welcome dolphins swimming with the boat, especially at night when their popping gasps and sudden splashes send me to the bow pulpit. These carefree creatures bob and weave and roll in the bow wave as always, but at night the bioluminescence illuminates their sleek torsos streaking through the dark water. Powerful thrusts of their flukes propel them towards and under the boat in glittering streams of light, like fairies, or sprites, or the balls of celestial energy swirling across the canvas in Van Gogh's painting *Starry Night*.

Flying fish are by far the most common night visitors, and the sudden arrival of one on board is always startling. The flying fish are surely startled as well, after launching themselves out of a wave for whatever reason they launch themselves, and discovering an instant later that instead of the two-hundred meter flights we watch so often during the day, they've smashed into the hull, or the sail, or the dodger, or the coach roof, or the side of your head. After the thudding impact, you hear them flopping around on the deck, and sometimes, especially if you're Ioan and don't mind the fishy stink on your fingers, you flip them over the side before they batter themselves to death or suffocate. Even with the most determined rescue efforts, however, come morning the dawn watchman will pick up ten to twenty dead flying fish, most only a few inches long but some a foot or more in length. Once Jelle found a flying fish had flown through the upper cabin hatch all the way into the head and landed behind the toilet. Willi on *Whirlwind* fries up the big ones and eats them like trout, but we've never tried them.

Dolphins, flying fish, and seabirds are our most numerous visitors, but the largest are the whales. Neither Ioan nor Jelle has seen a whale before this trip, and one calm morning Jelle spots a low, dark shape that he thinks is a half-submerged log until it blows a burst of water and vapor. "WHALE! WHALE!" he shouts, and Ioan is on deck in an instant. I'm an old whale hand, so I follow at a more leisurely pace, and for the next few minutes we watch a southern humpback about fifty meters away blow and sound while it swims an oblique course away from the boat. Ioan climbs to the spreaders for a better look, but by then the whale's gone. Long after I return to my cabin, I can hear them talking about the sighting. "Did you see how big it was? How about that tail? I wonder how fast they can swim."

The Indian Ocean passage yields another dozen humpback sightings, usually a solitary whale, and twice we encounter pods of small pilot whales. In almost every encounter I've had with whales or their smaller distant cousins, the orca, I've been struck by the creatures' apparent indifference to our presence, always continuing on their ways without regard to us, unlike the porpoises and dolphins that can't wait to frolic with the boat. Jelle, however, is convinced that our green and blue light-air sail, the drifter, somehow attracts the giant cetaceans, and calls it the "whale sail." Though most of our sightings come when the drifter's up, I'm inclined to believe it's because at such times the seas are calm and the whales are easier to spot.

One day in the western Indian Ocean we have indisputable evidence of a whale's attentions. Jelle is on the foredeck, carefully rationing his last pack of cigarettes, and sings out the by now familiar cry of "Whale!" The sky is clear and we're making about four knots in light winds, with the drifter and main set on a beam reach to keep the sails full. I spot a small humpback swimming a parallel course thirty or forty meters off in the two-meter swells. He (she?) blows and sounds a few times, and I expect him to disappear for good at any moment, when suddenly Jelle is shouting, "He's right next to the boat!" I hear the blast and suck, and there's the whale only six or seven meters from the starboard quarter. His entire flank is clearly visible: the distinctive paddle-like pectoral fin, the long smile of his baleen-lined mouth, and a large, unblinking eye. It's a juvenile, only about eight meters long, probably barely more than a calf. We all run for our cameras.

The whale glides alongside, scarcely seeming to move his tail, then there are a couple of quick thrusts and he's gone. The next time we see him is a few minutes later, thirty meters off again, keeping on a parallel course. Several times he eases closer to the boat and rolls his body to one side as if to get a better look, then silently slides beneath the waves and disappears, only to reappear a few minutes later thirty or forty meters away. Ioan climbs to the spreaders so he can keep closer tabs on our companion. "He's coming!" he calls, and the whale executes a series of fast charges beneath our stern, circling and swimming under from the other side, all visible in the clear blue water. After a few passes, he retreats and blows, then gradually eases his bulk towards the boat again. I've never seen anything like it.

Jelle is now pressed against the stern pulpit, pointing his camera straight down. "He's back here, he's back here," he cries, oblivious to his bare feet grinding his sunglasses to bits where he set them down a few minutes before. The whale is following directly in our wake, a half-meter below the surface, the tip of his nose (do they have noses?) only centimeters from the rudder. Once or twice I feel a gentle shudder, as if he's given us a probing nudge, but I can't be sure. He keeps his distance perfectly, and though we're making four knots, the movements of his flukes are imperceptible. After a few minutes he veers off with a sharp kick and speeds away for another series of blows.

He stays with us for forty-five minutes, his favorite spot being directly behind the rudder. Occasionally he swims parallel to us, as close as three meters away, twice rolling onto his side and waving his knobby pectoral fin in the air, and another time swimming completely upside-down. He no longer departs for breaths, and his fishy spray wafts onto our faces and tingles our arm hairs when he blows close by the windward side.

Even though he's only about two-thirds the length of *Atlantean*, I'm aware of the damage he could do if he were so inclined; one flick of the tail and we'd be stove. The big whales run about a ton per foot, and that makes him over twice our weight. My main concern is that he might come up under the relatively flimsy Aries servo-rudder and snap it off, but this little fellow is in his element, as unlikely to bump into us as we are to stumble into parked cars when we stroll down a sidewalk. He's content to swim along and check out this strange blue and white whale-sized object, as curious and friendly as a puppy. He finally tires of us, or maybe he hears his mamma calling, and we're disappointed when we can no longer spot him in the swells.

Sleep

Another day is drawing to a close. I've savored another sunset (and once again failed to see the green flash), recorded the sextant sights to be calculated later, listened to the Indian Ocean weather broadcast out of South Africa, made entries in the ship's log, and written a couple of pages in my journal detailing the day's events. It's almost full dark and I'm in my cabin, my body braced against the leeboard on my bunk while I search for a few hours of sleep. Tonight I have the midnight watch, and my alarm will beep ten minutes before it's time to go on. I'll likely find Jelle already dozing in the cockpit. Four hours later I'll be winding down myself, and will wake up a sleepy Ioan before making my way back to my bunk.

"Whale!" Jelle calls down the companionway hatch, but not loudly, and a few moments later I can hear him talking with Ioan about a couple of whales that have surfaced close enough to spot in the fading light. This time I don't join them on deck, but amidst the usual slosh and gurgle of the waves washing against the boat, I make out a chorus of plaintive whines and sighs and percussive glottal clicks reverberating throughout the hull. I'm hearing the songs of the humpbacks, strangely delicate for such mammoth creatures, like the whimper a child's toy makes when it's turned upside-down. It's said that the whales' voices carry hundreds of miles beneath the waves, and I think of them calling to one another, reassuring themselves that they are not alone in this vast expanse of ocean. Nor am I alone, and soon their otherworldly melodies have lulled me to sleep.

AUSSIES

COFF'S HARBOUR, NEW SOUTH WALES, is a pleasant little town several days' sail from Sydney, up Australia's east coast. The well-protected marina is nestled behind a massive haystack rock and a jetty that guard the entrance to the bay. After I take a slip there, bad weather sets in, closing the harbor for several days. The young Canadian I picked up in Sydney to crew for me grows restless and buys himself a bus ticket onward, so I put up signs advertising for crew in the local backpackers' hostel and around the marina. I amuse myself during the day with books, boat projects, and too much Game Boy, and at night I walk or taxi into town, where I've discovered the wonderful world of Australian "Clubs," which as a non-resident I'm invited to join free of charge. Prices are much cheaper than in regular restaurants and pubs; the club I join offers half-liters of beer at $1.55, and steak/salad bar/dessert for $8.50. It also has slot machines, which I avoid, and a dance floor full of spirited locals twisting and shaking to Nashville Network standards.

The weather at Coff's Harbour continues to deteriorate, and one day I'm sitting below, glad to be safely tied to the dock in this howling wind, when I hear a sharp crack. On deck, I find the ¼" marine-ply paddle on the Aries windvane has snapped off at the base, for which I fortunately have a replacement. All the rest of the day the winds blow at fifty knots or more, and there's talk around the marina of a

175

disabled U.S. cruising yacht offshore, the husband and wife crew of which have been rescued by a Coast Guard helicopter. Some of the local fishermen grumble that the harbor's closed—there are three-meter breakers pounding the entrance—because the drifting yacht could prove a valuable salvage for whomever finds her first.

My third evening in Coff's Harbour, I meet a young Australian couple with their three year old daughter who are out walking the docks in spite of the wind. They're not sailors, but the man, Warren, wants to talk about boats. "Been sailin' a few times, small boats, nothin' like this, o'course," he says, referring to *Atlantean*. "Rather fancy havin' one m'self." He asks what they'd need for overnight trips and how much it might cost.

I invite them aboard for a tour and tell him about the little Pearson 26 I learned to sail on, the likes of which would be inexpensive and adequate for a small family. "But if you really want to know what it's like to be out overnight," I say, "you could sail up the coast with me. I'm looking for crew as far as the Gold Coast. I wouldn't charge you and you could take a bus back in a couple of days."

Warren says he's tempted to "give'r a go," and the next day while the storm continues to rage, he shows up at the dock in his Akrubra and Driza-Bone—the typical Aussie hat and duster combination—and says he's decided to come along. When I tell him I'd like to wait for the weather to ease, he says, "What? Little wind got you shook?" We take his car into town, where I stock up on fresh produce and a few other items, then join him and his family for dinner at their apartment. There are religious posters and knick-knacks around, and we join hands for a long blessing before the meal, but the subject of religion doesn't otherwise come up.

The weather breaks and Warren and I leave with fair winds out of the east-southeast. It's an easy sail, though our broad reach has us corkscrewing through the still heavy seas. Warren is soon bored with his steering lesson, so I hook up the Aries autopilot, and we make ourselves comfortable in the cockpit, enjoying the fine day. My shipmate's a character, the first Aussie I've spent much time with, and he yaks away about whatever pops into his head. After we've been out a couple of hours he stands up in mid-sentence and says, " 'Ang on, right?" He climbs down the companionway ladder and soon I hear him vomiting in the head toilet. He comes back to the cockpit looking none the worse for it, and when I ask him how he feels, he laughs it off. The conversation picks up where we left it, only to be interrupted every hour or so when Warren casually gets up and visits the head, as if chundering into porcelain is such an integral part of Australian manhood that it hardly merits a mention.

After the third or fourth trip below, Warren sticks his head out of the companionway and says, "You got a shower in there." I explain to him that I never use it, because the entire head—the walls, counter top, cabinets, and toilet—must be wiped down afterwards, and how the cockpit shower is simpler and quicker. "Yeah, right," he laughs. A few minutes later I hear the water running and see Warren's clothes in a heap on the cabin sole.

"What are you doing?" I shout, and pound on the head door.

It opens a crack. " 'Avin' a shower, Mate," Warren says. "Gotta problem with that?"

"I told you not to use it. Use the one in the cockpit."

Warren looks confused. "I thought you was 'avin' me on. It's only a bleedin' shower." He finishes up quickly and dries everything to my satisfaction.

During the course of the day, I hear about Warren's life. He dropped out of school at age sixteen and went to South Australia to be a surfer bum, where he got into drugs and wound up in jail, serving a year on a one-to-three sentence for beating a crooked drug dealer to within an inch of his life. It was in the slammer where he found Jesus and cleaned up his act. He's now been married for five years and supports his family with odd jobs, lately by selling Electrolux vacuum cleaners door to door. He likes his work. "I tell 'em I'm 'ere to give the Hoover a free suction test," he says, then explains to me how he goes over a freshly vacuumed area with the clean Electrolux, showing the prospects how much their own vacuums missed. When the customer says he or she doesn't care, that the old Hoover is just fine by them, he'll say, "Then you won't be mindin' all the bits the Hoover's been leavin' behind," and he dumps the contents of the Electrolux back onto the carpet. The customer is shocked, and of course Warren cleans it up, slowly and thoroughly, which gives him time to make his full pitch. He doesn't sell many, but apparently enough to get by.

Early in the second day we round Cape Byron, Australia's easternmost point, and that night make Surfer's Paradise, where we take a mooring buoy outside of Sea World. The next morning Warren helps me move the boat to a marina, after which I treat him to breakfast in town and buy his bus ticket back to Coff's Harbour. Away from the sea breeze it's hot and muggy, and I'm glad to put away my fleece pullover and long pants in favor of my normal cruising attire of shorts, tee shirt, and sun visor.

The so-called Gold Coast is forty-three miles of overbuilt high-rise beach resorts reminiscent of Atlantic City or south Florida, full of tourists, families on holiday, and college-age revelers looking for sun, sex, and surf. Universal Studios, Planet Hollywood, the Hard Rock Cafe, McDonald's, KFC, Pizza Hut, and the other transplanted manifestations of America's culture of instant gratification don't interest me, and after two days of fruitlessly searching for crew, I decide to move on to Brisbane. My Queensland cruising guide points out how I can do this without venturing out in the ocean, by sticking to a maze of tidewater estuaries known as the Broadwater, all the way to Moreton Bay and the navigable Brisbane River. On the Broadwater side of the beach on the way out of town, I motor past a crowd bungee jumping from the top of a crane, with the cord measured to dunk the jumpers' heads into the lagoon before launching them skyward. "It's not *real* bungee jumping," I tell myself, though I'm disappointed New Zealand's Shotover River was too low during my own jump for a similar dunking—as if the adrenaline rush wasn't shock enough.

According to the cruising guide, there are only a few routes through the Broadwater that lead all the way to Moreton Bay, and none has a high tide least-depth of more than two meters, still enough for *Atlantean's* draft of five and a half feet if I figure the tides correctly. It's all shallow, however, and I have to wind around so many sand bars and islands that it's easier to motor than to rely on the sails. At around 1000 I have my first encounter with shallows in an unmarked channel, plowing the keel into a mud bank at about four knots, the first time I've ever put *Atlantean* aground. I'm stuck for about an hour with the tide nearing the end of the ebb until an Aussie Coast Guard launch comes along and pulls me free. "G'day," they say when they arrive, and "Call us anytime," when they leave.

By 1500 that afternoon I'm far from tourists and waterskiers. *Atlantean* motors down increasingly narrow channels lined with dense snarls of broad-leafed bushes and low, gnarled trees, where all kinds of birds flit and splash around me, as if this were some scene from *African Queen.* There are no mangroves, which I would have expected, and I wonder if perhaps the water is too fresh, or maybe not clear enough—it's a uniformly opaque, silty brown—which may also explain why there's no mention in my guidebook of the fearsome saltwater crocs. Around the time I've figured for high tide, I come to the most serious bottleneck of the journey, where *Atlantean's* keel again slips into the mud. I've been keeping my speed below two knots in the more extreme shallows, and am able to back out and try again a little farther over in the narrow channel, all the time watching the depth sounder, which consistently reads under six feet. Twice more I come to a halt in the mud, so I radio the Coast Guard—they said call anytime—who advises me to wait about an hour before trying again, since high tide comes late deeper into the Broadwater. I drop the anchor with about ten feet of rode and shut down the engine.

The silence I expected is disturbed by the sound of a generator. Tucked back in a brushy little cove not a hundred feet away, I spy a flat-bottomed houseboat, looking like a floating shoe box, the kind people rent for lake fishing or partying in comfort. The shades are drawn against the blazing afternoon sun, but a door opens and from it emerges the driving thump of a stereo playing seventies rock tunes. A middle-aged man with a substantial belly protruding through his unbuttoned shirt steps out to take a leak over the rail, unleashing a stream a draft horse would be proud of. "Ahoy," I call, as he's finishing up. "How do you get through here?"

The man waves and climbs into a little dinghy. "Got a keeler, eh?" he says when he rows alongside. "Shallows up here. You'll be right when the tide's up. Seen lottsa keelers goin' by. Come 'round to our place an' we'll rip open a few tinnies."

He rows me to the houseboat, where I step into Aussie male heaven. There are four of them, all married men from Brisbane, on holiday for a week. The air conditioner is roaring, cigarette butts overflow the ashtrays, and piles of empties are scattered among the full beer cases and numerous bags of crisps and other party snacks. Fishing poles and tackle boxes lie ignored in a corner. It seems these fellows are happy spending their week drinking, smoking, and swapping lies, and have no intention of budging from this spot until the rental is up.

It's my first exposure to Australian male comradery, mateship, as it were. They don't so much speak to one another as exchange insults. Even the most innocent of remarks is punctuated with "You fuckin' wanker," or "God rot ya," which they say with enough of a smile that no one takes offense. In short order I've ripped open my own tinny ("None of that Victoria Bitter pisswater here," they tell me, "only good old Foster's"), and bummed a smoke (since each of them has one and sometimes two cigarettes going all the time, I figure it might help). Between their insults and yarns, I insert a few of my own stories, and their running commentary has us all howling.

I'm thoroughly enjoying my visit and after a while venture outside to take a leak of my own, when I see a sailboat chugging past. It's another keeler, about the size of *Atlantean*, and it doesn't even hesitate at the spot where I ran aground. "Take me back to my boat!" I yell. "I'm gonna stay on that guy's ass!" I figure the safest way to avoid running aground again is to follow somebody else. One of my new friends rows me back to *Atlantean*, where I hurriedly start the engine and pull in the anchor. "See you later, Mate," I say, "and thanks for the beers."

I make it almost all the way out of the Broadwater before calling it a day. My cruising guide directs me to a lovely little anchorage behind Russell Island, in the approaches to Moreton Bay. I drop anchor for a late supper and a peaceful night, with the mosquito netting in place to keep out invaders. The next morning a steady breeze from the south blows me into Moreton Bay. I run on just the headsail, not bothering with the main, and make good time, entering the Brisbane River as the tide changes to flood and riding it fourteen miles into the heart of the city.

The day after my arrival in Brisbane, I wander around for several hours, as is my wont in a new place, but it proves to be disappointing. Though it's a large city, Brisbane doesn't seem to have many self-contained districts or neighborhoods like King's Cross in Sydney, or even an identifiable downtown core. It's hard to get much of a feel for the place. Brisbane reminds me of Houston in the States, an unplanned hodge-podge sprawling every which way, with high-rise office towers next to churches next to workshops and houses.

On the positive side, the marina where I'm staying is part of a new condominium development on the river, walking distance to the center of Brisbane and complete with a gym, sauna, spa, swimming pool, locker room, laundry, white-tablecloth restaurant, pub, and shops—the sort of place designed to attract up-and-coming young professionals, who most of the residents seem to be. The developers are selling boat slips, but until the marina is full, they're renting them to yachts in transit for only a few dollars more than I'd spend on an inconvenient pile mooring farther up the river.

I adopt a daily routine consisting of an hour of early-morning stainless polishing on *Atlantean,* followed by several laps in the pool and a shower, then breakfast, coffee, and a few rounds of Game Boy Golf. Afternoons are for reading, touring, and boat projects, such as having a spare paddle cut for the Aries windvane. One morning at the pool I meet an Englishwoman, Mau, who's been in Australia for twenty years. She's a television producer for a game show, an Aussie version of *Jeopardy,* and over the next few days she invites me to lunch, a play, and two cocktail parties where she shows me off to local celebrities. Mau is friendly and generous with me and her colleagues, but her overall attitude is a sort of upper-crust boredom with the whirl of her professional and social life. Her demeanor may have more to do with her native English reserve, because the similar attitude is only mildly apparent in her fellow Aussie celebs and yuppies, most of whom seem self-conscious of "tall poppy syndrome" and are happily bemused by their success.

Mau drives me around Brisbane and one day loans me her car to visit a game preserve outside of town, where I admire kangaroos and emus wandering freely about the grounds among caged wombats, echidna, snakes, turtles, lots of birds, and of course, koalas. At the visitors' center, I watch a film on the destruction of the koalas' eucalyptus tree habitat, and afterwards a handler lets me hold Snowball. Koalas are every bit as cute and cuddly as one imagines (they sleep twenty-three hours a day), and I send a souvenir photo of Snowball and me home for Mother's Day.

Looking at a map of the country, I'm struck by how sparsely populated Australia is—when I was sailing here from Sidney it was sometimes a hundred miles between towns—and it's difficult to imagine the vast and empty interior. The only evidence of what lies beyond the coastal hills comes at sundown when I'm treated to one spectacular sunset after another—cottony puffballs and wispy horsetails, all of them peach or purple or incarnadine red—the dry and dusty air over the deserts to the west enflamed by the flattening of the sun's rays. The country is the size of the continental United States but with less than ten percent of the population, and most of that is concentrated in the few large cities. This uncluttered and sun-saturated landscape has surely forged the national psyche in the same manner as North America's mountains, forests, and wide prairies have shaped our own. With so much untamed Outback challenging them, it's as if the Australians feel compelled to attack life in furious bursts of confidence. I've heard said there's no one better than an Aussie when there's a job of work to be done, so long as there's plenty of beer afterwards and no hurry to get on to the next task. I also have to wonder if the expanse is what drives them to congregate in cities—Australia is said to have the most urbanized population on Earth—as if there's simply too much open space, and without each other's reassuring presence, its scope would be too dispiriting.

Though I'm slowly developing a feel for Australia and the Australians, I don't know much about the continent's original inhabitants, the Aborigines, other than what I've read from Paul Theroux and Bruce Chatwin. It appears the whites here were more thorough in their attempts at extermination than even we Americans with our own indigenous peoples, and the prejudice against the "Abos," as I generally hear them called, remains near the surface. Mostly the whites refer to them with contempt, citing their filth, laziness, and alcoholism (traits that are hardly absent in the white male population), but even sympathetic Australians complain that the Aboriginals don't seem to want to improve their situation.

Australia has other people of color—in the cities I'm aware of small but significant minority populations of Asians, South Seas Islanders, Indians, Africans, and other indeterminate combinations of brown skin and black hair—but the Aborigines I encounter are hard to mistake. They're the ones wearing dirty and torn tee shirts or thin print dresses, with leaves and dirt in their matted hair, their skin black as tar, barefoot groups of them boozing in the park or passed out alone on a sidewalk. Now and then when I go to a shop to buy my newspaper and Velvet Crumble, I'll see one working as a clerk, cleaned up in the colored smock or jacket the manager makes them wear. Beneath that wild, flaring hair is the confused and wary stare of a zoo animal that can't quite figure out how it ended up this way. Life may be somewhat better in the Aboriginal homelands that have been set aside, but I can't imagine that the Aussies or the Brits before them were any more generous than our government was when it forced the Native Americans onto marginal reservation lands.

One evening in Brisbane I attend a movie, a bleak and somber film about death and dying, and when I come out I feel the need to surround myself with the living to pull myself out of my melancholic funk. There's an open-air, multi-level block of shops that's not quite closed for the night where I wander around looking at display windows, while the few remaining shoppers hurry past with their purchases and children. As I'm going down a concrete ramp leading to the parking lot and exit, I come upon a group of a dozen or more children and their accompanying adults who are engrossed in some street performer's act. The busker is an Aboriginal man kneeling on a greasy blanket spread out against a dimly lit wall, telling a story directed primarily to the children. I slip into the fringes to listen.

The story is about animals in the bush under a moonlit sky, except it's not really a story, it's more of a painting, the evocation of a scene. After the man names each animal, first in his native tongue, then in English, he tilts back his head, opens his mouth, and we hear the animal. But what we hear isn't some human approximation of bird song or a dingo's bark, *we hear the exact sounds of the animal:* a hissing snake slithering in the grass, a kangaroo bounding past, a kookaburra's cackling laughter followed by the rush of air from flapping wings. With each of the sounds of the night, the man contorts his body and gestures with his hands and arms—deft, swooping movements—and for a fleeting moment *he becomes the animal.* It goes by so quickly I'm hardly able to believe or recollect what I just saw, but I've never been so convinced by an illusion in my life.

We're all mesmerized, not just the children, but we adults as well. While we're under his spell, a didgeridoo appears in his hands, as if conjured out of thin air. It's about four feet long, and three inches in diameter, a rough hollowed-out branch or log painted a dull red. He cradles it for a moment, and then sweeps it before our eyes in long, graceful arcs before sitting back on his blanket. With the instrument at his lips and its open end between his bare feet, he begins to play. A music like none I've ever heard pours out of this most primitive of flutes, only a single droning note, but with shifting shapes and textures as complex and mysterious as the Outback itself. The music rises and falls, pulses with a complicated rhythm I can't quite grasp, and weaves a melody out of a monotone. I've heard of the Aboriginal technique of circular breathing—inhaling through the nostrils while blowing from the cheeks—but this is the first time I've seen it done, and the man plays his one-note symphony without breath breaks or pauses. While he plays, his free hand spins stories in the air with gestures that are both incomprehensible and utterly clear in import. No one in his little audience moves, and most of us scarcely breathe. Then the narrative hand slowly closes in on itself and settles to Earth, the drone fades away to silence, and the man releases his hold on us.

We blink ourselves back to reality, aware once again of the carpark around us, of the sounds of traffic rumbling past in the night, and of this human being before us whose appearance could only be called down and out, more destitute than the filthiest homeless person I've ever encountered, his hair a mass of dirt and tangles, his clothes rags, his few possessions tied in dark bundles lying on the tattered blanket. Parents wrinkle their noses and jostle their children, pointing them towards the car and home. A few people toss some coins onto the blanket before hurrying away. I dig a five-dollar bill out of my pocket and step closer. The man's acrid smell fills my nostrils and I'm instinctively repelled, but I want to say something, to somehow tell him how much his performance has moved me. When I hold out the bill, he looks at me, looks into my eyes—no, he looks straight through my eyes and into my soul. It's as if I suddenly have no secrets, as if he already knows everything there is to know about me, and that any words I might speak would be useless and wasted, merely the cheap and meaningless lies I tell myself to preserve my fragile hold on what I call sanity. The man holds his gaze for a second or two—though it might as well be an eternity—then turns when someone else offers him money. Somehow the bill is no longer in my hand when I leave, though I have no memory of his taking it.

All I can do is hurry home in the night, back through the streets of the city, back to *Atlantean*, back to whatever it is I call my life. Is it possible I have seen why the white race seems so intent on the obliteration of every native culture it encounters? Because the indigenous peoples of the world are not only closer to—more at one with—the Earth, plants and animals, but also their fellow human beings? Because when we are in their presence, *they are fully present with us*? Forcing us to acknowledge our kinship in ways that make us uncomfortable, that call attention to our objectification of the world, to our separation of ourselves from whatever or whomever serves us as means to our selfish ends?

The Aboriginals' culture developed in a relative vacuum, cut off from the rest of humanity for as long as 40,000 years, according to some anthropologists. For the Aboriginals, such keen awareness of the land, the plants, the animals, and other humans, was probably a survival mechanism, an absolute necessity in a place where rainfall is a rare blessing and death can lurk behind any rock, beneath any bush, or creep into your bed at night. White Australians, in the two centuries since they were unceremoniously dumped as penal convicts and guards at Botany Bay, developed other means of insuring survival in a far-flung land, means that today are manifested in their relentless urbanization, their dependence on a world economy, and their mateship with its alcoholic release and self-deprecating laughter. The white way will undoubtedly prevail, here and elsewhere, but so much of the collective wisdom and lifeways of the Aboriginals and other indigenous cultures will one day be lost forever. I feel we will all be diminished thereby, even as I admit it will never be possible for me to penetrate the Aboriginals' wisdom and make it part of my own.

Sleep is slow in coming that night, but the next morning, I'm up at the usual hour. The sun is shining, the air is fresh, and the stanchions are waiting for their scrubbing pads and Lysol Toilet Bowl Cleaner (the best solvent I've found for removing tarnish). My quotidian rituals may not exactly put me in communion with the natural world, but they're how I've learned to make it through each day. Perhaps there's a limit to how much truth I can handle, especially when it's the truth about myself and my kind.

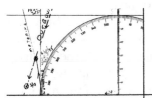

THE NEW
SOUTH AFRICA

THE DOCK OF THE SMALL BOAT BASIN at Richards Bay, in South Africa's Kwazulu-Natal Province, just below the Mozambique border, is the first place I set foot on the continent of Africa. I would like to have explored Kenya and Tanzania as well, but time and my dwindling cruising budget are working against me, forcing me to confine my adventures to post-apartheid South Africa. Mozambique could have been a convenient stopping place; before the Portuguese colonial city of Lorenzo Marques was taken over by the revolutionaries and renamed Maputo, it was one of the great travelers' crossroads of the world. But the United States hasn't been a particularly good friend to the unstable areas of Africa in recent years, and the State Department has issued a warning against U.S. flag vessels visiting Mozambique, saying they may be subject to seizure. It's a shame that our government's policies are fueling so much of the rest of the world's animosity towards us.

The last several hours before our arrival were spent battling one of the "Cape of Storms'" infamous southwest gales. Other cruisers in the harbor were monitoring our radio transmissions with Richards Bay Port Control, so when we finally make it in, there are helpful hands to take *Atlantean's* lines. As is usually the case, a gale at sea is little more than a blustery inconvenience to shore dwellers, and clearance procedures with the customs, immigration, and health authorities

185

are completed throughout the remaining afternoon. Each team of uniformed officials that visits us includes a junior black member who keeps his mouth shut and defers to his white seniors. Foreign yachts and tourists once avoided South Africa because of its apartheid policies, and watching the officials in action is my first indication of how the whites and blacks are getting along these days.

One of my two crew members departs for Johannesburg and his flight home to Holland a few days after our arrival, and I move *Atlantean* to the nearby Zululand Yacht Club, where other cruisers I know have already tied up. The place is far from fancy, but the terms for international yachts are good: two weeks' free moorage, unrestricted use of the facilities, and a complimentary bottle of South African champagne. There's serious work to be done over the next few weeks, both on *Atlantean* and its skipper. I tell my other crewman, the Welshman Ioan, that he's earned a vacation from boat work, so he shoulders his backpack for a tour of the surrounding countryside. He's already promised to stay on until Cape Town, and is as eager as I (but not nearly so apprehensive) to sail around the southern tip of the continent.

After he leaves, I sign up for hauling out on the club's marine ways (a rail-mounted cradle on a boat ramp) and consult a doctor about the persistent cramps, watery bowels, and low grade fever I've been running since a couple of days out of Madagascar. The doctor diagnoses common amoebic dysentery, and prescribes five days of massive doses of metronidazole and Kaopectate, along with the BRAT diet (bananas, rice, apples, and toast). By the end of the fifth day the cure has almost killed me, but the diarrhea abates and I'm able to start rebuilding my strength with normal food.

The boat work proceeds with typical frustration. I discover the leaky transmission seal requires a professional rebuild that will have to wait until Cape Town. The propeller shaft can be trued and its cutlass bearing replaced, but removing the shaft is an all day job that nearly defeats me. And the only bottom paint I can get is white, which the layabouts in the boatyard tell me attracts whales, and that I'll be lucky if I'm not rammed and sunk in the Atlantic. Like the treatment of my intestinal disorders, the various repairs are effected somewhat less elegantly than I had envisioned, but well enough to permit the journey to continue.

The harbor and yacht club are miles from the municipality of Richards Bay, and there's no public transportation, so I hitch rides when I need to shop for something, or want to catch the latest Tom Hanks flick at the local cinema. Richards Bay isn't much of a town, but it offers a modern shopping mall where most of the customers are white. Without much imagination, I can pretend I'm in an almost identical mall in Spokane or Milwaukee, instead of a country in which more than 80% of the population is ethnic African.

The de facto segregation seems a large part of "the new South Africa," as I've heard the country ruefully called by many of the whites. There's plenty of it around the yacht club with its all-white membership. Black employees arrive by bus in the morning to perform the menial labor—gardening, maintenance, and cleaning the ablutions block—and are taken away in the evening. They're distinguished by their "uniforms," dark blue coveralls for the men, and light blue dresses and scarves for the women. For the most part, they keep their heads lowered and only mumble when I say hello. While I'm working on the boat, I'm approached by other Africans asking for any work I might offer for $5/day. They rarely look me in the eye, speak quietly and humbly, and don't seem surprised when I tell them most of what I'm doing is a one-man job, and if they were working, I wouldn't be.

While the vast majority of South Africa's population is black, most of the whites are Afrikaners, descendants from the Boer (Dutch) settlers of a few hundred years ago. Their language, Afrikaans, resembles Dutch, but has evolved into a pidgin-language without a lot of formal rules, and is supposedly easy to learn. I can't understand it, but most Afrikaners I meet also speak English without much of an accent. The yacht club members are largely Afrikaners (the native English-speakers are concentrated around Cape Town to the west), and while they are outgoing and hospitable with me, they seem to be a relatively bigoted lot, at least to my way of thinking. They're not as openly critical as the white Aussies are about the Aborigines, but then the Aussies aren't outnumbered by the blacks eight to one.

The Richards Bay area is only moderately prosperous, and the yacht club is hardly a white shoes/blue blazer haven of leisure and luxury. The liveaboards who hang out in the club's smoke-filled bar are a motley crew who don't seem to have gotten it that apartheid is over. Many make a point of sardonically referring to blacks as "our new South Africans," and when I ask about life in the modern era, they'll typically preface a comment with, "I don't mind the coons, but..." They order the blacks around and call them "boy." The blacks, however, seem to accept it. Most are fawning and docile, almost fearful, and rarely make eye contact with whites. Their place has been hammered into them through hundreds of years of oppression, the last fifty of which were by far the most brutal. The bar is managed by Pete and his wife, who employ a lone black man to bus the dirty dishes and clean up the messes. "He's too stupid to do anything else," Pete's wife tells me, drink in one hand, cigarette in the other, and loud enough for the poor man to hear. "I don't know how many times I've told him to use the employees' toilets. I'm always catching him up here, using the members'." The employees' (i.e., blacks') toilets aren't even in the same building, and I don't bother to ask her which toilets she and Pete use. The anachronistic and potentially suicidal attitudes on matters of race notwithstanding, everybody has a friendly, helpful disposition towards us Americans. It's as if the whites' legacy of political incorrectness kept them too long separated from western civilization, and though they urgently want to stop being the world's pariahs, they don't really know how to go about it.

Fortunately, the majority of the yacht clubbers are neither bar flies nor layabouts, and on Sundays there's a communal *spit braai* where the atmosphere is more genteel (the spit braai is the Afrikaners' elevation of the art of barbecue to levels surpassing anything Americans or Aussies do over charcoal). The whites of a more educated or professional bent seem cautiously optimistic about the country's new regimes, and all rest their hopes on the near mythic respect commanded by Nelson Mandela among both blacks and whites. Most whites support the minority liberal party, the Democratic Alliance, but Thabe Mbeki's ruling African National Congress party is showing worrying signs of yielding to pressure from impoverished blacks for nationalization and property redistribution. The whites have witnessed the backlash and land-grabs against the former colonists in Rhodesia/Zimbabwe, Mozambique, and Congo/Zaire, and many consider South Africa to be the last bastion of European life on the continent. The newspapers carry daily reports of violence and unrest among blacks throughout the country, and the vaunted Truth Commission's disclosures of past outrages further inflame passions against the whites. The whites have so long enjoyed a privileged lifestyle at the expense of the blacks (almost everybody, even those of less than modest means, speaks of growing up with black servants in their homes), that it's by no means clear whether the various races (including Indians and other "coloreds") can peacefully and justly coexist, while maintaining South Africa's relative stability and economic prosperity (South Africa's GNP exceeds the combined remainder of the continent).

Many whites are hedging their bets. Colin, who runs the yacht club's chandlery, is of English descent and has ties with the old country that would permit him to return. He also owns an ocean-going sailboat, which he admits could become a means of escape should "the Chicken Run" (i.e., leaving the country permanently) become necessary. He's squirreling away as many U.S. dollars as he can get his hands on—partly by offering substantial cash discounts to foreign yachties—in order to circumvent government restrictions against outflows of wealth. But for almost all of the whites I meet, they make it clear that South Africa is their home, and they would prefer to keep it that way.

All is not work and worry at Richards Bay. I join Willi and Lou from *Whirlwind,* and Chantal from *Beckoning,* in renting a car for a three-day outing at the game preserves a few hours away. Our drive begins on a modern highway, the N2, through gently rolling hills punctuated with pastoral farms and deciduous forests, looking far more like parts of Ohio or Kentucky than darkest Africa. The hills are soon followed by an extensive plain where there are more farms and thousands of acres of eucalyptus plantations. Willi says eucalyptus wood is fast growing and highly resistant to ants, but the trees are so tall and spindly that I can't imagine they would be good for building anything except fence posts.

It's easy to tell the white man's land from the black man's. White land is the best land, and it's fenced, mostly flat, neatly cultivated, with picturesque farmhouses and well-maintained out buildings. The black land is overgrazed and narrow, on rocky and eroded hillsides, crowded with traditional rondevel huts and tumbledown shelters, and is home to too many cattle. The venerable 80/20 rule is very much in effect, or is it the 90/10 rule?

We drop onto a more rural road, and another turn-off takes us up a steep ridge. A sign near the top tells us the Mkuzi Game Preserve is another two kilometers, and also points to a small village off the entrance road. The village is typical of what we've seen of native settlements: shacks and rondevels, animals grazing the hillsides to a stubble, children in tattered clothes playing in the dirt, women carrying large water jugs on their heads, men doing not much of anything. There's a small store amidst a cluster of dwellings, identified by the ubiquitous Coca-Cola sign. Since our guidebook says no provisions of any kind are obtainable in the preserve, we decide to stop for cold drinks and anything else of interest the store might offer.

We park and go inside. It's only a few hundred square feet, and the shelves are stacked with the usual limited quantities but diverse variety of items: canned foods, household dry goods, sacks of rice, flour, and sugar, auto parts, tools, and an assortment of junk snack foods. A refrigerated cooler, one of the old horizontal kind with the lifting lid, stands to one side. Ten native Africans, mostly women and children, are gathered around the counter, some playing a card game and the others watching. All conversation ceases and everybody turns to stare when we walk through the door.

As we smile and nod and say hello, an enormous woman detaches herself from the group. "My friends!" she shouts, and flings herself at us in an effusive outpouring of greetings, throwing her arms around each of us in our turns. We laugh and return the hugs enough to appear polite, while the woman launches into a non-stop barrage of questions, her voice nearly a bellow. "Where you from? You tourists? USA? You going to Mkuzi? My brother work at Mkuzi. I not from here. I from Soweto. You hear Soweto? I visiting my brother. Why you come here? You buy drink?" She follows us around while we select our soft drinks and browse through the shelves of goods, with Willi or Lou now and then squeezing an answer into the garrulous flow. After a few minutes it's apparent there's nothing else we need at the store.

The show is entertaining, up to a point, and the woman is clearly enjoying her loud monologue. She exaggerates her gestures and struts around like a puffed-up prairie chicken. The other people watch quietly. I slip up to the counter to buy our drinks (I'm holding the communal purse for the weekend), and when the woman at the register gives me my change, she looks up with an apologetic grimace that tells me she's embarrassed by all of this.

We maintain our polite smiles as we edge our way to the door, but our self-proclaimed friend isn't ready to let us get away. "Photo," the woman shouts, "you take my picture!" "Okay," Lou concedes and reaches for her camera. "No, take photo you too," the woman insists, and gathers us all together. Lou shows one of the bystanders how to use the little point-and-shoot, and we line up with the woman, who shrieks and sprawls in front, clowning for the camera.

After the photo we head for the door again. "Wait!" the woman says. "You buy me drink, too!" I look at Willi. "Sure, buy her something," he says. She follows me to the cooler, but when I take out a Fanta, she heaves her considerable bulk against me and grabs a liter bottle of beer. "You buy me this," she says. I ask the woman behind the counter how much it is. Six rand.

It's annoying—our own drinks were two rand each. I reach for one of the small cans of beer, then think, no, this woman's not going to get started on her drunk at our expense. "No beer," I say, "only soft drink," and offer her the Fanta. "No, you buy me this," she says, holding the big bottle in front of her and shifting from foot to foot like a petulant child.

I put the Fanta back. "Sorry, no beer," I repeat, more loudly this time, and turn to walk out the door. When I do, the other people in the store break into applause and cheer. I stop in my tracks, completely surprised, while they laugh, shout, and clap; they're pleased to see someone finally stand up to this pushy, obnoxious woman, who no doubt torments them as well. "Thank you," I say with a little bow before I leave. "Good-bye!"

Willi and the others are waiting in the car with the engine running. As we pull away, the woman bursts through the door waving the bottle above her head. "Five rand!" she shouts. "She sell it only five rand!"

Wildlife viewing in the South African game parks is done mostly from vehicles or from camouflaged shelters ("hides") situated near water holes ("pans"). The 35,000 hectare Mkuzi Game Preserve is a viewer-friendly mix of grasslands and bosky thickets, and by mid-morning the next day we've seen hundreds of impala, several wildebeest, a herd of zebras, and a couple of warthogs. Lou has a field guide and identifies the various species of antelope: kudu, nyala, and duiker. Hulking rhinos, the world's second-largest land animal, graze contentedly near the road, indifferent to our presence. Our guidebook tells us these magnificent creatures will likely be hunted to extinction elsewhere in Africa, uselessly slaughtered for the supposed aphrodisiac properties of their horns, and that their best hope for survival is in a peaceful, stable South Africa. The highlight of the morning comes when we find ourselves in the midst of a dozen giraffes, gentle, elegant creatures, with long eyelashes and big soft eyes. Tall males hide their heads in the trees, and two juveniles stand opposite one another rubbing necks.

Dung beetles are everywhere, all different sizes, from huge flying ones with fierce mandibles, to tiny ones less than a centimeter long. Many are pushing dung balls, some nearly as big as golf balls. It's not clear where they're taking them, but there's no shortage of dung to work with. Vervet monkeys gather along the side of the road like inner-city street kids with nothing much to do; two mothers look on with their young clinging to their chests. A tortoise starts a slow plod across the pavement; Willi stops and picks it up while Lou snaps a picture.

At a large pan we identify stilts, ducks, peeps, egrets, spoonbills, and plovers. Buzzards and eagles circle in the updrafts overhead as the sun heats the land. We come to the Mkuzi River, where there are hippos and crocodiles, pelicans, and more eagles. The hippos stay mostly under water, occasionally raising their heads and bellowing menacingly, while leggy white birds peck at insects on their exposed backs. Willi tells us more people are killed by the fiercely territorial hippos in Africa than by any other animal. Crocs, two or three meters long and looking plenty mean, sun themselves on the shore. Ducks stroll among them, completely ignoring any danger they might be in.

In the afternoon we visit a "cultural village," an uninhabited tourist installation on the reserve grounds. Inside a circular kraal are five rondevels arranged around a more sturdily constructed inner kraal. The outer kraal is made of closely-spaced unfinished five foot stakes, three to four inches in diameter, sawed even at the top and stuck in the ground with no wiring, lashing, or other lateral support, not even leaning against adjacent stakes. The inner kraal is maybe thirty feet in diameter, not so tall, but its stakes are tightly bound together with weaving vines, and the area is evidently used for storing livestock.

The rondevels are about fifteen feet across, with round tops and straight sides, and look like big, thatched beehives. The single door is only about three feet high, so we have to bend low to get in, a helpless posture supposedly intended to prevent any kind of aggressive behavior by a visitor. There are no windows, and the floors are packed earth (our book says packed dung). The construction is more intricate than I expected: an internal framework is supported by two central poles, with a circular lattice work radiating out beneath the roof's concentric cross-thatching. The rondevel we enter is stocked with Zulu and Xhosa handcrafted items for sale—woven baskets and mats, and smoothly carved sticks, figurines, trays, and utensils—shown to us by two native women. I consider buying my father a nicely decorated walking stick for $7.00, but don't because he might not appreciate the implication, and because I'm generally not the type to buy souvenirs of any sort, no matter how finely wrought. Willi selects a walking stick and Lou picks up a basket to go with the dozens of baskets she's accumulated from all over the world; where they find room for them aboard *Whirlwind* is beyond me.

At the park's interpretive center we buy cold drinks, ice cream, biltong (similar to jerky), and postcards. We also inquire about the cattle we've seen within the park boundaries. "They are from the villages outside the preserve," the Zulu woman at the information desk tells us. "The village children used to watch over them, but now all the children go to school, and we do not have enough guards to keep the cattle out." It's an ironic reminder of how improving the lives of people often comes at the expense of our planet's other life forms. Parks and nature preserves worldwide are becoming isolated oases, threatened on all sides by the press of an increasingly populous and desperate humanity.

Outside the visitors' center the sound of drumming leads us on a short walk to the settlement where the park's African staff and their families live. A group of seven boys is going through dance practice in the sweltering heat of mid-afternoon, under the stern tutelage of an old man and a drummer. The boys are stripped to their shorts, barefoot, and each carries a stick adorned with three or four pom-pom tassels. The dancing is aerobic and energetic, with lots of kicking and knee lifting and thrusting the stick in various phallic gestures. The old man, speaking in growling Zulu, stops them from time to time to correct their steps and routines. One of the younger boys looks our way and smiles, but that brings a shout from the man and the boy turns his attention back to his dancing.

In the year 1488, a northerly gale lasting thirteen days blew the Portuguese explorer Bartholomeu Dias and his two caravels, from the tropics to a point "150 leagues" to the south of Africa. Finally turning northward, the crew had all but given themselves up for dead when they spotted the mountains of the south coast. The storm enabled Dias to accomplish what no European before him had managed, rounding the tip of Africa and entering the Indian Ocean. Now, over five hundred years later, Ioan and I make the trip in reverse, sailing from Durban on South Africa's east coast, and battling three less fearsome gales along the way. The final gale is at our backs, sending us flying under our shortest possible rig, and blows itself out just as we reach the Cape of Good Hope, an impressive rocky monument towering majestically above the entrance to False Bay, south of Cape Town. The setting sun bathes the sheer cliffs of the Cape in burnished gold, while Ioan and I pose for pictures and congratulate ourselves on a memorable accomplishment.

We drift northwards through the night, and at 0600 I awaken to a picture-perfect spring morning. The sun is not yet above the mountains, and the hillsides are shrouded in a dewy haze. Ioan hands me the chart and points out we're still about ten miles from the entrance to Cape Town Harbor, the city not yet visible behind Signal Hill. We start the engine as the sun sneaks over the lip of Table Mountain, the 3,500-foot edifice that looms behind Cape Town. Ioan's been chilling our bottle of South African champagne in the cold Atlantic Ocean waters, towing it with a fancy knot he's learned from my rigging book. We pop the cork and toast Cape Town, *Atlantean,* and each other.

With the chart we're able to identify Lion's Head, an impressive pinnacle near the sea, its ridgeline leading to Signal Hill, Green Point, and the turn into Table Bay. The mist begins to burn away, and the elaborate homes of Sea Point and Clifton take shape, perched on the slopes of Lion's Head. We round Green Point as the morning sun washes down on the basin of Cape Town, spread across the foot of Table Mountain. It's a picture-perfect moment, and at once I understand why this is said to be one of the world's most beautiful cities. Arriving here at dawn only makes it better, a dream come true, and is one of those awe-inspiring sights I'll never forget. Cape Town Radio puts us in touch with the Royal Cape Yacht Club, located inside the breakwater to the harbor, and soon we're safely moored.

As its name implies, the Royal Cape Yacht Club is a far cry from its poor cousin in Richard's Bay. The dining rooms and bar area are sumptuous and elegant, and the club's many docks are lined with gleaming white yachts. *Atlantean's* finger-pier berth includes water and a power hook-up, though the latter is 220 volt and not much use to me. The price is a little higher than I'd like, but still far below what I'd expect to pay for comparable facilities in the States. We don't even have to supply our own towels in the well-appointed men's locker room. The Club Secretary greets us enthusiastically, and tells me *Atlantean* is the first cruising yacht of the season to take a slip, though he's heard of a few other boats at Haut Bay, a half-hour car ride to the south. It's normally a twenty-minute walk to downtown, but a woman from the club office offers us a lift. I need to check in with the various authorities, so Ioan takes off on his own after agreeing to meet me this evening back at the boat.

The delight I've been feeling since our arrival continues throughout the afternoon. Cape Town is a city of over a million, but the central area is compact and pedestrian friendly, and reminds me of Auckland, San Francisco, or one of my favorite cities, Vancouver, B.C. There's more mixing of the races than I saw in other South African cities, more blacks and Asians wearing business attire and looking important, but the prosperity curve is still tilted heavily toward the whites. I ask an attractive young woman for directions to the post office, and when she hears my American accent, she offers to walk me there herself, though it's six blocks out of her way. I rave about how much I'm liking Cape Town, and she says, "It's the best city in the world. I think you should live here."

Back at the boat that evening, I find Ioan packing up. "You don't have to leave right away," I tell him. "Relax, save yourself the price of a bed."

"I'll be needin' work," he says while he folds his clothes and arranges them in his backpack. "The hostel's in a good spot—plenty of cafés and pubs about. I've waited table before."

"How about making the Atlantic passage with me? You'd like the Caribbean, maybe get a charter skipper job."

"One ocean's plenty for now," he says. "Mum wants me home. I booked a flight for the end of January."

Ioan's been the best crewmember I've ever had: dependable, conscientious, and orderly to a fault. We've been a good team, and he knows *Atlantean* almost as well as I. "Don't be a stranger," I say when we shake hands on the dock. "I'll be here for awhile."

"You reckon they'll let me in the front door?" Ioan's already decided the Royal Cape Yacht Club is too posh for a working-class boy like him.

We've arrived on a Wednesday, which is race day at the club, and after Ioan leaves, I join the post-race party on the patio outside the bar. Eric, the club's race organizer, and his wife Jillian, the kind of statuesque blonde I'd expect at a Hollywood pool party, have already heard of my arrival, and they introduce themselves. "We'll have to put you with a race crew," Eric says. "The Rothman's coming up and boats are always looking for an able hand." The Rothman Cup is South Africa's premier racing event.

"I'm afraid there's a big difference between cruisers and racers," I say. "I might not be much help."

"Nonsense. There are two classes, one for the captains who think they know what's what, and the other for the rest of us who don't give a rip. Whichever suits you." For the next Wednesday races, Eric invites me to join him aboard *Touch and Go*, a handsome Oyster 39 owned by his friends Dave and Veronica. There are ten of us on board: Dave is at the wheel, Veronica manages the cockpit, Eric is the tactician, and I stay out of everybody's way. On an upwind leg, we get into a furious tacking duel with another boat, changing tacks a dozen times, with bodies and lines flying. After we've rounded the mark a full length ahead of our competitor and can finally relax, I say to Dave, "You know, on *Atlantean,* if we're going to tack we usually talk about it for a day or so first."

One of Dave's Rothman crew cancels, so he invites me on as the ninth hand. For the next week sailing takes all my time, and we run eight races, including a long overnight event. We're in the "B" class, and though we place well down in the standings, our crew of able-bodied twentysomethings (only Dave, Veronica, and I are older) has more fun than most. Dave isn't an ego-stoked tyrant and never once raises his voice in anger, though his commands sometimes come across as gruff. When that happens, Victoria steps in and says, "What he really means is would you mind awfully trimming the starboard sheet? Here, let me fetch you the winch handle." Dr. Dave, as he's called by the crew, is a retired geologist for Anglo-American, the South African mining giant, and when I idly mention during the overnight race that I don't know much about the tectonic forces that have shaped South Africa, he's happy to spend forty-five minutes filling me with more information than I can possibly assimilate.

In addition to my geology lesson, the Rothman Cup teaches me a great deal about racing, including convincing me that it's something I'd never put *Atlantean* through. While I'm trying to preserve my boat for as long as it will last, racers push their crews and equipment as hard as they'll go. Over the course of the week there's one dismasting, a few minor collisions, a broken bone or two, and plenty of equipment breakage and blown-out sails. The captains seem to take the damage in stride. Once when our foredeck crew is raising the number one spinnaker, the pole gets loose and tears a gaping hole in the sail. Everybody looks at Dave in horror, but Dave says, "All right, take down the number one and put up the number two." I can't imagine I would be so calm watching one of *Atlantean's* precious—and expensive—sails being torn to shreds.

Being part of the racing team improves my social life, though it doesn't rate me any dates with beautiful women (Jillian laughs good naturedly when I ask her to fix me up, as if who in her circle would give up the good life for a spartan existence on a sailboat?). The retired Commodore of the yacht club, Ken and his wife Molly, invite me to their home for Christmas dinner, which, as in New Zealand, is a start-of-the-summer party. Molly is a distinguished sailor in her own right, and organized the first all-woman crew for one of the Cape Town-Rio races years ago. Before dinner I join a few of their guests for a lovely walk through the Newlands Forest near their hillside home.

I mention to my fellow racers that I'd like to get to the top of Table Mountain for the view. I've heard there are trails up the backside of it, and Jody, an architecture student at Cape Town University, and the only woman on the crew besides Veronica, offers to make the hike with me. Unfortunately one of the frequent fogs blankets the windward side of Table Mountain, and we see nothing from the viewpoint. We're caught in "table cloth" conditions, when the southeasterly winds stack up the clouds on the back of Table Mountain, which then spill over the edge of the sheer Cape Town face like a fluffy white cloth. The winds themselves are highly variable and unpredictable, and can go from flat calm to gale strength in a matter of hours. When the wind is especially strong, the townspeople call it the "Cape Doctor" for blowing away the pestilence and disease that once lurked in the city.

Another race crewmember, Andrew, offers to drive me to Cape Province's Franshoek and Stellenbosch wine regions for a day. The scenery is first rate, and reminds me of the wine country north of San Francisco: warm, relatively dry, with gently undulating plains surrounded by forested mountains. We stop at a winery and restaurant, *Petite Ferme*, owned and operated by the family of one of Andrew's friends from university. Although they're booked solid, Andrew's former classmate shows us to a prime garden-side table, where we enjoy a multiple-course lunch and a fine bottle of Riesling. Wine prices are ridiculously low—a third or less of what their comparable California counterparts would cost—and I buy two cases of reds and whites from a dozen different labels, paying at most only about five dollars a bottle.

Though I'm not averse to solo-sailing the Atlantic, I decide to try my luck with placing an ad for crew on the yacht club bulletin board. Following one of the Rothman races, I'm approached by a young man, Geoff, who's a foredeck crewman on another race boat. He's recently graduated from Cape Town University with an engineering degree, and has applied to several schools in the States for his MBA. He knows his sailing and nobody else applies for the job, so after Christmas I tell him he can come with me on the usual terms: passage across the ocean and splitting provisioning costs.

Geoff's engineering skills come in handy with boat maintenance, and his car is useful for running errands and picking up provisions. He lends a ready hand for the most expensive and frustrating project of my entire trip, removing *Atlantean's* transmission to fix the persistent leak and replace the drive train pressure plate. Another disheartening problem arises when I'm rebuilding the marine toilet; I overtighten the bolts on the plastic flange that connects the body of the pump to its discharge pipe, and the flange snaps off. Replacing it will require a new pump assembly, which is unavailable in South Africa. It takes us a few days, but Geoff and I eventually fashion an aluminum plate, hoses, clamps, and PVC glue into something that doesn't leak, but which also doesn't inspire much confidence. I send a fax to my sister with a diagram of the toilet and the model number of the broken pump assembly, and ask her to ship me a new one c/o the American Express office in Trinidad, our next destination. Some people might not mind using a bucket aboard a boat, but I prefer flushing and overboard discharge.

I set my departure date for January 8, which should allow us enough time to cross the Atlantic and arrive in Trinidad in time for Carnival. But shortly before we're ready to leave, the U.S. Embassy decides to be uncooperative when it comes to Geoff's visa application. Apparently the embassy staff thinks a young white South African from a prosperous family, who's recently graduated from university and is continuing his education in the U.S., and who doesn't have a job or own property in South Africa, is somebody who might not want to return.

"You are coming back, aren't you?" I ask Geoff.

"Sure," he says. "Well, maybe."

"I'll see what I can do," I say, and we drive to the embassy.

The mid-level State Department bureaucrat to whom we're finally shuffled is a clean-cut young Southerner with a receding hairline and a skinny tie. After he tells me there's nothing he can do, I step into my lawyer persona. "Look," I say, "I'm a United States citizen. It just so happens I need a crewman to help me get my boat back to Miami." I'm not going to Miami, of course, nor am I so helpless, but since when does this fellow need to know my particulars? "If you're not going to let me hire a South African, maybe you'd better assign me one of those Marines you've got standing guard out front." The man disappears for an annoying length of time, and when he returns, he tells us he can issue Geoff a transit visa, one that will permit him to go from the boat directly to the Miami airport. When we go, I say to Geoff, "This will at least allow you to leave South Africa. But I'll bet we can get it upgraded somewhere else, maybe at the embassy in Trinidad."

I've thoroughly enjoyed my stay in Cape Town, but I can't really say I've gained much insight into the challenges that face the country as it tries to craft a viable future out the ruins of apartheid. As happens too often, the focus of my stay has been on my own amusement and the problems of boat maintenance. My extra-cultural experiences have been almost exclusively among the privileged whites. The homes I've been invited to for dinners and parties—Dave and Veronica's, the retired Commodore's, Eric and Jillian's—are all like fine English country houses, in hillside neighborhoods where the streets aren't rectilinear, safely hidden behind ivy-covered walls topped with razor wire and broken glass. Most of the whites I've met in Cape Town have been of English descent, and I'm relieved that none of them exhibited the thinly-veiled racism I experienced among a less prosperous class of Afrikaners in the eastern provinces. "Race was never a problem in Cape Town until the Afrikaners enacted the apartheid laws," Eric told me one night in the back garden while he tended steaks on the spit braai. "What choice did we have?" Of course, the yacht club membership is again glaringly white, and at the social gatherings where such tolerant attitudes are expressed, the one or two black or mixed race couples in attendance bespeak a certain tokenism.

The young people from our racing crew are the most optimistic. "It's stupid, really, that it went on so long," Andrew tells me. "We'll learn to live together. Nobody wants to see South Africa end up like the rest of the continent, with everybody killing each other." All of them are openly praiseworthy of the legacies of Nelson Mandela and Desmond Tutu, whose reputations remain untarnished even as the age-old animosities surface among their fellow blacks in almost daily reports of corruption and violence. A major hurdle facing South Africa, Andrew says, is impatience and unreal expectations. He tells me that shortly after Mandela took office there were reports of blacks being swindled by other blacks, who told them that for a fee they could be granted title to any white-owned land they desired—an empty promise that cost many their life savings.

In spite of the optimism, I suspect it will be a long, slow process to achieve any meaningful level of integration and general economic justice. The black townships are still home to many atrocities, now perpetrated by blacks on blacks rather than at the hands of the white security forces. The scourge of AIDS threatens South Africa as in nowhere else in the world, and many of the difficulties in combating the dread disease seem to be cultural as much as economic. But the people I've met here are among the most friendly and hospitable I have ever known, and the land is beautiful and fruitful. I wish all South Africans well in their struggle.

The only ethnic African with whom I've had regular dealings is Henry, who is the yacht club's dock manager. When it's time to pay my final bill, I show up with eight hundred rand, the amount I've calculated I owe from the rate sheet posted in the club office. Henry looks at my account card and asks for only five hundred rand. I don't question him, and count out the bills, but when I ask for a receipt, Henry says, "It's five hundred if you don't want a receipt. For a receipt, you have to pay eight hundred."

I hope Henry didn't pocket the cash, but it's really none of my business.

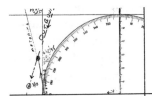

Maintenance: Boat, Body, and Soul

THE BOAT GREMLINS have stolen my duct tape. I last saw it in Mexico when I taped the corners of the solar panels so the edges wouldn't snag the sheets. Everything is fair game for the boat gremlins, who can strike in an instant. While working on the engine, I'll set a wrench within easy grasp, and a moment later it's gone. After groping around hopelessly, I'm forced to unscrunch myself from the engine compartment and won't find the wrench until I've searched for several minutes; it's always somewhere I know I didn't put it. Part of the gremlins' game is to always return what they've taken. Two days after *Atlantean* set sail for Alaska, they pinched the charger for the electric screwdriver. Four months later it was lying on the cabin sole in the forepeak, in plain sight.

I've torn the boat apart looking for that fat silver roll no man can live without. At night in my bunk, I think of places I haven't looked. Without duct tape, how will I fix anything?

I find a small hardware store in Taiohae, on the Marquesan island of Nuku Hiva. My pocket-sized French dictionary has no word for "duct," but provides translations for "tape" and "adhesive." Two Frenchmen man the store, which stocks plumbing, electrical, and building supplies. While I search through the aisles, the men ignore me, arguing and poking one another as if they're in a Left Bank bistro. I find masking tape, cellophane tape, and electrical tape, but no duct tape.

"Do you speak English?" I ask at the counter.

"A little," one of the men says. The other sniffs and peers at me down his long nose.

"Do you know what duct tape is?"

"Duck? You mean like a bird, *un canard?*"

I try to explain what it is, a cloth-backed adhesive tape, but he's not following me. He shows me the shelf with the other adhesives, and can't understand when I tell him these simply won't do the jobs duct tape can. He dismisses me with a Gaulish shrug and mumbles something to his partner, who nods. They've found something on which they can agree: Americans are fools.

After the constant exposure to sun and salt, and the heavy use on the ocean, there's much to fix aboard *Atlantean*. The mainsheet traveler is frozen in place, and no amount of WD-40 or hammering will break it free. The jib's roller furler also seizes up, but with a fellow cruiser's help, I'm able to get it apart. The bearings are badly corroded and should be replaced, but I have no spares and no way to get any. I clean and lubricate the furling assembly and remount it on the bow.

The digital readout on *Atlantean's* primary depth sounder works only intermittently. I have the backup sounder, but it's a bulky graphic display unit, difficult to read, and can't be moved to the cockpit for use while we're picking our way through the coral. It will likely have to be replaced.

The sails took a beating during our passage from Mexico to the Marquesas, and several seams have opened or have broken stitches. Restitching them is tedious, sweaty work. One of my cruising friends inspects my mainsail, pronounces it worn out, and tells me I'll have to replace it when I get to New Zealand. I cringe at the thought of the thousands of dollars it will cost, in addition to the new dinghy I'll need because the one I have is fading away in the sun. I had to patch it after a pontoon deflated from rubbing against the sharp concrete on the pier.

One of the stainless steel solar panel mounts breaks a weld. With duct tape I could at least hold it together, but until I find some way to get it welded, I'll have to disconnect the panel and store it below. The man at the post office tells me where to find Neti, who has a welding shop. With the broken solar panel mount in hand, I follow a dirt road over a low ridge east of town until I come to a heavy equipment yard enclosed by a chain link fence. Off to one side—beyond the two tractors, three massive dump trucks, and an aging back-hoe

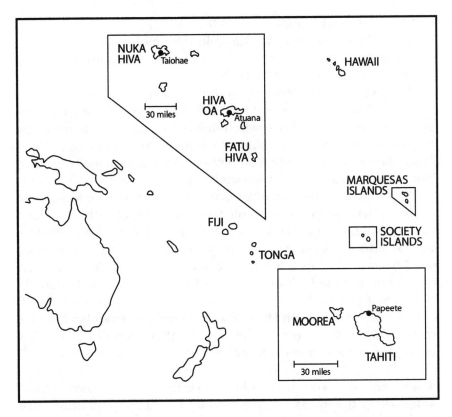

with its hydraulic lines disconnected—are some small warehouses and shop buildings. The place is nearly deserted and radiates heat and oil fumes in the heavy afternoon air. I nose around for several minutes until a man comes out of a building and directs me to the open door of Neti's shop.

Inside, Neti is lounging on an old lawn chair, carrying on a relaxed conversation with another Marquesan, a younger man, who props his elbow on a stack of threadbare tires. Neti's a grizzled old fellow, and his arms and hands are tattooed with purple-pink burn scars. Welding equipment, steel plates and beams, and bits of scrap iron are scattered haphazardly throughout the shop. In spite of his profession, Neti wears only an unbuttoned short-sleeve shirt and shorts. Like all Marquesans, his feet are as wide as dinner platters, and bare.

I show him the broken mount. Can he weld it? He studies it for a moment and shakes his head. *"Inoxidable,"* he says. Stainless steel. He has no stainless welding rod.

I tell him I only need it to hold until I get to Papeete. Will a normal weld work?

Yes, but it would rust.

That's okay, I tell him. Will he weld it for me?

"Not today, " he says. "It's too hot. Come back tomorrow morning at ten."

The next morning I show up at the appointed hour. Neti's shop is open, but Neti is nowhere to be found. After waiting a few minutes, I go in search of somebody who might know his whereabouts. The only person around is the younger Marquesan from yesterday, who's in another shop, working on an old Renault. "Neti's gone to town to buy salad," he says. "He'll be back soon."

I seat myself in the shade. After another half-hour, the Marquesan goes into Neti's shop and helps himself to a couple of tools. "No Neti?" he asks when he comes out. I tell him I need the mount welded to-day, because I'm leaving tomorrow for Anaho Bay. "I can weld it for you," he says. He puts down the tools, fires up Neti's arc welder, and in five minutes the job's done. When I offer to pay him, he laughs. "Pay Neti if you see him."

I return to *Atlantean* and paint the fresh weld in lemon-yellow zinc chromate so it won't rust in the salt air. After taking care of a few more jobs, *Atlantean's* ready to sail again.

Anaho Bay, on the north side of Nuku Hiva, has no river flowing into it. Instead of the murky green water of the other bays on the island, Anaho Bay is clear and blue, and supports an extensive coral reef. While I'm snorkeling along the reef, enjoying the Technicolor display of fishes and corals, a large, silver-gray shadow swims into my field of view. It's a shark, the first one I've seen in the wild, broad in the body and about five feet long. A shot of adrenaline reminds me I'm an interloper in his element. I stop swimming, my breath shallows, and my eyes rivet on the shark. The dive knife strapped to my ankle, with its angry eight-inch blade, suddenly seems puny.

Ever since hearing there were schools of hammer heads off the coast of Baja, I've wondered what my reaction would be when I finally confronted a shark. "Don't worry," is the common advice, "they're almost always harmless." The reminder brings little comfort. Every sense, every muscle in my body, is attuned to the shark. Though my rational mind tells me the shark is too small to attack, for the mo-ment I contemplate the image of fighting for my life. Somewhat to my disappointment, the shark ignores me. He's patrolling his reef, and goes about his business. I watch him for a minute or two before he disappears in the distance.

During the hour I'm in the water, I see the shark three more times. Growing up on *Sea Hunt* and *Jaws* has given me the wrong impression of these animals. The shark belongs to the reef, as much as the coral, the tubeworms, and the parrotfish. The sharks are predators, to be sure, but their prey doesn't include humans. The reef provides all the shark needs to live. Why would they tangle with an unknown creature as large or larger than they are?

They don't know how helpless I am.

After we've returned to Taiohae Bay, I wake up in the middle of the night; somebody has jammed a crowbar down my ear and is prying my head open. In a feverish sweat, I stagger to the head (bathroom) to take my temperature. The thermometer reads 102°. I choke down three aspirin and return to my bunk.

In the morning the ear is plugged and throbs with a dull ache. I find the health clinic in town, a long, single-story building that looks like a dying Route 66 motel in the American Southwest. Inside the main entrance, where the motel office would be, are several Marquesan women, their massive bulk overflowing out of blue plastic chairs. Most have sick children on their laps or beside them, and the room is filled with quiet worry. Another woman sits at a desk flipping through a ragged issue of *Paris Match*, to whom I explain my problem. She writes my name on a note card, along with a sentence or two, then walks the card through the door at the rear of the room.

"Please sit down," she says in French when she returns. "The doctor will see you as soon as possible."

"I would like to know how much this will cost," I say. "I may have to cash a traveler's check."

She shakes her head. "It costs nothing."

I wait for an hour, during which most of the women and children are called and treated. Oddly, no other patients come in after me. Before the waiting room is completely empty, a young European with frameless glasses appears at the back door. The white lab coat over his flowered shirt and drawstring cotton pants confirm he's the doctor.

"Are you Gregory Smith?" he asks, in English. "From the yachts, yes? Please come with me." He introduces himself as Alain, and asks me to describe my earache. When I'm finished, he looks in my ears with an otoscope, and tugs painfully at my outer ear. "Your ears are full of wax," he says. "You do a lot of diving? Swimming? I thought so. The saltwater does not drain properly. You have what you call swimmer's ear. It is common in tropical areas." He explains his assistant will clean out the wax, and gives me some antibiotic drops. "Stay out of the water for a few days. When you swim again, be sure to dry your ears completely and rinse them sometimes with a mild boric acid solution."

He asks about my boat and where I'm going. "I, too, am traveling by sailboat," he says. "Perhaps you have seen *Virus* in the bay?"

I recall the small, steel-hulled sailboat. "An appropriate name for a doctor's boat," I comment.

Alain laughs. "People think I gave the name to the boat, but it already has that name when I bought it. I decided to keep it."

"You speak excellent English," I say.

"I was an intern in New York City for one year. There I met my 'significant other,' as you Americans say. She is a public health nurse. We are sailing now for three years. We work where France needs medical people. They pay us a little. We are one year in Guadeloupe and two years here."

"Your partner is an American?"

"Yes, she is for two weeks working on the other side of the island. Otherwise, I am sure she would enjoy to meet you." He tells me she's permitted to stay with him in Polynesia without a bond or visa through the French convention known as *concubinage*. "It comes from colonial times when Frenchmen had native women," Alain says. "The idea is a lot of shit, but for us, it works. A companion is very important when you are traveling, yes?"

That evening, Barrett and I drink cheap boxed wine aboard his boat, *Serendipity.* He's a retired fire chief and sailing solo, something I've been thinking about trying when my crew gets off in Papeete. I'd like Barrett to tell me how wonderful it is, having the boat to yourself and the freedom to go where you choose, but he doesn't give me the encouragement I'm looking for. Like me, Barrett never planned on taking this trip alone. When it came time to leave his hometown of San Diego, his long-term ladyfriend refused to give up her career, though she agreed to spend vacations with him while he traveled across the Pacific. He hasn't seen her in three months, and won't for another month, when she's flying to Papeete. Barrett's lonely and discouraged. "I'm thinking after two weeks in Tahiti, she'll finally make up her mind to join me," he says. I recognize the feeling. It's called false hope. After my evening with Barrett, I'm lonely and discouraged, too.

A few days later I go snorkeling (my ear is feeling much better), diving to about twenty feet to see if I can spot lobster antennae poking out from among the rocks. When a shadow passes over me, I think *shark!* and snap my head around. Something massive and dark undulates slowly above me, like a blanket gently waving in the wind. The unexpected sight sends another jolt through my stomach, before I realize what it is: a giant manta, nine or ten feet across. Despite its fearsome visage and large size, these plankton eaters are completely harmless. I surface for air, then swim as fast as I can, following it. Its measured wing beats are remarkably graceful, and it soon outdistances me. Later in my swim, I see it again, this time in the company of a smaller ray, perhaps its mate.

That evening, sitting alone in the cockpit, I hear several loud splashes. The two mantas throw themselves out of the water, breaching, for sheer joy, like whales.

Hiva Oa is the other major island in the Marquesas, and its main town is Atuana, with a few thousand residents. The anchorage is narrow, crowded with a dozen other sailboats, and we're soon joined by more. On our private radio net with friends back in Nuku Hiva, we hear that the westward cruiser migration is in full swing, and new boats are arriving every day. My friends Brian and Mary Alice, on *Shibui*, show up in Atuana the day after we arrive. I borrow Brian's roll of duct tape, on pain of death if I don't return it, so I can show the shopkeepers what I need. There are two hardware stores in Atuana, and at the larger of the two, the Frenchman in charge is impressed with the duct tape.

"*Très utile*," he says, unrolling a foot-long strip. I can almost feel his male hormones surging at the thought of the countless jobs he could dispatch in a snap. His Marquesan assistant's eyes grow large. "Sorry," the Frenchman says. "We don't carry this. We would sell a lot if we did." Later that morning when I'm returning to the harbor, my mission unfulfilled, the Marquesan from the hardware store stops me in the street. He points to Brian's roll of duct tape. "*Changez?*" he asks. He wants to swap for it.

"Sorry," I say. "Not mine to give." When I hand over the tape to Brian, I tell him, "I've found something the Marquesans want as much as bullets and Bob Marley cassettes. If you know anybody who hasn't left yet, tell them to pack a case of duct tape."

Another important project is refilling one of *Atlantean's* two propane bottles, which is empty. At the hardware store I discover the only available propane (actually butane, which is interchangeable) comes in large tanks—three times the size of each of *Atlantean's*—that are filled in Papeete and shipped to the outlying islands. In defiance of the rest of the world, the French have their own system of gas fittings and regulators. I can't hook a French canister to *Atlantean's* propane lines, though I'm assured the necessary adapters are available in Papeete for refilling my own bottles.

In Atuana I meet an Italian, Frederico, from the yacht *Toti*, who has the same problem. Armed with a cumbersome French bottle and various bits of hardware, we set up shop on a concrete ledge in the shade of a mango tree, and struggle with jury-rigging a system to gravity-feed the gas out of the French tank and into our own. A group of Marquesan boys hovers around us and offers useless advice, until their attention is diverted by the nearby girls' school letting out. While the girls parade by, one of the boys demonstrates his tree climbing prowess and tosses large, ripe mangoes to his friends below, who employ the fruit to entice the girls into conversation. The girls, however, aren't interested in either the boys or the mangoes, so the boys share them with us. They're delicious, and Frederico and I make a sticky mess of ourselves. Somehow the boys eat theirs without smearing a drop of juice on their faces or hands. After several hours, I give up and take my now only nearly-empty propane bottle back to *Atlantean*. It's enough work for one day.

My final mission in Atuana is to find Paul Gauguin's grave, which Paul Theroux writes about in his thoroughly depressing book, *The Happy Islands of Oceania*. The French Impressionist painted his most famous works in Polynesia, and died on the island of Hiva Oa, where he's buried in a cemetery on a hill outside of town. It's a long walk to the cemetery in the stuffy afternoon heat, on a meandering one-lane road past houses with pamplemousse trees and little garden plots of taro and tomatoes. The weedy cemetery contains hundreds of gravestones and monuments, arranged in no discernable order. I wander aimlessly for several minutes, and then seek out two Marquesans who are listlessly chopping brush near the outer fence.

"I'm looking for the grave of Paul Gauguin," I say in French.

They look at each other and shake their heads.

"The famous painter. He's buried here."

They shrug their shoulders. As I walk away, they put down their machetes and watch me from the shade of a tree.

After a twenty-minute search I find a well-tended grave with an ornate carved stone and plenty of fresh flowers. It's Jacques Brel's final resting place, which I didn't realize was here; no longer Alive and Well in Paris, it appears Brel died a happy Frenchman in paradise. Fortunately Gauguin's grave is close by. A gnarled tree grows over the grave, upon which a simple round stone says, "Paul Gauguin,

1848–1903." There are no fresh flowers on the grave, only a vase of faded plastic daffodils.

I want a photo of myself sitting on the rocks next to the grave, like Theroux has on his book jacket, but I'm all alone. There's nobody to take my picture.

The depth sounder eventually gives up the ghost, and I call my sister in Seattle to ask her to send me a new one. It's supposed to be waiting for me when *Atlantean* arrives in Papeete, the largest city and the capital of French Polynesia, but American Express has no record of its delivery. I make several trips between American Express, the customs office, and the airport freight office before the package is finally located and released. The depth sounder takes a significant bite out of my cruising budget, mainly because *Atlantean's* previous owner installed 120-kHz hull-mounted transducers that are incompatible with all but the most expensive sounder units. My sister, who handles my finances back home, charges my account $700 for the sounder and another $215 for the DHL shipping, all for something that will show me the bottom a thousand feet down, when what I really care about is the five and a half feet I need for the keel. At least I'm able to convince the French I'm a yacht-in-transit and don't have to pay the customary 100% duty. Another disappointment is discovering the package doesn't contain the duct tape I requested.

The next morning I'm changing the engine oil and performing other routine maintenance when I notice a trail of dried salt leading to the weep-hole on the cooling system's raw water impeller. I take the housing apart and discover the shaft seal is leaking, for which I have no replacement. It's a garden-variety engine part, easily replaced, were I back home.

I spend another hot, sweaty day trekking through the outskirts of Papeete searching for the seal. Each place I visit directs me to another hardware store, auto parts store, or repair shop. Along the way, I inquire about duct tape, and though every other kind of tape is available, duct tape is not. I wind up at the maintenance facility for the Port of Papeete, at the ocean-going shipping wharf. The man behind the counter looks at my defective seal and jots a few notes as I describe the make and model of my engine's raw water pump. He disappears into the back room and returns with a small box.

"We do not have the rebuild kit for your pump, but this one contains the seal you need."

"Can you sell me only the seal?" I ask.

"Oh, no. You have to buy the whole kit."

I ask how much it is and gasp at the price: eighty dollars, just to get a four-dollar seal. But I have no choice, not unless I want to wait for another package from home. On the way back to the boat, late in the day, I stop at a bookbindery, where for ten dollars they sell me a roll of cloth-backed bookbinding tape. The roll is so small I can close my fingers around it—scarcely the fount of all-purpose abundance I'm used to—but it, too, will have to do.

It's been a typical day in the life of a blue-water sailor. Fix one problem, discover another. The setbacks we encounter along the way from "problem identified" to "problem solved" are like friction in an engine. The more friction, the less efficient we are. But in part it's this problem-solving that distinguishes the traveler from the tourist. The tourist wants a quick fix, because in two weeks he's on a plane back home. If he can't fix it, he'll do without; anything is tolerable if the end is in sight. For the traveler the solution usually involves time, time to learn the processes of a place, time to let those processes unfold. Most of the world moves at a much slower pace than Americans prefer. To time, add money, usually more than I would like to spend.

We persevere, day in and day out, one problem after another, a to-do list that never gets done. It's enough to drive a person crazy. Some cruisers call it quits and sail for home. Others sell the boat or load it on a freighter for transport back to the States. Many simply park the boat and fly back for however long it takes to get sane again, to be with friends and lovers who've promised to visit but never come, to drive around in a car and enjoy the cool, fresh air, and to be where they know what stores sell replacement seals and duct tape and how to ask for them. For the rest of us, when the problems of cruising begin to feel overwhelming, we retreat to our boats, as close as we come to having a home. There we bar the hatch against the outside world of strange customs, dangerous animals and diseases, and people who don't look like us or speak our language.

My friends and family think I'm a long-term tourist on some sort of extended vacation. They write to me, "What a wonderful time you must be having!" How can I explain to people who have only been tourists how much work it is to be a traveler? I can't. Nobody wants to hear me whine about sailing around the world: the constant maintenance required to keep the boat running, the importance of guarding my health and safety, or the battle to keep despair from loneliness and helplessness at bay. The folks back home all want their dreams safely intact.

My fellow cruisers joke about the titles of books we'll one day write summarizing our trips. One is *Cruising: The Most Expensive Way to Take a Third-Class Tour of the World.* There's the venerable mantra, *B-O-A-T: Break Out Another Thousand.* After days like today I prefer, simply, *Working On Your Boat In Exotic Locations.*

One afternoon shortly before I'm ready to leave French Polynesia, I'm sitting in the thatch-covered open-air bar of the Bali Hai Hotel on the island of Moorea, enjoying a Happy Hour beer with a young American known among the cruisers as Surfer John. "Where's your wife?" I ask. Surfer John's wife is Polynesian, and they have a two-year old daughter. He came to Moorea from Los Angeles at age seventeen, when his father took a job selling time-share condominiums. John fell in love with the surfing and a young Polynesian maiden, and stayed on. He lives with his wife's extended family on a nearby stretch of land, where his in-laws grow fruits and vegetables.

"She's in L.A. with the baby," he says, "doing the grandparent thing. They'll be back in a couple of weeks."

"How often do you get home?" I ask.

"Never. I'm a carpenter. I have to keep an eye on my tools."

"Can't your wife's family look after them?"

"Are you kidding? That's who I'm worried about." When it's clear I don't understand, he explains. "Say Uncle Louie needs a hammer. Since everybody knows where mine are, he helps himself. When Louie's done with the job, he's done with the hammer. He drops it wherever he is and walks away. A week later, I'll be looking for my hammer and ask Louie. 'Oh, yeah, I think I was using it out by the back fence.' That's if he happens to remember."

After another round, I ask the question that's been bothering me. "So why can't you buy duct tape in French Polynesia?"

"Think about it," Surfer John says. "You can do anything with duct tape, right?"

"Of course. That's why I need it."

"The French aren't stupid. The locals would use it for everything. They'd hold their cars together with it. They'd patch the plumbing. They'd probably build houses with it."

"Your saying it's a conspiracy by the French government? To keep duct tape out of the hands of the people?"

"You got it."

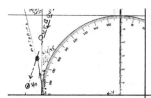

TRINIDAD
AND TOBAGO

THE ATLANTIC PASSAGE is a long one for two people on a thirty-nine foot sailboat: the GPS tells me the rhumb line distance from Cape Town, South Africa to Trinidad's Port of Spain is 5,272 nautical miles. Adding another five hundred miles for sailboat meandering and dividing by *Atlantean's* average passage record of 125 miles per day, it amounts to more than forty days of sailing. Not as far across as the Indian Ocean, and certainly not the Pacific, but then there were stopping places along the way.

Fourteen days out of Cape Town we arrive at the South Atlantic's one convenient landfall: St. Helena, a dispiriting piece of barren rock suitable for an exiled Bonaparte and his few loyal sycophants to endure the former emperor's final days. Our water, fuel, and food are in good shape, so I decide we'll keep moving. As we sail past the one narrow harbor in a niche on the island's lee, a radio call finds my cruising friends from *Isa Lei, Silk,* and *Skerryvore.* "But you have to stop," Clive on *Isa Lei* tells me. "Where else will you see Napoleon's toilet?"

The remainder of the passage goes by without undue difficulty, partly because with only two of us standing three-hour watches, Geoff (my South African crewman) and I don't see each other enough to get on one another's nerves. Late in the afternoon of our forty-second day at sea we spot Galera Point on Trinidad's northeastern corner, and set the sails wing-to-wing for the fast run down Galleon's Pas-

213

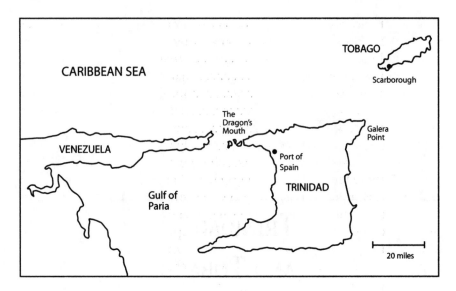

sage between the northern shore of Trinidad and the smaller island of Tobago to the northeast. With the current and wind in our favor we arrive in the night at the Mouth of the Dragon, named by Columbus himself, and heave to until daylight.

Dawn arrives clear and windless, and we motor through the entrance into Trinidad's Gulf of Paria. A general hail on VHF channel 16 directs me to the local cruiser's net, where I ask for advice on checking in. We're told to divert to Chagauramas Bay, and there we tie up at the customs dock at 0800. *Atlantean* is one of six boats checking in this morning, the others all being Caribbean cruisers from the U.S. arriving for Carnival season. I'm the first one to collect my rubber stamps and finish my business, perhaps because I supply the right answers to the most important questions ("Nothing to declare!" "No firearms!") and know that filling out the paperwork with 100% accuracy isn't essential. The loosely-uniformed Trinidadians, who are various shades of brown and betray no European descent in any ascertainable degree, are typical of civil servants the world over in their self-important and unhurried approach to meeting our needs. I keep smiling, partly because I think they'll appreciate it, and also because I'm happy to be back on land. Only when the building sways too much or the roof over my head feels too claustrophobic do I have to step outside to catch my bearings.

I've heard the Caribbean has gotten ridiculously crowded in the last few years, and the anchorage in Chagauramas Bay confirms it; there are at least seventy-five boats here, not counting the dozens that are tied up at various docks and boatyards on the shoreline. The water is stagnant and green-brown, inhabited by countless three-inch jellyfish, little self-propelled sandwich bags that no doubt feast on the effluvia of so many overboard-discharge marine toilets. The boatyards offer haul-out facilities, coin-operated laundries and showers, a few lunch-counters and bars, and their proprietors don't mind if we tie our dinghies to their docks when we come ashore.

After forty-three days at sea we're ready for a dose of civilization. There's a bus stop on the road outside the boatyard, but the cruisers gathered there tell us they're waiting for a "maxi-taxi" to come by, one of the several mini-busses that prowl the streets picking up fares into Port of Spain. They're more expensive than the public busses—which are scarce and unreliable—but far less expensive than private cabs. It's only a few minutes before one shows up, a salt-eaten Dodge van with four rows of worn-out seats, and Geoff and I each give the driver US $1, equivalent to the TT $5 fare, since we don't have the local currency. The ride into Port of Spain lasts forty-five minutes and follows an incomprehensible route, up side streets and into disorderly pockets of rough local dwellings, until all the seats are occupied. Then it's a straight shot into town, or as nearly straight as traffic, road construction, and the whim of the driver will allow. Once we divert down a dirt road where the driver stops to flirt with an ebony-skinned woman hanging laundry in front of her shanty.

In outward appearances Trinidad reminds me of Mexico. Though it's an island, it's so large that sea breezes don't have much effect where we are, and one isn't aware of the constant presence of the ocean. In the countryside there's the same feeling of relentless sun, and the humid, bursting verdancy that all but swallows up the isolated shacks with their little gardens and scratching chickens. As the city approaches, the quality of the housing improves from squalid to merely decrepit, and the city proper is a mishmash of concrete buildings in various states of construction or disrepair, painted every imaginable sun-bleached and faded tropical pastel. Enclaves of well maintained homes with their gates and high-walled gardens face otherwise empty streets, and are interspersed seemingly at random with neighborhoods of tenements and chuck-holed roads that teem with people.

My only Caribbean experience to date was years ago, a weeklong sailing charter in the British Virgin Islands, but the sleepiness of those locales can hardly compare with the noise and vibrant chaos of Port of Spain. Downtown is crowded with people, traffic, and the bustling commerce of countless small shops. Trinidadians appear to be a mix of all races: African, Indian (both Asian and American), Chinese, and European. Many have eyes with an exotic upward slant, and loud, colorful dress is the norm. I've read very little about Trinidad, except for V.S. Naipaul's *The Middle Passage*, and in that book it's hard to get past Naipaul's underlying racism and his animosity towards the land of his birth. He says there are complex hierarchies within Trinidadian society based on subtle gradations of skin color (black at the bottom, white at the top), but Trinidad's lack of an oppressive slave heritage has produced a tolerant, if unproductive, populace among whom almost any eccentricity will be applauded, particularly if superior results are achieved through clever artifice or fraud.

Our first objective is American Express, where only a little mail awaits, but which includes the happy notice that my replacement toilet pump is waiting at the nearby United Parcel Service office. After we exchange money at a bank, we find UPS (multinational corporations sometimes come in handy) and pay US $50 import duty to retrieve my package. The UPS woman says I could hire a customs agent for a refund, but it would cost almost as much as the duty. She is delighted, however, to tell us about Port of Spain. "You are here in time for Carnival," she says. "You simply must see the Kings and Queens competition, and of course the pan orchestras." She gives us a copy of the special newspaper that lists the events, venues, and ticket prices. We also ask her where we might enjoy some authentic Caribbean cuisine, and she directs us to the Breakfast Shed. "Try the callalou," she says, "and a mauby is most refreshing."

We find the Breakfast Shed, but it's already closed for the day, so we stop at a little Chinese restaurant for a passable but uninteresting meal. Another hour is spent walking through the downtown area, orienting ourselves, stretching our legs, and idly poking through the shops. Geoff buys himself an African cap, a colorful poncho-like cape, and a blue bandanna, and I buy nothing, as usual. It's hot and we're both tired, so we catch a maxi-taxi back to Chagauramas Bay.

I've attended various Mardi Gras festivities before, from Fastnacht in Basel, Switzerland, to Carnival in Nice, France, and even Fat Tuesday in Seattle, so I'm expecting outlandish costumes, drunken rowdiness, and anonymous, promiscuous behavior. The Catholics take their Lenten abstinence more seriously than we always-abstemious WASP-types, so they're more willing to go overboard during the pre-Lent party. But here in Trinidad, and in spite of the religious name—Britain was the colonial ruler here, and the official language is English, though the

Spanish and French were here earlier—I can't see much evidence of Catholicism, not like one would expect in Rio or other Latin countries. Mainly it appears that whatever turbulence might simmer beneath the surface of this multi-ethnic society, it finds its greatest release, and therefore its greatest expression in Carnival. If Naipaul is correct, the energy isn't expended towards much else.

At the heart of Carnival are the individual bands, groups that range in size from maybe a dozen to several hundred participants. The bands, each with its own unique costumes, march together during the "J'ouvert" parade that begins at 0200 Monday morning and ends at sundown the Tuesday evening before Ash Wednesday. A band has a king and a queen, and their costumes, many of which involve an entire year's planning and making, are by far the most elaborate.

Our first Carnival event is the Kings and Queens Competition held one evening at the Carnival grounds. Following the UPS woman's recommendation, we buy the cheap seats in the rowdy south grandstand, rather than the more expensive reserved seats on the north side of the stage. We arrive an hour early and the festivities start an hour late, so there's plenty of time to observe families of Trinidadians in the bleachers with their coolers of fried chicken and beer, and to listen to recorded *soca* music: a driving, rhythmic blend of pan-African, calypso, reggae, and salsa, composed specifically for Carnival and blasted without interruption in the grandstands and everywhere else one goes in Port of Spain during the weeks leading up to Carnival. Soca is get-up, get-down, party-hearty, dancing-in-the-streets music, with happy-to-be-here lyrics about feeling nice, peas and rice, swing and sway and dingolay, and "mas," which I gather involves the culmination of events at the J'ouvert parade. There are only a handful of official soca tunes each year, and they get played over and over—short versions with only the sung verses, and dance mixes that go on for twenty or thirty minutes—all of it so loud it can't be ignored. By the time we arrive at tonight's event, we've already heard the tunes so many times we can sing along with some of the lyrics.

When the competition starts, the music volume is turned down only long enough to announce the band names, then it's right back up to around a hundred decibels for each king's and queen's solitary sashay across the stage. The queens' costumes defy belief and any reasonable notions of restraint. They're like human Rose Bowl floats: complicated arrangements of light-weight structural material covered with a blizzard of fabrics and decorations, from shimmering sequins and silks, to Spandex, Lycra, and shiny lamés, to plumes of ostrich and peacock feathers, all of it bristling every which way and sometimes extending to fifteen feet in height and width. In the middle of this assemblage is the unfortunate woman whose honor it is to transport it across the stage, often with the help of small wheels hidden within the framework. The kings are more contained and therefore more mobile, but their costumes always incorporate some hugely exaggerated effect: an elaborate top hat, a giant hand or sword, or long legs on stilts. Each king carries a ritual weapon and displays the band's iconography, usually involving skulls or devil masks. The participants who reap the most vigorous cheers from the crowd are those who manage a shimmy or a shake inside all of that costume. Though the kings and queens exude a certain sensuality and mystery that could be described as erotic and alluring, none of the costumes is brazenly obscene; there are no priapic phalluses or simulated humping. We sit through the first sixty or eighty participants, which takes almost three hours, but at 11:00 pm the parking lot behind the stage is still full of royals waiting their turns, organizing their regalia, and jostling for space. We give up and catch the early bus back to the anchorage, where our ears ring all night.

My project for the next day is to join a band so I can participate in the J'ouvert parade. On an earlier maxi-taxi ride into town, I met two cruising couples, Dan and Jeanne from *Far Reach*, and Don and Heather from *Far Niente* (the similarity in boat names was purely coincidental; they didn't know each other before Trinidad). Dan and Jeanne are a couple of middle-aged junior high math and science teachers who travel the world teaching at American schools abroad. Their most recent gig was St. Thomas in the American Virgin Islands, where they acquired a cruising yacht that they'll store in Florida when they take off on their next assignment in Shanghai, China. They've learned we cruisers can join the Desert Rats band for TT $100 a head, which gets us a costume and participation in all the festivities, including as much free alcohol as we can pour down ourselves.

Geoff, my South African crewman, doesn't drink, nary a drop, and isn't interested in joining the band, so he stays behind on *Atlantean* studying his economics text (he got a letter from his mother telling him he's been accepted to the Cornell MBA program, and he says he wants to get a leg up). The maxi-taxi takes the rest of us into town where we find the Desert Rats International Headquarters operating out of a modest house in a residential neighborhood. We plunk down our money and each receive a costume: a Fred Flintstone tunic of orange cloth and black leopard spots, with matching waist, arm, and head bands. We're told not to miss the party Friday night, and get a map with directions to where it's held, at a Country Club outside the city.

Thursday night we're back at the Carnival grounds for the annual Pan Orchestra World Championships, also known as "Panorama." Pans are the steel drums supposedly invented by Trinidadians, originally made from the oil barrels the U.S. Navy left behind after World War II. There have been weeks of preliminary competitions, and the judges have narrowed the finals down to twenty groups.

I've heard steel drums plenty of times, usually in a group of six or eight musicians—one or two of whom might actually be from the Caribbean—playing for tips in Seattle's Pike Place Market, or in some park, where they pound out lengthy, bouncy tunes to appreciative passers-by. They're loud but not obnoxious, and the chromed treble pans can be quite melodic in skilled hands. I'm expecting something similar after our customary soca-addled two-hour wait, but am taken completely aback by the mob of musicians who finally cart and drag their hardware onto the stage, pouring in from the wings until there are over a hundred of them before us. After several minutes of fussing with their instruments, the blaring sound system is finally shut down, and the announcer says, "Please welcome Phase II Pan Groove, tuned by Lincoln Noel, playing Kitchner's *Heavy Roller.*"

The blast that follows is as loud as a seventies Led Zeppelin concert; the stage trembles and shakes, and even the grandstands vibrate from the collective outpouring of this vast sea of players. The energy isn't just aural, it's visual as well, with more than two hundred sticks flailing at the drums while the musicians rock and bob to the music. Pretty girls in startling Spandex shake their breasts and buttocks, and carry the group's banner around the stage, while ecstatic teenagers run in circles waving colorful flags, fueled by the exuberance that comes from five minutes of fame. As my ears grow accustomed to the din, I begin to make out a vague melody over the thrashing polyrhythms and thumping bass beats. There's no conductor, only a lead treble pan player whom everybody seems to watch. He cues sudden breaks throughout the piece's complex syncopations that echo in our throbbing ears before the almost cacophonous roar starts again. Then it's over and time for another fifteen minutes of canned soca music, while the one orchestra leaves and the next one hauls its mass of instrumentation into place.

We stay for eight bands, until around midnight, but to my untrained ear the music starts sounding the same. It's all loud, it's all complicated, it's obviously highly rehearsed, and probably represents the apotheosis of pan music, but I've gotten the idea. I find it interesting that the tuner's name is always announced with the orchestra, recognition that it isn't easy to turn an oil drum into an instrument that produces specific notes with any degree of accuracy. The names are also worth noting: the Amoco Renegades, Exodus, WITCO Desperadoes, Neal & Massy Trinidad All Stars, Arcadian Nutones, and my personal favorite, TCL Skiffle Bunch/Tropical Angel Harps, perhaps a combined orchestra.

The next night is the private party, and to get to it we have to hire a real taxi. The Desert Rats aren't the only band participating; there are at least four other bands, one dressed in sailor suits, another in turbans and veils, another in gaudy police uniforms, and a smaller group dressed as doctors and nurses in surgical masks, gowns, and caps. Probably five hundred people have turned out, and perhaps because we're at a Country Club, the ratio is about 2:1 white to the various shades of brown. It's interesting to hear white Trinidadians speak with the same musical, lazy-diction English we hear on the streets—dropping subjects, referents, and verb endings from their sentences—as if a surfeit of discussion topics requires economizing whenever possible. But the party is loud and I've never been adept at conversing with strangers, so I spend most of my time with my fellow cruisers, swapping sailing stories, and drinking too much beer and the rum punch that's dispensed freely from the back of a flatbed truck in the parking lot. There's no shortage of gorgeous local women, and they're mostly unencumbered by accompanying males, but no matter how much alcohol I consume, I can't imagine what I'd say to them. At least I'm able to dance with some of the cruiser wives, and we spend much of the evening on the dance floor, shuffling our feet and pumping arms and shoulders in our pseudo-uninhibited white people way (doing the sixties-freestyle), until it's time to go home.

Sunday at midnight we put on our costumes again and take a maxi-taxi into town to where our band has been assigned its staging area. There are probably five or six hundred Desert Rats in all, only a tiny fraction of whom are cruisers. Hundreds of different bands have turned out for this year's event, and the organizers have placed us throughout the city, where we'll march in endless and sometimes intersecting loops. The largest bands, of which ours is one, have flatbed trucks dispensing free beer, soft drinks, and rum punch, and are led by the biggest mobile sound systems I've ever seen, massive semis towing open trailers filled with stadium-size speakers boxes.

Everybody lurches forward at 0200, with the sound trucks booming the by now too-familiar soca tunes so loudly the ground pulsates with the thumping bass notes. We have our drinks in hand and shake to the music when the spirit moves us, but it's too loud for conversation. The cruisers don't know the ground rules for lewd behavior, so we don't participate in the alcohol-fueled sexual euphoria going on around us: women baring their breasts, throwing themselves into passionate kisses, and rubbing strangers' crotches, and men being equally brazen. It's as if those who are able to pull off such stunts know when and with whom they can get away with it, and that doesn't include us. Nor do we participate in the hooliganism, the scamps running through the crowds with buckets of tar or mud, splashing and slapping it on the unwary, others showering everybody with handfuls of sparkles or confetti. Of course I'm never unwary and don't allow anybody to catch me with a direct hit. There's mass insanity going on all around, and I'm not one of the crazy people. Geoff isn't either, though at least he's come along, wearing his African hat and cape like some liberal college professor at a civil rights rally, dancing to the music on the edge of our band, not really belonging but not caring, since nobody else is caring about anything but the Bacchanal.

By 0600 our procession has brought us to a part of town where I know I can catch a maxi-taxi back to the anchorage, so I call it quits. I lost Geoff hours ago, but he lasts longer than I do and stumbles in that afternoon. I sleep through the rest of Monday, and then head out again on Tuesday afternoon, without my costume, to see the last of the stragglers dragging themselves to the end. There aren't many of them, and those who are still in costume look considerably worse for the wear. The music booms as loud as ever, but there's not a whole lot of shakin' going on.

Carnival Heals

(Excerpted from the Trinidad Guardian Carnival Souvenir)

More than a century gone, and we still trying to assert some power in every year's carnival.

We want, in a calypso, to bring down the power.

But a calypso is no praise song.

And the carnival is not pretty pretty. It more powerful than that: like SuperBlue's Lara voop, it have subtelty and skill, wildness. And where you least expect, it reveals great beauty.

So, yes, we wining back into chaos, we going down in order to come up again, to breathe the rain and dance the light.

So, watch how we waving, we wailing, we playing, and we playing we playing. We ent paying no notice of nutten but the beat of we blood and the boom in our veins. But we ent really devils, we ent really bad, we just feeling to feel so we know we not dead.

Is nearly the end of the wining season . . .

So doh waste no time: *we on the trail of a bumsie...*

The biggest bambam in town ka-ka-lay-laying on them who does feel is only to sit down on: she ent turning the other cheek—no sir—each one moving independently. Is ah art in support of our Africa behind, what was before we. We perfecting the art of how we moving ahead . . .

And if you can't wine, *breathe in, breathe out,* left, right, in, out, Sparrow gone and Machal take over...

Is a wine is a wine to make you lose your up-rightness...

And when you think you really lost in this dense city of confusion, is to find the soul-saving sweetness of the riffs some night on the hill next to the highway, where the heart of John John beats in a bass pan.

"Robbery" is the cry of all them who didn't win this round of the battle for *liberté*—not freedom from chains, but we freedom to think and to feel—for the power is here in the voice of the band, in the turn of the hand on the stick on the pan.

And if is not pan, go be bottle and spoon, biscuit tin and raucous iron, ringing the heat on the j'ouvert trail, with horn and pointy tail, black and grease and pitchfork, to jook the night and wake up the day.

Is not just *any* day waking, is carnival, and we *on the road* from sun up to las lap, feeling so sweet, so empty, so full.

Gone from your head is the buzz of the ol' talk, for and not for, against and again, this word is mine, that shout in the mas' cannot be praise, the un-holy notion that the sacred is clearly not another side of the profane; or that the words of some men carry more weight than one tiny wine, one good deed of a carnival jammer.

In the passing parade, we coulda bring back Short Pants long-time calypso: where Minshall? You see him?

What is this? Is Carnival, all right. And after we bring down the power and take it in, and refresh weself with it, how will we use it, this truth we have in song, in dancing, in *playing*?

Hallelujah!

A week later I'm sitting under an ancient mimosa tree in Courthouse Square, in the town of Scarborough. This is the administrative center of the island of Tobago, the sleepy brother of Trinidad, and the other half of this nation with two names. We arrived in Tobago a few days ago after a forty-hour sail against wind and current, though we're only fifty-five miles from Port of Spain. *Atlantean* is anchored in the farthest upwind shelter on the island, Man o' War Bay, opposite Charlotteville, a little fishing village where, as in the rest of Tobago, not much goes on. Except for the stereo sounding from a shop window at the corner of Courthouse Square—thankfully playing old Motown numbers rather than throbbing soca music—the scene before me is likely little changed over the years. Tobagons congregate under the large shade trees, sit on the hard stone benches or low rock walls, and chatter amiably among themselves about everything and nothing. The local *patois* is barely discernable as English, though with concentration I can follow it.

I'm waiting for a maxi-taxi to take me back to Charlotteville. The road between here and there is pot-holed, narrow, and winding, steep along the cliffs and rocky headlands of the rugged coast, and is far enough that a regular taxi would be too expensive. There's talk of a bus, but nobody can tell me when it might arrive. I came in this morning to check-in with the local authorities, which went without a hitch, the officials treating my forms and clearances with the usual languid indifference. Afterwards I strolled through the confusion of streets that make up Scarborough, until I'd had enough of heat, dust, and disorder. Lack of room has pushed the town up the slopes and ravines surrounding the bay, and this little park I'm now in is perched atop a hill, where it catches the breeze and offers a nice view of the harbor.

Chickens, belonging to nobody in particular, peck at the ground near my feet, or roost in the plumeria bushes scattered throughout the park. It's the first time I've seen chickens sitting in bushes, which they reach with a squawking flap of their nearly useless wings. Vendors hawk a few handicrafts and fried snacks from small stands set along one side of the square, and a little while ago I bought myself a tasty tidbit and an iced glass of mauby, a kind of spiced tea I've grown to like. It's a hot day, and the air is thick with smells, of grease and greenery.

Life in the Caribbean may be heaven on earth for some, but for me it would only be so in proximity to contrast, and prolonged contrast at that. I imagine this heat would be a blessed relief if I were stepping off a plane that's just flown in from frigid Minneapolis. But this is only one of dozens of tropical isles I've been on over the past two years, with no Minneapolis in between: another warm, sunny place with lovely water and beaches and too many people with whom I have almost nothing in common.

I know I should be savoring each and every moment of this wonderful sailing-around-the-world life, but my willingness to experience wonder and awe has been drained by the absence of a soulmate with whom to share it. I've used that excuse so many times I feel I should get beyond it, but it's the explanation that makes the most sense. Whatever the cause, the symptom is loneliness. Fortunately these years have also increased my capacity for solitude. Or is it creeping middle age that's made me more jaded and reduced my ability to feel deeply? I hope not.

I've been murking around lately in my W.H. Auden collection and came across the following stanza:

The waters long to hear our questions put
Which would release their longed-for answer, but.

But what? Maybe I'm asking the wrong questions. Or maybe I'm not even asking the questions anymore. I'm living a day at a time, looking at the horizon ahead of me, thinking about the Pacific Ocean, and wondering whether flirting with hurricane season might lead to disaster. Home is still a long ways off.

My friends whose letters catch up with me say not to be in any hurry to come back. The U.S. continues its disturbing lurch to the right with Republicans wreaking vengeance on the Democrats for everything from school prayer to abortion to welfare. It's as if the entire country is suddenly obsessed with security, afraid they'll lose it all—whatever "it all" is. The rich are getting richer and the poor are willing to allow it; maybe the poor think one day they'll strike it rich themselves, and it's that faint hope that sustains them. As far as I can tell, it doesn't matter which party is in power, they're all captives of the special interests and corporations. On the other hand, violence is also escalating, much of it fueled by drugs and desperation. All of it means I'll have to figure out some new way to stay sane when I get home. But that's the great lesson of cruising, learning to adapt to whatever is thrown at you.

A Scandinavian couple arrives in our park, husband and wife I'd guess from the ring on her finger and the familiar way they relate to each other. We speak briefly when they ask whether I know anything about the maxi-taxi headed for Charlotteville—they're staying somewhere along the road—and after I tell them I'm waiting for it as well, they move off a polite distance, as I would if I'd been doing the asking, typical westerners who don't want to impose their uninvited presence on others. Now they're standing in the shade, voicing their confusion and complaints to each other, looking both worried and impatient. They should bow to the inevitable and accept that they'll have to wait an unknowable amount of time for the maxi-taxi to show up. "It will be here," say the locals, and I believe them. Where do two Scandinavians vacationing on Tobago have to go in such a hurry? What choice does any of us have?

It's too hot to do anything except sit in the shade and watch the molasses-slow ebb and flow of Caribbean life as it eases past. And slow it is, indeed, though perhaps too slow for escapees from WTO service-and-software economies looking for diversions and entertainments. Many Tobagons have little to occupy their time that I can see, except for the keepers of the tiny shops and dark bars, or the always-harried Indian merchants operating the few prosperous businesses—hardware, textiles, appliances—that the town has to offer. Needs and wants are not great in this environment, to those accustomed to idleness. Cruising accustoms one to patience, if not idleness, and I've learned that watching life go by is not necessarily wasted time. This is a public square and offers much to observe, mainly an interesting cross-section of individuals from what one might consider the lower-echelons of *homo economicus*.

A fat island woman squeezed into this year's Carnival tee shirt and impossibly tight pink Lycra exercise pants flops heavily onto the other end of my concrete bench. She carries on a pleasant and pointless conversation with the driver of a private taxi parked nearby under the shade of the trees. The man's windshield is a shattered mess; an eight-inch slightly off-center hole, probably knocked out with a hammer, affords the driver a view of the road. After a few minutes the Scandinavian couple can wait no longer and agree to the man's expensive "tourist rate" fare to take them back to their bungalow, wherever it might be. They climb into the back seat, uneasy about not having seatbelts or a better taxi at their disposal.

With nobody to share her conversation (she knows I have nothing to talk about), my bench companion takes out her lottery cards and surveys her picks. She also has a collection of number grids, probably betting pools on the local cricket matches. She glances up to see if I'm sneaking a look at her bets, and catches me watching her. "Waiting for the maxi to Charlotteville?" I ask. She smiles impersonally and nods before turning back to her studies.

A bag-lady, barely distinguishable as a woman, shuffles past. Toothless, and swathed in layers of dark men's clothing in spite of the stifling heat and humidity, she incongruously wears a pair of fancy black pumps, polished to a shine, with gold buckles and two-inch heels. She drops an empty rum bottle wrapped in a brown paper bag, and discreetly nudges it under a plumeria bush with her elegantly shod toe, before continuing her slow plod up the hill.

A dangerous-looking fellow with Rastafarian dreadlocks sets up a little stand onto which he spreads an assortment of ragged and out-of-date magazines, presumably for sale. He painstakingly mounts a cardboard sign over his wares, and then walks away, leaving the stand unattended. He stops and looks over his shoulder a few times to survey the arrangement, before disappearing down the hill towards the harbor. I stroll over to examine the plain cardboard sign, which is a foot wide and two feet tall. With a broad-tipped marker, he (or some more educated colleague) has written the following:

THE Ruler
IS A THIFE
BISNESS   B
PlACe IS   E
BEFOR   F
SATAN   O
BLiND AND   R
PARRALiSE
CRiPPLE CRAMP
VANiSH Dead Hell

The exact meaning escapes me. From the context, I assume he'd rather people didn't steal his magazines while he's off to wherever. Nobody does, and after ten minutes the vendor returns and squats in the shade near me, where his sweat and urine smell wafts in my direction and tickles my nose. The man takes out a greasy pouch of tobacco and rolls himself a smoke. He bums a light from another taxi driver, and then resumes his place, from where he can keep an eye on his shop.

Bells sound, and a group of bright-eyed school children pour out of a building and skip past. The boys wear uniforms consisting of powder blue short-sleeved shirts and khaki shorts, and the girls wear dark blue jumpers over white blouses, with pretty ribbons tied into their kinky hair. All the children are varying shades of brown and look happy and healthy, beautiful with their gleaming smiles. They are well behaved, playing cheerfully but not noisily or meanly. *If only there weren't so many children!* I think to myself. We can assure the survival of most, but the world lacks the resources to provide a meaningful and healthy life for so many. As is happening in Haiti, I fear these lovely islands will be spoiled by overpopulation and its scourge of ecological suicide. Naipaul suggests many of these tiny Caribbean nations may one day succumb to rampant poverty and be abandoned by the rest of the world to stew in their own misery, isolated behind a kind of *cordon sanitaire* that keeps the squalor out of sight and out of mind.

My dour thoughts are interrupted by a flurry of activity centering around another taxi. A young Japanese couple arrived a few minutes ago and negotiated a cab ride. After they got in, the driver decided—much to his Japanese passengers' surprise, I'm sure—to take everybody else headed in that direction, which happens to be Charlotteville. My hefty bench companion figured it out, along with another woman of equal bulk and stature, and they're motioning for me to join them, though I can't imagine where we'll all sit. Somehow we all squeeze ourselves and our belongings onto the seats, which are clearly designed for fewer and/or smaller bodies. The driver fires up the rattling engine, and the cassette player kicks out the distorted and by now nauseatingly familiar soca tunes from this year's Carnival. After forty-five aromatic minutes, we arrive in Charlotteville, where *Atlantean* bobs peacefully in the gentle swells of the bay. I pay my share of the fare and say good day to my companions.

I've survived another day in paradise.

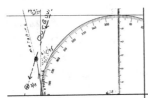

CLIMB ABOARD

Fᴀᴛᴜ Hɪᴠᴀ ɪs ᴛʜᴇ ʟᴀsᴛ ɪɴʜᴀʙɪᴛᴇᴅ island in the South Pacific's Marquesan chain, all of which are the peaks of geologically recent volcanoes. They comprise the northern component of French Polynesia's three principal island groups, the other two of which are the Tuamotu Archipelago and the Society Islands, to the southwest. We've been cruising these emerald jewels for a month—myself and the two eighteen year old Canadians who share expenses and crew for me in return for a ride to Tahiti—beginning with our first landfall at Nuku Hiva after twenty-three days at sea. Fatu Hiva is the most dramatic island yet, its central volcano sharper and steeper, its jungly vegetation wilder and more impenetrable, than what we've seen elsewhere. On the hillsides around *Baie de Vierge,* where we're anchored, are vertical volcanic plugs, some knobby, some spiked, inspirations for the Polynesians' phallicly-oriented tiki religion. Missionaries with hammers may have eliminated most of the statuary genitalia, but they couldn't alter the landscape.

Joel and Luke have gone ashore to look around while I keep watch on the anchor. I'm about to settle into my afternoon laziness—starting a new bonehead book I borrowed last week from Larry aboard *Restless*—when an interruption arrives in the form of two Marquesans paddling a small plywood outrigger. I noticed them earlier making the rounds among the other four sailboats in the bay: two French, one Italian, and one Danish, none of which I recognize. Visits from the locals aren't unusual. I suppose they're curious about the sunbaked, saltburned yachties who show up on their islands uninvited, who tramp around the villages with cameras and pockets full of colorful French Polynesian francs looking for a cold Heineken and a lobster lunch. Under other circumstances, I might welcome native visitors, but not today.

I'm tired from the overnight sail and in a lousy mood. As *Atlantean* came into the lee of Fatu Hiva just after dawn, the wind disappeared. I started the engine and tightened down the main sheet, only to rip out another seam in the aging mainsail, which will take us hours to stitch back together. Adding to my distress is the deep and narrow anchorage, the only reasonable shelter on the island. The other sailboats have appropriated the prime anchor space close to shore, leaving me farther out than I'd like and unconvinced that I've set the anchor properly on the steeply sloping rocky bottom. The constant low-level anxiety about damage to the boat from combinations of equipment failure, human error, and the vagaries of wind and waves is wearing on me.

The two natives pull alongside, banging the canoe into *Atlantean's* hull harder than seems necessary. I wince, thinking of the scuffmark I'll find when they go. The forward man stands to grab the rail. "Bonjour," I say, smiling to indicate I'm somebody they should have no reason to actively dislike.

They're both good-sized Marquesans, probably six feet tall and broad-boned, well muscled in the way of people who spend most of their time outdoors, but soft enough in the belly to indicate that life isn't a hardscrabble struggle. As is usual for me in the tropics, I can't determine their age. If I were judging by American standards, their missing teeth, squint-lined eyes, and pockmarked cheeks would indicate late forties or fifties, but there's no gray hair, so they're probably younger. Both wear only color-print pareus wrapped around their loins. The forward man is heavily tattooed on his chest, face, and right shoulder with the elaborate geometry of purple-blue swirls, bands, and arrows comprising traditional Marquesan body art.

"*Monter?*" ("mon-TAY") the tattooed one asks. He wants to come aboard, a request that catches me off guard. At the other islands the locals were content to visit from their canoes.

"No," I tell them in French, "I have work to do. Perhaps tomorrow." Because I don't want to tell them my intended work consists of entertaining myself (and only myself), I manufacture some business around the cockpit, straightening lines and stowing gear. Though we've lost nothing since arriving in the Marquesas, sailors dating back to Captain Cook have told of the Polynesians' willingness to help themselves to attractive doodads. I'm careful not to leave anything lying about. Even if I were inclined to invite the two men aboard, I'd want to keep an eye on them.

The hint to leave doesn't work and the men remain in the canoe, watching me. I don't wish to appear as impolite as I'm actually feeling, so I ask them if it's going to rain. It's a stupid question, since it rains every few hours in these islands, after enough puffy trade wind clouds stack up on the mountain, snagged like baseballs in a catcher's mitt. The Marquesans puzzle over this for a long moment, perhaps to confirm to each other that I really asked what they thought I asked, then nod silently. So much for conversation.

Not that we'd have much to chat about. It's been my experience that very little happens in the Marquesas. Few people seem to work, which I can certainly understand. This close to the Equator—about 10° south latitude—the heat and humidity produce a languor and indolence that makes one think twice about physical activity. I frequently see the men lounging around in the shade of the palm trees, swilling two-liter bottles of Coca-Cola and munching Cheeze-Puffs out of jumbo-sized blue canisters. From the meager offerings of the grocery stores, it appears the locals supplement these dietary staples with frozen chickens, cans of corned beef, ice cream, and the occasional green vegetable, all brought in by the French on the copra boat a couple of times a month. If the Marquesans bother with traditional pursuits, such as fishing, I have yet to see it. But all of that could be happening behind the scenes, work the women are doing, along with raising the children.

I imagine a conversation I'd like to have with the Marquesans, were we to have each other's language and the candor to speak our minds. "Why have you forsaken your traditional culture in favor of unhealthy and decadent western consumerism, which has made you lazy and destroyed your teeth?" I'd ask. Although rude, it's what I wonder.

"Because we've never had to work," is the answer I assign to them. "The fruit has always been in the trees. The French only made it easier for us. Their ships bring us delicious salty foods and beer. The four-wheel drive vehicles they let us buy with loans we will never repay are fun to drive, though there is nowhere to go. What would you suggest we do? Build a Nike factory?" Of course the more appropriate response to my contempt for the natives' apparent interest in western commodities would be, "Who the hell are *you*, Round Eye, to be talking about *us*?"

Sweltering in the tropical heat and uninterested in apologizing for the poverty of my thinking, I coil another line. One of the Marquesans points to it and asks, "*Changez?*" Do I want to exchange, trade? It's a request I've been hearing a lot lately. *Atlantean* has an abundance of rope—genuine Dacron Polyester double-braid—each length of which has its own essential purpose. The Marquesans on these outlying islands must have few, if any, sources for good rope. Their plywood canoes are lashed together with crude plastic twine that looks like it's spun out of shredded Hefty bags.

When I decline to part with any of *Atlantean's* precious sheets and halyards, or the spares, which I have safely stowed below decks, the men shrug. At least they're not asking for bullets, which was a regular request on the main islands of Nuku Hiva and Hiva Oa. At first I didn't know what the French word *cartouches* meant and merely smiled and shook my head, but when I filled out the French customs forms and saw a question about *armes à feu et cartouches*, which I interpreted to mean weapons and answered in the negative, I realized these people had been wanting cartridges: bullets. Specifically, .22 long rifle shells, a fellow cruiser explained to me, which the French ration out at the rate of a dozen per family per year. The wild goats on the mountainsides, introduced by European sailors as a source of fresh meat, mean dinner, though you have to be a pretty good shot. The French treat the islands as a colony, one of several politically incorrect outposts throughout the world's tropical zones where the French go to be French without having to apologize for themselves. Too much weaponry in the hands of the locals might prove dangerous.

After a few minutes, the man in the canoe grunts for my attention and points to my river sandals sitting in the cockpit. "*Bien,*" he says.

"Yes," I agree, "they are very nice."

"*Changez?*"

"No, I need my sandals." I use the English word "sandals" because I have no clue what they might be called in French. The man nods blankly.

Since they want to barter, I ask them what they have for trading fodder. "*Des fruits,*" the spokesman says. He gestures at an ugly pamplemousse and a couple of mangoes sloshing around the bottom of the canoe. We're already well stocked from the last island, Tahuata, where a friendly family loaded us down with a gunnysack of pamplemousse and oranges, plus a huge stalk of bananas. The little green-orange bananas (one of dozens of varieties growing on the islands, all of which are more flavorful than the uniform yellow paste-pods multinational agribusiness has declared fit for mass consumption) are hanging from our stern pulpit and threatening to ripen all at once, which will have us each eating dozens a day before they turn into a mush of sticky-sweet goo.

I fetch the bag of trinkets I bought at the Dollar Store in San Diego. It's full of cheap kid toys, costume jewelry, disposable lighters, and a few packs of stale Marlboros. The men poke through it, but they're not interested in anything it has to offer. The tattooed man shakes his head and sets the bag back on the deck. It's too hot to go below again for the little bottles of Nescafé and vanilla I bought in Mexico for trading.

The man points to my sunglasses, dangling from a strap around my neck. *"Changez?"* he asks. I'd never part with my sunglasses, which keep me from going blind out on the ocean, even if the terms were close to *quid pro quo*. I put them on and say, *"Sûr la mer, il y a trop du soleil."* "Too much sun," though it's somewhere behind the clouds at the moment. The man nods, and the scenario repeats itself: my tee shirt, my pocketknife, a bucket and brush. Each time I decline, and explain these are items I need. They nod, unperturbed, and ask for something else.

After rigging a canvas tarp over the open hatches to keep out the rain, there's nothing more to do on deck. With the boys ashore and conversation going nowhere, I'd like more than anything to get back to my book. It's easier to make up a lie than to sit in front of the Marquesans and ignore them. "I have to go below to work," I tell them. *"Au revoir."* I grab my sandals and close the hatch behind me.

Joel and Luke return shortly after the two Marquesans leave, ending my hopes of a peaceful afternoon on the boat. As I suspected, they didn't find much to interest them in the village: no fast food, no video parlors, no decent surf for their boogie boards. It's my turn to take the dinghy to shore, and I walk a mile or two up the dirt road leading across the island, happy to be alone and stretching my legs. I'd like to find a path up the mountain, but I've learned attaining the high ground for a Petrarchian vista of my surroundings is a western aspiration rarely shared by the Polynesians.

The island itself is like a vast tropical greenhouse, bursting with vegetation, the air redolent with the warm, wet smells of earth and chlorophyll. All around is the almost palpable rustle and pop of greenery pushing its way towards the sun. Fruits of all sorts—mango and breadfruit trees with their spreading canopies; pamplemousse and orange trees, their branches heavy with round green orbs; spiral-trunked bananas with their elephant-ear leaves—line the roadway and look to be minimally tended. I might be tempted to help myself, but I understand the land is governed by complicated ownership rules, and it pays to ask first. Beyond the road are numerous palms and other waxy-leafed trees I can't identify, thickly trunked and reaching for the sky, though each seems a mere platform for the wild profusion of vines and foliage, dozens of varieties, that twine around them. Plants I've seen potted and groomed in offices back home—schefflera, crotons, bromeliads, spider aralias—grow in reckless abundance. I'm reminded of that first morning after our nighttime arrival in Nuku Hiva, when I opened the companionway hatch and nearly fell backwards from the assault of color on my eyes. Green, green, green everywhere, after more than three weeks of nothing but the blue of the sea and sky, and for months before that the sere brown hills and rocks of Mexico. I'd forgotten what an intense color green could be.

On my way back to the anchorage, I catch up with a Marquesan carrying a 4' x 8' sheet of plywood. I ask him if he can use a hand, and he lets me take the back half. We walk for ten minutes, neither of us saying anything, until he steers us to a palm tree where he props up the plywood and sits in the shade. He takes out a tobacco pouch and rolls himself a cigarette, then hands the makings to me, which I decline. I reach for my water bottle and offer him a drink, which he declines. After these mutual gestures of kindness, we smile and nod through my entire vocabulary of French pleasantries, until there is nothing more to say. Since he's in no hurry to reshoulder his burden, I eventually excuse myself and continue on my way.

The frustration I feel in my encounters with the Marquesans is similar to what I experienced with the locals in Mexico. I find myself thinking there must be something that would make life better for these people, but I have no idea what that might be. More education? Paved roads? High-speed internet? Or merely leaving them alone? Though many of my countrymen would surely consider this island an earthly paradise, building a tourist hotel would only turn the locals into poorly paid chambermaids and beach boys.

It offends my self-centered American idealism that I can't come up with a solution to their lives. Perhaps my helplessness is one of those great lessons of travel, realizing that my inability to relate to the locals doesn't arise so much from the lack of a common language as from an unbridgeable cultural gulf. My background of relative wealth and privilege has afforded me opportunities for education, travel, and expressing my frequently naive opinions on how best to solve the problems of the world. As a prisoner of my culture, however, I've probably compromised my ability to forge close connections with nature, the land, and other people, which the Marquesans who are confined to this small island must share in abundance.

The United States has an unfortunate history of imposing its view of right living on other peoples, as if our idealized notions of the boons of free market capitalism, representative democracy, and Judeo-Christian theology automatically trump anybody's alternatives. Too often our efforts at cultural enlightenment are accompanied by the guns that we're too happy to supply to the thugs who pay lip service to our ideology (and who are also lining their own pockets), while the general populace is seduced with the empty blandishments of material goods, junk food, trash culture, and wage-paying sweat-shop jobs. Small wonder the rest of the world both envies us and hates us. Wouldn't it be better if our country's emissaries instead addressed these people as adults, and said, "These are the resources we're prepared to offer," so the locals could choose for themselves? But really helping other countries would involve suppressing our own greed, since weapons and the trappings of instant gratification are by far America's most profitable exports.

The next morning I'm up early to work on patching a chafed mainsail batten pouch. I'll need Joel and Luke's help to repair the main's torn seam, but they're sleeping late, something they do with increasing regularity. I'm in much better spirits after my own good night's sleep, and a hard rain before dawn has brought a welcome freshness to the air.

I sip my coffee in the cockpit and watch a tall, rail-thin man come out of the cabin of the Danish boat fifty yards off. He wears only a pair of faded shorts, and his blond hair and beard glow like a halo in the morning sun. Except for my own shock of sun-bleached red hair, to the Marquesans he must look a lot like me. He balances momentarily at the rail, then dives gracefully into the water for his morning swim. As the Dane climbs back on his boat and rubs himself dry, there's a commotion on the beach. We both turn to watch as seemingly the entire male population of the village—probably forty men and boys—piles into four large outrigger canoes and several smaller ones. They fire up the boats' smoky two-stroke outboards, and roar off around the point.

An hour later I'm sewing on the mainsail's batten pouches when a girl in a little blue outrigger paddles alongside. *"Monter?"* she asks, careful not to bump into *Atlantean*. Asking to climb aboard is beginning to sound like a Fatu Hiva custom. The girl is young and pretty, with silky black hair, wide eyes, and—most unusual for these islands—all of her teeth. A flowered pareu is wrapped around her waist, over tight-fitting shorts and a stretchy top. I immediately wonder if allowing her to board the boat risks offending some of her large male relatives. Since they've all gone away, I decide it can't hurt to keep her in the cockpit, in plain sight of anybody who might be watching. A long piece of twine serves as the canoe's bow line, which I secure to a cleat. Before she climbs through the gate, she hands me a small cassette player she carries in a plastic bag.

Her name is Angelique and she speaks passable French. Unlike her fellow countrymen, she's tiny, certainly not over five feet tall. She tells me she's eighteen, "almost nineteen," and declines my offers of coffee or tea. After several attempts to start a conversation with her, it becomes apparent she only wants to sit in the cockpit and play her single cassette of poorly recorded French disco music. Every few minutes she flips the tape over, presses the record button, and says something into the player's built-in microphone. She speaks in Marquesan, and when I ask her to translate, she giggles and shakes her head, before starting the music again.

I go back to patching the mainsail, pausing every few minutes to ask her questions as I think of them.

"Where did the men go?"

"To the other village for a soccer game."

"How far is the other village?"

"Not far."

"How often do they play?"

"Every week."

"Does the other village come here for soccer?"

"No, the only field is in the other village."

"Do you like soccer?"

"No."

And so on.

Later I ask, "How do you like living on Fatu Hiva?"

The look she flashes is a language I've learned to understand: it's the unmistakable teenage Grimace of Disgust. "Are you kidding?" it says. "I'm bored to tears by the place." Joel and Luke offer me the Grimace of Disgust regularly, though its meaning is variable, depending on context. The common theme is that the question I've asked or the observation I've made is incredibly lame and will not be dignified by a civil response.

Does she get off the island much?

"I have been to Atuana twice," she tells me proudly, referring to the administrative capital on Hiva Oa. "I am going there to live. A man on a sailboat has promised to take me there when he returns."

It's all the information she's willing to offer, and leaves me imagining some randy French sailor taking advantage of the poor girl (of course I assume he's French; Frenchmen have no shame). I don't blame her for wanting to leave. If I offered her a ride to Papeete, the South Seas metropolis on Tahiti, she'd probably pack her bags and be on board in an hour. But I don't offer, and the hour slides by. The young Marquesan sits contentedly with her music, while I sew on my mainsail and contemplate Angelique's unpromising future.

A rustling below decks indicates the boys are rousing themselves from hibernation. Joel, no doubt having heard the female voice, appears in the companionway and stretches expansively, puffing his bare muscle-bound chest. "Well, hello," he purrs, acting surprised and running a smoothing palm across his micro-length buzz cut. Luke follows him up the stairs, tall and slender, his straight blond hair tied in a ponytail. There's scarcely an ounce of fat between them.

The emergence of my crew perks Angelique's interest considerably. She shuts off her cassette player, sits up straight, and smiles prettily, fluttering a particularly flirtatious eyelash towards Joel. Though my middle-aged ego suffers for a moment, it occurs to me the boys are the likely objects of her visit. She must have noticed them wandering through the village yesterday and watched where they were headed when they got back in the dinghy.

I explain to the boys what little I know of Angelique, leaving out the part about her desire to run away to Atuana. Once that's out of the way, conversation evaporates. I put away my sewing kit while Joel and Luke furl the mainsail, then we lapse into our typical mode of dealing with locals: sitting silently, smiling, and nodding. The boys seem a little bemused by our unusual guest; she's the first unaccompanied female to come to the boat uninvited.

The sudden gargle of outboard engines throws Angelique into a panic. As the returning outriggers round the point, she springs to her feet and jitters around the cockpit searching for a place to hide. When the boats draw to within a hundred feet, she leaps into the water and swims behind *Atlantean,* away from her fellow countrymen. The boys and I stare at each other in amazement while Angelique splashes around noisily. "Too weird," Joel says.

"Maybe she doesn't want them to see her," I venture.

"Sure, like they couldn't see the humongous splash."

"Or her little blue canoe," Luke adds.

A small outrigger with two men and a teenage boy swings around us, its occupants having obviously recognized Angelique. She sees them, gasps for air, and dives under *Atlantean*. When she resurfaces, they've also gone around the boat, and she dives again. The canoe idles alongside. "*Visitez?*" the lanky teenager asks. He's wearing only gym shorts, and a pair of soccer shoes with the laces tied together hangs from his neck.

"Sure, climb aboard!" I call out in English. "We're having a party. Bring your friends." I know they don't understand what I'm saying, but I want to see how this plays out. Angelique grabs another noisy gulp of air and dives under the water. Rather than climb aboard, however, the men say something to the teenager in Marquesan. Their tone is critical, and the boy shrivels in his seat. "*Returner,*" he calls as the driver revs the engine and pulls away.

After they're gone, we drag sopping Angelique back onto *Atlantean*. From her sparse and evasive answers, I gather the boy has a crush on her. Another Grimace of Disgust indicates she can't stand him. I'm mildly relieved we're not in trouble with her elders for compromising her virtue.

Fifteen minutes later the teenage boy paddles alongside in a small outrigger, accompanied by another adolescent male and a fat boy about six years old. The child is stark naked and crouches in the canoe, hiding his private parts, and refuses to join us aboard *Atlantean*. The other two boys hoist themselves into the cockpit, each wearing unbuttoned print shirts they've put on for the occasion. We identify ourselves with names all of us immediately forget, after which I pass around a bag of hard candies.

Angelique's suitor doesn't speak much French, and the princess herself sits on the cockpit coaming with her back to us and her nose in the air, braiding her wet hair and refusing to participate in the festivities. Without the benefit of conversation to ease the tension, the Marquesan boys sit silently and uncomfortably, sucking on their sweets. The one lad is obviously love struck, and looks rather glum. The other stares at Joel and Luke in open envy of their impossibly cool raiment: baggy shorts reaching to their knees, faded surfer-logo tee shirts, and Joel's John Lennon sunglasses.

After a few minutes the absurdity of the situation gets the best of us, and the boys and I are cracking jokes in English at our poor guests' expense. "I don't think this guy's going to get lucky tonight," Joel says. The young Marquesans eventually leave, except for Angelique, who's in no hurry to go anywhere. I'm tired of this game, so I turn her over to Joel and Luke, and search for something better to do in the cabin.

Within minutes I hear the three of them giggling shyly, engaged in some universal boy-girl chitchat that transcends the lack of a common language. In another fifteen minutes Joel and Luke are showing off, taking turns paddling the little outrigger. Angelique dances around the deck, clapping her hands and shouting encouragement. I'm a little put off that things didn't loosen up while I was around, but I'm aware enough of my age differential to realize it took my stepping out of the way to let the young people's natural instincts take over. They're enjoying themselves, not dealing with heavy issues, not worried about what the future may hold either for them or for Angelique's culture. They're simply three young people exploring the kind of extraordinary chance occurrences that life throws at us every day.

After Luke makes lunch, Angelique wants to clean up, perhaps to show us what a good little wife she'd make. I refuse her offer, since disappearing below decks for more than a few minutes might raise some attention. Her tongue loosens further as the afternoon wears on, and she chatters away in French like a coquette, though the boys scarcely understand a word. The little I catch seems obvious enough to not need translating.

It's nearly dark when she announces she has to leave. Before she goes, I dig out a snapshot I have of Joel, and call him down to the cabin. "Sign it," I say.

"Why should I?"

"She'll treasure it," I say. "Write, 'To Angelique, my Polynesian Princess. I'll remember you forever. Love, Joel.'"

"I'm sure," he snorts. He scrawls his name across the back of the picture and shoves it to me.

"Not me, Stud. *Give it to the girl.* You can do this." We go back on deck where Angelique sits with her hands in her lap, sighing and making herself as available as possible. I turn to Luke. "Let's go below and give these lovebirds some time alone."

"I hate you guys," Joel says, as we close the hatch behind us.

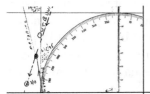

THE SLEIGH RIDE

WHAT IS IT ABOUT SHIPS going to sea that has made generations of sailors kiss their loved ones good-bye and venture at their peril into the vast unknown? After all, we're not born to travel upon the ocean. Life may begin in the sac of seawater in our mothers' bellies, but after we land kicking and howling in the world of air and solid ground, saltwater is forevermore an alien environment. It's the fresh stuff we prefer and in fact depend upon (heavenly in its cloudy origins), so long as it comes in manageable quantities and we have the security of the Earth beneath our feet. On the other hand, its saline counterpart is a bother, a substance of little apparent use, except for dabbling in its margins as beach vacationers, fisher-folk, or surfers. Yet the sea has always been a magnet for wanderers, adventurers, fortune hunters, and countless others who search for fulfillment and escape from the commonplace.

In times past, part of the attraction must have been the nature of the ocean as a barrier, separating the known from the unknown. Because barriers were difficult to surmount—whether they were vast oceans, impenetrable mountains, dense jungles, burning deserts, or, like the Steppes of Russia, simply great distances—they were what gave the world its breadth, and in the process gave breadth to people's imaginations, their curiosity, and their hunger for adventure. They crossed the barrier for what they might discover and bring back (knowledge,

241

treasure, fame) or perhaps because they hoped to stay for what the other side had to offer (farmland, religious freedom, escape from persecution). For the last several hundred years, and until just recently, a ship going to sea represented the only means by which one could tackle that earthly environment for which our bodies were least adapted, the oceanic barrier. But with the advent of modern air travel a person can go virtually anywhere on the planet simply by climbing aboard an airplane, which reduces geophysical barriers to the price of a ticket and a few hours' or days' time. Of course not everybody flies or can afford to, and people still join the navy or the merchant marines as a way to see the world.

The attraction nowadays for adventure seekers must involve the barrier itself. We climb a mountain, trek through the wilderness, or sail across an ocean because of the challenges they present. It's not to say we aren't curious about what we may find on the other side, in which case traversing the barrier can become a kind of rite of passage preparing us for what we're about to encounter. But as I'm fond of telling people who say they dream of going to Tahiti, "If it's Tahiti you want, buy a plane ticket. Don't sail to Tahiti, unless you want to *sail* to Tahiti." I say this because when you're sailing the open ocean, being on the ocean is what it's all about. Where else do we face such distances, so many unknowns, and such potential helplessness?

Barriers are by their very nature inhospitable to humans, and our experiences are perforce reduced to a more elemental level, involving nothing less than survival itself. Stripping ourselves of the clutter of the comfortable and familiar sharpens our senses and our wits, enabling us to see more clearly that which we don't know and can't control, and spurs us to expand our capabilities. At sea our physical limitations are most obvious, and without the vessel to which we entrust our fragile bodies, we die. Small wonder the boat becomes so intimately woven into the fabric of any sea-voyager's experience. Sailors feel every inch of the journey sliding away beneath them, and at a pace that makes the sight of land all the sweeter.

It's a chill morning in late August, and I'm about to begin my around-the-world journey in earnest. Three of us are aboard my thirty-nine foot sailboat, *Atlantean,* as it pulls away from a small marina in Astoria, Oregon. We yield a wide berth to a black and red freighter steaming beneath the towering cantilevered lacework of the Columbia River Bridge, en route to Portland or Longview or Camas to pick up a load of logs, or perhaps wheat, or paper pulp. The air is thick with the iodine tang of the estuarine mudflats and marshes. Gray and white gulls squawk and squabble around us, and mugs of steaming coffee warm our hands and stomachs.

Twenty minutes later I'm in the galley stowing two weeks of provisions when George calls down the companionway. "We're abeam of the number one entrance buoy," he says. That means we've made it over the bar, an area once known as a graveyard for sailing ships, where they'd ground on its shifting shoals and be pounded to driftwood by the storm-driven waves (even now, the Coast Guard ranks the Columbia as one of the most treacherous entrances on the North American coast). For us there's been an almost disappointing lack of drama. The sky is overcast, the wind light, we left according to the recommended tidal current schedule, and we're following a well-marked channel. *Atlantean's* dependable diesel soon putters us into the uncharacteristically gentle swells of the Pacific. It's time to raise the canvas and prove we know how to sail.

I'm glad to have George and his friend Steve aboard. During my just completed shakedown voyage to Alaska (with other friends and family joining me as crew), I ventured onto the open sea a few times, including sailing three days and two nights from the Queen Charlottes to Nootka Sound on Vancouver Island's rugged outer coast. But there was nothing like the passage we're about to undertake. George is *Atlantean's* former owner, and he got in touch with me when I was in Juneau, saying he'd like to join me for the trip down the West Coast. He's an avid armchair sailor who's read everything from accounts of the square-riggers rounding the Horn to the adventures of modern cruisers—Slocum, Chichester, Tristan Jones, and even William F. Buckley's sailing memoirs. This will be George's chance to taste the salt-breeze and feel the roll of the waves. "Forget about stopping in San Francisco," he said when I told him I'd pick him up in Astoria. "We might as well go all the way to San Diego."

"You don't want to sail under the Golden Gate?" I asked. It was my original plan, to be followed by short hops from harbor to harbor.

"Damn it, Greg," he said, "when I told you I wanted to go to sea, I didn't mean some little piddly-ass jump down the coast. I want to go to *sea!*"

Even before making up my mind to quit work and sail around the world, I started researching offshore-capable "blue water" sailboats. I wanted something with space to comfortably accommodate myself and a sailing companion, plus guests and everything necessary for years of travel. The boat had to be sturdy to withstand heavy weather, yet small enough for two people, or even one, to handle. It was hard to know what kind of boat to look for. Other than my two boat-partners, with whom I jointly owned *Puffin*, a little twenty-six foot sloop, I knew few other sailors. I belonged to no sailing club, had never raced except in Seattle's Lake Union Duck Dodges, and could count on one hand the number of other boats I'd sailed aboard. I wandered the docks and read a book about buying a sailboat. Brokers showed me whatever they had and spouted empty promises.

One wintry day in February, around the time I planned to begin serious boat shopping, George gave me a call. His wife was out of town and he repeated an invitation I'd been putting off, to crack a bottle of vintage port with him at his house, a nineteen-twenties mansion perched atop a bluff overlooking Puget Sound. Though I didn't normally socialize with clients, especially wealthy ones whose priorities rarely coincided with my own, he sounded lonely and I accepted.

George and a brace of black dogs greeted me at the door, and led me to a stone fireplace where a log fire crackled. We settled into deep leather armchairs with our wine, and after obligatory exchanges about its fine quality, the day's stock market performance, and the sorry state of the world, our conversation came around to George's frustration with his wife's lack of interest in sailing. It was the first I'd heard George was a sailor, though it shouldn't have been surprising. "Yachting" fit my tweedy, old-money image of George perfectly.

"I've had the goddam boat twelve years," he said. "I took Jeanne for a sail after I'd bought it—sun shining, fifteen knots of breeze, a perfect day. Afterwards she said, 'George, enjoy your new toy. Just don't expect me to come along.'"

I shook my head and tutted appropriately.

"We could have gone anywhere," George continued, "seen the world together on that boat. Now all I do is sail in and out of the marina, and not very damn often at that."

"What kind of boat is it?" I asked.

"A Fast Passage 39," he said.

I'd never heard of the make, and told him.

"Damn fine boat, even if she is made of Tupperware."

"Tupperware?"

"Fiberglass. Nobody makes a decent wooden boat anymore."

Several minutes went by while George wandered off to some other astral plane. His three big Bouviers—Arcturus, Regulus, and Procyon—sprawled at our feet. I watched the fire, sipped the too sweet wine, and chewed over whether I should reconsider fiberglass. Wooden boats supposedly required a hellish amount of upkeep.

George returned to the planet with a decisive nod. "That's what I should do," he said, "sell *Atlantean* and get myself something with a little class. An old wooden boat from the glory days of yacht racing. Bring her back to Bristol."

"Tell me about *Atlantean*," I said. After listening to his description, I decided to take George into my confidence. I told him about my thoughts of sailing offshore and the plans I'd shared with only my family and closest friends. He immediately warmed to the idea.

"*Atlantean* could be the boat for you," he said. "She's built for heavy weather, but she's not a plodder." We agreed to go sailing the following weekend. A few months later George had bought himself a museum piece—the legendary but decaying racing yacht *Carib-bee*—and *Atlantean* was mine.

This morning George is well prepared to go to sea. He's dressed in his red Stearns foul-weather suit with its built-in safety harness and self-inflating life-vest. Although there's no sign of the sun, he has a glob of zinc oxide on his nose, bracketed by a pair of Ray-Ban aviators, beneath a fisherman's cap with a dark green bill that sticks out about a foot. His colorless hair, slight build, and sallow indoor complexion remind me of Edwardian photos of overbred English gentry.

The third member of our company is Steve, in his forties, whose solid physique, shoulder-length black mullet, and bushy mustache give him a swarthy ruggedness that seems incongruous in company with George's doughy conservativism. He's a self-employed audio engineer, and his association with George, like mine, arose out of a professional engagement (George's profession consists of figuring out what to do with his money, which he earned the old fashioned way: he inherited it). As a longtime partner in some of George's projects, including co-producing a documentary about dogsledding Montana's Bob Marshall Wilderness, Steve is as familiar with George's idiosyn-crasies as he is with *Atlantean*.

Once we're safely out of the Columbia, George handles the wheel while Steve and I raise the mainsail. We soon have *Atlantean* on a port tack (the wind coming from the front left of the boat), beating into the light southerly breeze. The seas are calm and we set a course to the southwest to escape the heavy traffic around the mouth of the river. As with any long anticipated journey, it feels good to be underway, and all of us stay in the cockpit fine-tuning the rig and talking about what we might expect over the next ten or twelve days. For George and Steve this means reacquainting themselves with *Atlantean*, and discovering what it feels like to sail under conditions they've never experienced before.

I soon realize the rolling swells might have unpleasant side effects on those unfamiliar with the motion, so I put out a box of saltines to ward off seasickness. To further keep my crew's minds off their stomachs, I announce, "Steering a boat's for racers and day sailors," and make preparations to hook up the Aries windvane, which neither Steve nor George has seen in action before.

We have two autopilots on board. When *Atlantean* belonged to George, he equipped it with an Alpha 3000, which uses electrical power to steer the boat on whatever compass course it's set, and is the most reliable to use when motoring. I installed the other autopilot, the Aries windvane, which can be set to any angle on the wind and corrects the course when the boat strays from that angle. The Aries relies on the force of the water moving past a small servo-rudder to pull on lines that turn the steering wheel. It's an engineering marvel that draws no electricity, and is designed for long ocean passages.

Monitoring the Aries to keep track of our course and speed is an important part of plotting our position and measuring our progress. Ever the purist, George is my inspiration to navigate by sextant. "Any idiot can push a button," he says. Finding my way around the world using the stars has a certain romantic appeal, and at his urging, I've bought the best sextant I can afford, a used Tamaya Jupiter, a magnificent piece of precision machining and optics. I have no idea how to use it, and have a hand-held GPS aboard as a back-up and for navigating around tricky reefs (GPS stands for Global Positioning System, a network of satellites that provides nearly instantaneous position fixing anywhere in the world). For the San Diego passage, George has brought along the venerable Weems & Plath sextant he inherited from his grandfather, and I'm counting on him to teach me celestial navigation.

George takes his role as navigator seriously. Even before we're out of the Columbia he spreads his tools under the cockpit's canvas rain dodger: parallel rulers, pencils, spreaders, plotting paper, and calculation sheets. He takes bearings on every buoy we pass and notes minor course changes in the log, working earnestly on his notes. Unfortunately, concentrating on books and charts isn't the best activity for the first few hours on the open ocean, and George soon reaches for the saltines. By early evening he's stopped talking about sextant sights altogether. His normally pasty complexion has taken on a distinctly green hue, an interesting contrast to the bright white zinc oxide still adorning his nose. The winds ease further and back to the north, producing rolly, confused seas. While Steve and I are resetting the sails, George leaps from his seat and heads for the rail, where he's violently ill.

By 2100 it's full dark and we're all still in the cockpit. Seasick George lies stretched out diagonally across the bench seats, apparently sleeping, so Steve and I flip a coin to see who will stand watch. I lose, and Steve, who isn't feeling too well himself, heads below.

I stay up as long as I can, but at 0100 I'm exhausted, partly because worrying through my last night on shore didn't yield much sleep. George hasn't budged in five hours, so he must be well rested. "George," I say, giving him a little shake, "can you stand watch for a few hours?"

He sits up instantly, as if he's never been asleep, only lying in wait. "My turn? Okay." Lit by the soft red glow of the sailing instruments, the dark pupils of George's eyeballs wobble uncertainly.

"Are you sure you're all right?" I ask.

"It's my watch, and I'll stand it," he snaps, and rubs his face with his hands.

"Okay, George." I turn my back to him and point to port. "The Aries is holding us on a course of 190° magnetic," I say. "The light over there is a ship that came over the horizon about five minutes ago. It looks like we'll pass it well to the west." I wait for a grunt or some other sign of acknowledgement. "George?" I ask, and turn to find him sprawled at the leeward rail heaving his insides out, a process that takes several minutes to complete. "Maybe I'd better wake Steve," I say when he's hauled himself back to the binnacle.

"Dammit, I can stand watch," George says, so I leave him and go below. He manages to hold out for two hours, but by then the wind has quit entirely. He gets Steve out of bed to drop the sails, fires up the engine, and heads for his bunk, where he spends the next thirty hours in misery.

Thankfully I have never experienced the full brunt of *mal de mer*, having always been fortunate enough to suppress the queasiness that seems to accompany the first day or so of passage making. Seasickness is our bodies' proof of the inhospitable nature of the sea. The ocean is never still and even on the calmest of days there will be the irregular rise and fall of the swell. Adding waves to the mix makes the boat rock—back and forth, forward and backward, up and down—never the same way twice. It's like a cross between a wobbly rocking chair and a slow yo-yo, what a Dutch research study on the subject called "pitch and roll . . . combined in a non-linear fashion with heave," which I'm sure comes as no surprise to anybody who's felt it.

According to the experts (and there is no shortage of scholarly papers on the subject), it's not just the pitching, rolling, and heaving that leave people feeling puky, it's the combination of irregular motion and the confusion of our land-oriented sensory apparatus. In the cockpit our eyes register the apparent stability of the boat, a stability that is contradicted by the balance mechanism of our inner ears—the vestibular nerve—which tells us we're in motion. The brain struggles to process the conflict, and nausea is often the result, accompanied by cold sweats, dry mouth, and elevated levels of protein and sodium in the blood and saliva. At least in the cockpit we have the added advantage of fresh air. Deep breaths seem to help (Penn State University confirms what practically anybody who's been to sea can tell you), as does looking at the horizon, which moves up and down and provides a more compatible referent.

Going below, however, all bets are off, and in this the experts are also in agreement. The enclosed space of the cabin increases the illusion of stability. But the walls lean toward us or away from us, the ceiling and floor are no longer horizontal, and all are constantly shifting, hopelessly confusing the visual cues we normally rely on to keep ourselves upright. The air is close, sometimes musty with mildewy boat smell, and there's no horizon toward which we might extend a comforting gaze. Aboard *Atlantean* it's often the sight of the gimbaled stove canting back and forth at bizarre angles in relation to the rest of the galley that pushes somebody over the edge.

There are plenty of medical and folk remedies for seasickness, many of which have demonstrated, at best, "some efficacy." Scopolamine in transdermal patches is popular, though with interesting side effects, such as hallucinations; ginger root came off with high marks in a Danish study; and the University of Miami reported that "a ten week program of mostly home-based visual-vestibular habituation and balance training has been shown to be effective against seasickness." The same studies all point out, however, that nothing is guaranteed to work all the time.

The good news for most people is that seasickness passes within thirty-six hours, usually after the body is so exhausted that it collapses into a hard sleep. Something about sleeping through the rolling motion of the sea allows the victim to finally adapt. The bad news is that being back on land wipes away the adaptation. The next time you go to sea, you have the whole process to look forward to again.

While George is out of commission, Steve and I take turns on watch, though there isn't much to do. We motor through the next day and all night, using up half of the fuel we're carrying, during which I calculate our position by *dead reckoning*, plotting course and speed over a set period of time. Motoring makes it especially easy, since we maintain a steady course with the electric autopilot. I could use the GPS, but we're sailing southwest to put some distance between us and the coast, and there's nothing to hit.

Prior to our departure, George and I spoke by phone about the often-difficult stretch of ocean lying off Oregon and northern California. Cape Mendecino is the sharp kink about halfway down the California coast, and marks the turning point for the nasty southerly gales that can spring up any time of year and last for days. Between Astoria and San Francisco, the few safe havens are guarded by treacherous bars that can be impassible in bad weather, making running for cover next to impossible. The coast is also crowded with shipping traffic and fishing boats. To avoid the freighters there are two strategies: go out over one hundred miles, or stay close to land. Since we're not planning on stopping until San Diego, it makes sense to head far offshore.

By the third day George's seasickness has passed, and enough wind comes up from the north to resume sailing, lifting our spirits. George steels himself for his first noon sextant sight. For ten minutes on either side of the hour, he stares through the eyepiece at the filter-darkened sun and fiddles with the adjusting knob, barking "Mark" at us from time to time. Steve and I stand by with pencil, paper, and wristwatch, dutifully noting the precise times and sextant angles. After we've filled a sheet with numbers, George packs the handsome brass Weems & Plath sextant into its velvet-lined wooden case, takes our data, and heads below. For the next two hours he sits at the chart table pouring over his books and scribbling pages of calculations.

Steve and I are in the cockpit playing cribbage. After an hour goes by, I call down the companionway stairs. "Just a hunch, George, but we're guessing it's the Pacific Ocean." Steve snickers.

"Screw you guys," George says over his shoulder. "Do you want to know where we are or not?" His face is flushed and perspiring, as if he might be getting seasick again.

"There's always the GPS," I say.

Steve pegs a double run. "Next thing," he says, "George'll come flying up the ladder shouting, 'Turn left! Turn left!'"

When George finally arrives at a fix, it's only twenty miles off our dead reckoning position. Steve and I pronounce his efforts a success, though George grumbles the rest of the day about arithmetic errors. At sunset George and I practice taking sights with both of our sextants and find the Weems & Plath is consistently a quarter degree off from the Tamaya, which I had calibrated before I left. "Might as well throw the damn thing over the side," George says about his own sextant, then relents. "It'll make a good paperweight."

The prevailing winds along the West Coast are out of the north, produced by the clockwise airflow around the permanent mass of high pressure parked in the middle of the North Pacific Ocean. We soon have "fair winds and following seas," but that doesn't mean we can put the wind squarely at our back. We sail what's called a broad reach, with the wind angling across Atlantean's starboard quarter, or in other words, from over our right shoulder. This is necessary to keep the mainsail from "blanketing" the headsail, but it also means that waves strike the boat at an angle, producing an annoying corkscrewing motion that makes life belowdecks uncomfortable.

Being the most immune to motion sickness, I manage all of the cooking, strapping myself in front of the gimbaled stove, which remains level while we rock and roll through the waves. Eating becomes a hurried affair, with one hand steadying the plate lest a sudden lurch deposit the meal in your lap. In order to sit and read a book, I have to push myself into a corner and brace a foot on something solid. At night we slide around our bunks in our sleeping bags, chafing our hips, knees, and elbows as we search for positions that will hold us in place. Sleep eventually comes, however, and with our rotating shifts of three hours on and six hours off, we gradually adapt, and even begin to enjoy ourselves.

At noon of our fifth day at sea, George calculates we're south of Cape Mendecino, our first milestone. We celebrate with the expensive bottle of sauterne George brought along, chilled in the refrigerator. Our spirits are high. Later that day, I write in the log:

2040—What a beautiful evening. The boat slices through the water, smoothing out the swells, the air is starting to warm up, and the wind is moderate. Sunset is spectacular—clouds everywhere, except the western horizon, where it's all aglow—turning the water a sparkling black, with a sharp, clear horizon line. It's a surrealistic scene you would never see from land, like something out of Dante or Jules Verne's Journey to the Center of the Earth.

Everybody feels more rested, more used to the routine, relieved everything is working so well. We're sharing in a love affair with Atlantean and how well she cares for us. The miles pile up, hour after hour, as she brings us ever closer to the southland.

The next day the barometer shoots up, and the winds and seas build at our backs. At first we try running with only the big forward sail, the genoa, which substantially increases our speed but further unbalances the boat's motion. When the wind gusts above fifteen knots apparent (actual wind speed reduced by our forward progress) and the waves start breaking around us, we claw the gennie back down and put up a shorter rig. By nightfall the wind is over twenty knots apparent and we're down to a double-reefed main and the small staysail.

The heavy weather introduces a new dimension belowdecks: noise. The hull acts like a sounding board, and even under calm conditions there's a constant washing-machine gurgle and slosh inside the cabin. With the increased wind, however, the waves rushing past rise to a roar, almost as if we're running down a white-water river. The wet slap of a side-breaking wave is sometimes followed by *Atlantean* dropping into a trough, with a hollow boom that bounces our stomachs. Added to the din are creaks and groans as the hull twists and flexes under the force of the sea. More than once I come up from my cabin, where it sounds as if we're in the midst of a war zone, only to discover the noise is not nearly so apparent on deck, and that all is well.

During the first night of heavy weather, George relieves me, and I retire to my bunk in the aft stateroom (Steve and George sleep on opposite settees in the main cabin). Sleep is hard to find, but eventually I wedge my torso into the tight corner at the foot of the bunk and accustom myself to the mayhem. After an hour or so, my turbulent dreams are interrupted by an explosive crash and a precipitous drop in the stern that brings me flying out of bed. It felt and sounded as if we'd smashed into something solid, but *Atlantean* continues to surge through the waves. I burst through the door into the companionway, half-expecting the cabin to be awash, and collide with Steve racing for the cockpit. When we throw open the hatch, we find George on his feet, clutching the binnacle like Horatio Hornblower, and laughing gleefully. He's soaked and dripping in his foul weather gear, ankle deep in the seawater sloshing around the cockpit well.

"Out of bed you lazy bastards!" he roars. "This is what sailing's all about! It's a goddamned sleigh ride!"

"George," I shout into the teeth of the wind, "what happened?"

"Mountains of water! Gusts over thirty! It's great!" He points at the instrument panel. "YEE-HAH! Nine fucking knots—we're hauling ass!" I lean out of the companionway and check the knotmeter. Its needle hovers briefly beyond the nine, then backs down to a steady eight. It's the fastest I've ever sailed.

"The crash, George," I shout, "what was the crash?"

He tells us a huge wave broke over the stern, inundating the cockpit. "I turned around just in time," he chortles. "Twenty footer at least." Fortunately he had the foresight to close up the companionway earlier on his watch, so no water came into the cabin. Steve and I shake our heads, replace the hatch, and return to the warmth of our bunks.

For three days we fly down the California coast over a hundred miles offshore, surfing down fifteen-foot waves. There's no one else in sight, no fishing boats, no freighters, no airplanes overhead. With our boat speed consistently over six knots and thirty knots apparent showing on the wind speed indicator, we're in a fair-weather northerly gale produced by the compression of the mid-Pacific high against the coast. Standing watch means putting up with nearly constant spray in the cockpit, and every hour or two a wave dumps a significant amount of seawater over the stern, though never again as much as the one that caught George. It would be much worse if the boat had a flat transom, but *Atlantean's* rounded stern increases our buoyancy and parts the following seas. Nevertheless, after watch I go below and peel off my foul weather gear, feeling as if I'm covered in a sticky layer of salt.

By the second day of this we're all tired and irritable, as the rough seas make any task difficult, particularly cooking and sleeping. One night the lee cloth on Steve's bunk comes loose and he's thrown headlong into the corner of George's bunk. His bloodied lip and puffy cheek, added to the general scruffiness from a week at sea, make him look like a derelict who's been rolled in an alley.

Despite the good progress, the constant heavy weather makes me nervous, and I keep us on a short rig. My main concern is the Aries, which is mounted on the stern and is frequently submerged by the following seas. Without the Aries we would have to hand steer, which would be grueling under the circumstances. Fortunately it's designed to take far more abuse than what we're getting; it clings to the outer hull like a limpet on a rock and never falters in its duty. I sometimes watch in amazement as its wooden paddle windmills from side to side and the control lines spin the wheel. Like an old Gloucester schooner-man, the Aries always seems to know exactly when to bring the stern up to face a big wave, steering better than any of us could.

"Whoever Nick Franklin is," I say one day to Steve, "I hope he made his fortune off this thing." Franklin is the Aries' inventor and manufacturer, which I know because his name and telephone number (with international area code) are cast prominently into the Aries' aluminum frame, as if we could phone him up at any time with a question or a compliment. I've heard Franklin retired to go sailing, which explains why the only Aries vanes on the market are second-hand (I bought *Atlantean's* Aries from a Canadian who had already used it to sail around the world).

During the early morning hours of our third day of heavy weather, I have an unsettling dream. In the dream, I'm lying awake in my bunk, and hear women's voices outside my cabin door. Their tone is urgent and worried, and I can't make out what they're saying. Suddenly I realize the boat is no longer moving. *We're sinking,* I think. *The women are launching the life raft.* In a panic, I try to claw my way out of bed, but can't move, as if I'm caught in a straitjacket. I'm suffocating, unable to breathe, and awaken to find myself hopelessly tangled in my sleeping bag, sweating and gasping, lost in that netherworld between dreaming and consciousness.

I gradually come to my senses in the thin daylight and discover that *Atlantean* is indeed dead in the water, wallowing in the big swells. Without the usual roar of the waves I can hear the wind whistling through the rigging, muffling Steve's and George's voices on deck and giving them a trebly quality that accounts for hearing women in my dream. I head for the cockpit and find the two of them huddled over the folds of the mainsail, which lies in an enormous heap atop the dodger and binnacle. "Holy shit," I say as I clamber out of the companionway, "what's going on?"

"Geez," Steve says when he sees me, "are you okay?"

"Bad dream," I mutter, shouldering them aside and grabbing for the sail. The sight of my precious main hanging limply from the boom has come as a shock.

"Reefing line chafed through," George says, showing me the ragged end of the ½" line he holds in one hand. "When it gave, the bottom of the main blew out. I dropped it as fast as I could, but we've got a tear." My mind races as I sort through the piled sail, looking for the damage. We have no replacement for the main, and though I've reserved enough fuel to motor us to shore, losing the main would be both a major inconvenience and expense, and could put us in danger should the weather deteriorate further. I've never seriously damaged a sail before, and we're far away from the nearest loft where friendly sailmakers can work their magic and return the main to its former glory.

It turns out we've been lucky. I find the tear, fourteen inches along the lowest batten pouch where the fabric has partially shredded, but it's nothing I can't fix. I put Steve and George to work on running a new reefing line down the boom and rigging a preventer so it won't happen again, while I hand-stitch a patch on the sail using materials from the well-stocked ditty bag I purchased during a sail-repair class I took at the Hasse & Petrich sail loft in Port Townsend, Washington.

In two hours we're underway again, but I've been sobered, witnessing for the first time the effects of the tremendous stresses the equipment comes under from operating around the clock. It's the kind of failure that would never happen day sailing in Puget Sound, and I resolve to keep a closer eye out for wear and tear while we're underway. But on the positive side, we've handled our first potentially serious equipment failure at sea, and that's a major confidence booster.

We round Point Conception, still a hundred miles offshore, and turn to the east for the final run to San Diego. For days we've operated under the heightened state of awareness necessitated by the demands of a turbulent sea and a tumbling sky. It's almost as if we've been in another world, a world with *Atlantean* at its center, surrounded by the relentless forces of wind and water. The shifting cycle of the watch has defined these days, from the three hours in the cockpit, when we've borne the heavy responsibility of attention to the boat, to the six hours off, when we've hung up our wet gear and sought whatever respite we could find: in our bunks, in books, or in food. Our thoughts have never strayed far from the rush of the waves, the roll of the boat, or the demands of the moment.

The turn to the east spells the end of our fast sailing, and the winds ease steadily as we approach land. We shake out the reefs and put up the bigger headsails—the yankee, then the genoa, and finally even the spinnaker—in an effort to keep up our speed. As the seas calm we experience a letdown, almost a sense of disappointment that our trip is coming to an end. Without the urgency of the elements, watch duty consists largely of trying to coax more wind into the sails. Our minds have the freedom to wander, and eventually the ever-lengthening pencil line on the chart reminds us of the inevitability of that other world, the one we've ignored for over a week: people, automobiles, pollution, money. California is out there, waiting for us. Or as George puts it, "The land of fruits and nuts."

Our last full night out, we watch the sun set to the northwest through the smoggy Southern California sky. We've been trying to spot land all day, and though we calculate we're only thirteen miles from the 1,500 foot peak of Santa Rosa Island, we can see nothing in the haze. Eventually it's dark enough to barely make out the blinking red lights atop the island, distorted by the thick air to a dirty orange. "Land ho," Steve says unenthusiastically while George and I take bearings and study a chart by flashlight, verifying our position.

We creep through the night at only a few knots, and by dawn we're near San Clemente Island, a desolate hump of rocks and dirt the Navy uses for target practice. They aren't shelling today, and, as if to celebrate the peace, we're soon joined by dolphins. They bound over the waves to play with us, flying out of the water in synchronized leaps of two or three together. I've often seen their cousins, small black and white Dahl's porpoises, around the Inside Passage and Puget Sound, but generally only in small groups. Now as many as twenty or thirty swarm around *Atlantean's* nose, jockeying with one another for position on our minuscule bow wave. Their misty breath explodes in instantaneous blowhole bursts, followed by gasping inhalations. We crowd together at the bow pulpit admiring their sleek torsos and snapping pictures as they zip and dart through the water. Individual dolphins swimming alongside roll an eye towards us as if to say, "Is this the best you can do?" After twenty minutes they get bored with our leisurely pace and swim away.

The day is sunny and warm but eventually grows too calm for sailing. By mid-afternoon we're tired of bobbing up and down at less than two knots, and resign ourselves to motoring the rest of the way, about forty miles. "Might as well polish off the beer," I say when we've started the engine. We have a dozen cans left, which I load into the refrigerator. With the help of the alcohol, the five-knot push of the diesel pulls us out of our lethargy. We spend our last few hours at sea happily recounting the highlights of the ten-day passage.

The sweep of San Diego's Point Loma lighthouse guides us into the channel. It seems that half the U.S. Navy and San Diego's entire fishing fleet are putting out to sea tonight, an overload of sights and sounds after the peace and solitude of the open ocean. We focus our attention on the harbor chart, and soon find our way past the submarine pens and boat yards to La Playa Cove and the transient moorage at the Police Dock.

It's midnight in San Diego, a place that bears no resemblance to the peaceful coastal community of Astoria we left behind a week and a half ago. The nearly empty Police Dock, where we pull into the first available slip, is at the end of a skinny park-like strip of land called Shelter Island, separated from San Diego proper by La Playa Cove and Half Moon Bay. The air is warm and thick with smells, of damp freshly-cut grass and the sticky sweetness of peat moss flower beds, overlaid by the dead odors of car exhaust and creosote pilings from a nearby fuel dock. The screech, rumble, and swish of traffic isn't loud, but constant in the automobile-infested manner of American cities. Tall palm trees, their crowns groomed to look like stage props, stand silhouetted on the shore against the hazy glare of a million electric lights. Beyond, the night sky spreads out dull and featureless, revealing neither clouds nor stars.

We're exhausted, but at the same time energized, almost to the point of giddiness. Not because San Diego holds any especial attraction for us—we've all been here plenty of times—but because our arrival marks the successful completion of what only two weeks ago seemed such a daunting task, an ocean passage of over 1,300 miles. We've reached the finish line, though there are no crowds to cheer us. We wobble on our weary sea legs up the dock to a phone booth, where we call our families to tell them we're safe. They're relieved of their concern for our well-being, but nobody's nearly as delighted with our accomplishment as we are, certainly not the surly young policeman on night-desk duty who orders us to move our boat to a different slip, nor the indifferent multitudes living within a few miles of the harbor, all of whom have lives and cares of their own. After we've secured *Atlantean*, we enjoy a quiet celebration with George's last bottle of wine, then settle into a peaceful night aboard a boat that's not rocking anymore, knowing if we wake up, we can simply fluff our pillows, roll over, and go back to sleep.

The next morning I rise refreshed and eager to explore what will be my surroundings for the next several weeks, during which I'll advertise for crew and make final preparations for sailing to foreign shores and beyond. The weather contributes to my enthusiasm: it's California perfect, about 75° under pale blue skies, and the air is fresh with a morning sea breeze that deflects the sounds and smells of the rush hour commute. It's the kind of day that makes everything look clean and cared for, from the expensive hillside homes with their floor to ceiling views across the water, to the glass and granite office towers in the distance reflecting the morning sun.

We motor through Half Moon Bay past hundreds if not thousands of gleaming white yachts, to the San Diego Yacht Club, former home of the America's Cup and the area's most exclusive yachting address. George's membership in the almost as prestigious Seattle Yacht Club entitles us to three days' moorage, which should give me enough time to find a longer-term slip where I can wait for Mexican hurricane season to pass. Our immediate objective after checking in, however, is to treat ourselves to an old-fashioned greasy American breakfast with a bottomless cup of coffee.

Steve and I secure *Atlantean* along the yacht club's guest dock while George prepares to make his entrance. In a few minutes he emerges from the cabin wearing a pair of pink Japanese gardening pants, a button-down long-sleeved white shirt, and Top-Siders with lime green socks. "George grew up in Connecticut," Steve explains. "When you're yachting on the East Coast, you're supposed to dress like this." George reaches for his long-billed fisherman's cap sitting under the dodger. "No, George," Steve says, "not the hat." George ignores our laughter, twists the cap onto his head, and totters down the dock to announce our arrival.

Steve and I spend a half-hour hosing the salt off *Atlantean* and straightening up before we get impatient. We set out in search of George and find him at the Club Secretary's office, where a woman behind a desk coaches him in filling out his registration forms. He looks bad, pale and shaky.

"You'd better get some coffee into this man," she says.

"George," I say, "what's the matter?"

"Nothing's the matter," George says, irritably. "A case of sea legs, that's all. Perfectly normal after you've been at sea."

The formalities complete, the woman directs us to a diner a few blocks away. Steve and I tear into our bacon, eggs, hashbrowns, orange juice, and coffee, while George picks at a lackluster lox and cream cheese bagel. As we finish our meal, George lurches off to find the restroom.

The waitress comes by with more coffee. "What's wrong with your friend?" she asks.

"It's nothing. He's landsick."

"What?"

"It's hard to explain. Actually, he's always like this."

"Well, get him out of here, would you? He's making me nervous."

"We will. Don't worry, he's harmless."

"Tell him not to forget his hat," she says, nodding to where it hangs on a hook by our booth.

It's clear something is bothering George, something that goes beyond regaining his equilibrium after ten days at sea. When Steve decides to rent a car and stay on for a few days, George grumbles about having to "get back to work," though we all know there's hardly any hurry. The yacht club secretary helps me arrange a slip for *Atlantean* in nearby Half Moon Bay Marina, and George books the early afternoon flight to Seattle.

My guess is that George is disappointed to see somebody else living out his dream of ocean-going adventures, while circumstances he considers out of his control keep him at home. He's had his taste of the sea, and the seasickness notwithstanding, he reveled in it. Ever since he was hit by the wave, he's been raving about "the sleigh ride," and how it was the most exciting night of his life. I can understand his desire as well as his frustration. It wasn't easy for me to break away either, and George has more ties to bind him to his old life, including a twenty year marriage to a woman who hates sailing.

"You lucky bastard," George says when it comes time to put him in a taxi to the airport. "You'll be down in the tropics drinking rum out of a coconut, chasing bare-breasted babes, while I'm back home, stuck in the rain."

"Come sail with me anytime," I say. "I hear the Indian Ocean's great." I'm grateful to George, and not only for his companionship these last ten days. He sold me *Atlantean* for less than he could have gotten from somebody else because he supported my plans to use the boat as he'd originally intended. Feeding his fantasies is the least I can do.

But what I want to tell George, and can't, is that life is about making choices. It would be cruel to say so, because he's painfully aware of it, if not before our recent ocean passage, then certainly afterwards. The freedom to follow one's dreams is everybody's secret desire, though most of us keep our dreams bottled and hidden behind an often overwhelming sense of responsibility—to our jobs, our families, our homes, our consumerist economy—precisely the attitude a conservative society fosters and condones. It's as if we're trained to believe our wishes are the light at the end of the tunnel, and if we simply keep our backs bent to the tasks we've been assigned, we'll eventually make it into the light of day. We clothe our longings in the guise of present impossibility, safely out of reach, while we remain comfortable, secure, and perpetually frustrated. And yet: I'm visible proof that following one's dream doesn't require extraordinary circumstances or superhuman efforts. These past ten days have forced George to admit that he stays in the tunnel—in his marriage, in his mansion, in the entanglements he's knowingly or unwittingly created for himself—by choice.

The barriers are out there, whether they're mountains, oceans, or simply overcoming the inertia necessary to leave an unsatisfying job that pays the bills and keeps us in our comfort zones. Which shall we choose? To remain huddled behind the known, safe, and secure, or shall we test ourselves, shall we break loose from our self-imposed restraints and surmount the barriers around us? We're all ultimately free, and personally, I prefer spending this precious gift we call life finding out how much the world has to offer, over the horizon and not so very far away.

ABOUT THE AUTHOR

Gregory Newell Smith, from the Pacific Northwest, is a seasoned ocean sailor and de-livery captain with over 50,000 miles of blue-water experience, ranging from the coast of Alaska to the Cape of Good Hope, including a fifty-three day, 6,000 mile solo passage from Panama to Hawaii. In The Solitude of the Open Sea, he draws upon his three-plus years of offshore sailing aboard his thirty-nine foot Fast Passage cutter, *Atlantean*, to explore the importance of broadening our horizons beyond the known and commonplace, freeing ourselves from cultural self-centeredness, and achieving self-discovery through persever-ance, hardship, and solitude. The themes of the book's seventeen narrative essays are not unique to sailing, but rather are intended for a general audience of reflective readers who value travel and the insights it provides in helping us understand our place in the world around us.

ORDER FORM

QTY	ISBN	TITLE	US $	TOTAL
	1-892399-02-4	ABACO GUIDE	$29.95	
	0-9627562-4-5	ADVENTURING WITH CHILDREN	$14.95	
	0-9639566-5-5	ALWAYS A DISTANT ANCHORAGE	$15.95	
	0-9627562-3-7	BAHAMAS OUT ISLAND ODYSSEY	$14.95	
	0-333-56603-3	BAHAMAS REDISCOVERED	$38.95	
	0-9663520-1-7	BEST TIPS FROM WOMEN ABOARD	$14.95	
	1-892399-10-5	BOAT COSMETICS MADE SIMPLE	$14.95	
	0-9711911-1-5	CHARTRACKER FLORIDA KEYS COLORING BOOK	$9.95	
	0-9711911-0-7	CHARTRACKER FLORIDA KEYS NAVIGATION GUIDE	$74.95	
	1-892399-00-8	CHARTRACKER TO THE ICW: NORFOLK TO JACKSONVILLE	$39.95	
	0-9639566-6-3	CHASING THE LONG RAINBOW	$15.95	
	0-333-73538-2	CHILDREN OF THE SEA	$24.95	
	0-9618406-6-8	CRUISING IN CATAMARANS	$29.95	
	0-9618406-7-6	CRUISING K.I.S.S. COOKBOOK	$24.95	
	1-892399-16-4	CRUISING WITH YOUR FOUR-FOOTED FRIENDS	$19.95	
	1-892399-14-8	ELIMINATE ON COMMAND	$14.95	
	0-9639566-7-1	EXUMA GUIDE: 7th Anniversary Edition	$29.95	
	0-9675905-1-5	FRENCH FOR CRUISERS	$24.95	
	2-87923-152-3	FRENCH POLYNESIA GUIDE TO NAVIGATION & TOURISM	$69.95	
	1-892399-08-3	FULL AND BY	$14.95	
	0-9663520-2-5	GALLEYS OF WOMEN ABOARD	$14.95	
	1-892399-07-5	GEORGIA COAST, WATERWAYS & ISLANDS	$39.95	
	1-892399-15-6	GET RID OF BOAT ODORS	$19.95	
	0-9652356-1-0	HEALTHY CRUISER'S HANDBOOK	$16.95	
	0-9715640-1-9	HF RADIO E-MAIL FOR ""IDI-YACHTS	$29.95	
	0-9652356-1-0	HUNGRY BOATERS RESTAURANT GUIDE	$23.95	
	0-9644112-0-2	INDEPENDENT ENERGY GUIDE	$19.95	
	0-9709714-2-7	KNOT TYING: ADVANCED KNOTS	$24.95	
	0-9709714-0-0	KNOT TYING: BASIC KNOTS	$24.95	
	0-9709714-3-5	KNOT TYING: FISHING KNOTS	$24.95	
	0-9709714-1-9	KNOT TYING: SPLICING THREE-STRAND LINE	$24.95	
	0-9639566-0-4	LIGHTNING AND BOATS	$9.95	
	0-9715640-0-0	MARINE SSB FOR "IDI-YACHTS"	$19.95	

ORDER FORM

QTY	ISBN	TITLE	US $	TOTAL
	2-87923-174-4	MARQUESAS ISLANDS ARCHIPELAGO	$34.95	
	0-9639566-2-0	MEATLESS GALLEY COOKBOOK	$16.95	
	0-9659325-7-5	NORTHEAST BOATERS ALMANAC 2005	$19.95	
	0-9639566-9-8	ON & OFF THE BEATEN PATH: CENTRAL & SOUTHERN BAHAMAS	$34.95	
	0-9753887-1-1	ON THE WINDS OF DESTINY	$17.95	
	0-892399-09-1	PANAMA GUIDE: 2nd Edition	$44.95	
	1-892399-12-1	PUERTO RICO CRUISING GUIDE	$29.95	
	0-9676657-0-1	RACE TO FREEDOM	$19.95	
	0-9534379-1-4	RULES OF THE ROAD AT SEA	$59.95	
	1-929006-03-9	SAILING DESIGNS – VOLUME 4	$29.95	
	1-929006-04-7	SAILING DESIGNS – VOLUME 5	$39.95	
	1-58334-001-7	SAILOR'S GUIDE TO LIFE	$6.95	
	0-9627562-8-8	SAILOR'S MULTIHULL GUIDE	$29.95	
	1-892399-22-9	SOLITUDE OF THE OPEN SEA, THE	$14.95	
	0-9675905-0-7	SPANISH FOR CRUISERS	$24.95	
	1-892399-13-x	TRINIDAD AND TOBAGO CRUISING GUIDE	$27.95	
	1-892399-01-6	TURKS AND CAICOS GUIDE 2nd Edition	$27.95	
	1-892399-05-9	TWO AGAINST CAPE HORN (VIDEO)	$22.95	
	1-892399-03-2	WE FOLLOWED ODYSSEUS	$27.95	

SUBTOTAL	
SHIPPING*	
(Wisconsin Only)	
TAX + 5.6%	

Seaworthy Publications, Inc.
207 S. Park St.
Port Washington, WI 53074
Shipping Address

Phone: (262) 268-9250
Fax: (262) 268-9208
e-mail: publisher@seaworthy.com
www.seaworthy.com

_____
(Name)

_____
(Address)

_____
(City, State, Zip Code)

Please enclose check or money order. We also accept Visa, MasterCard, American Express, and Discover.

_____ - _____ - _____ - _____
Visa, MasterCard, or American Express Card Number
_____/_____ Card Expiration Date (_____) _____ - _____Phone Number